DISCARD

The Enterprise
for the
Americas Initiative

THE ENTERPRISE FOR THE AMERICAS INITIATIVE

*Issues and Prospects
for a Free Trade Agreement
in the Western Hemisphere*

Edited by ROY E. GREEN

Westport, Connecticut
London

Library of Congress Cataloging-in-Publication Data

The Enterprise for the Americas initiative : issues and prospects for
  a free trade agreement in the Western Hemisphere / edited by Roy E.
  Green.
        p.   cm.
     Includes bibliographical references and index.
     ISBN 0–275–94266–X (alk. paper)
     1. Free trade—America.   2. North America—Commercial policy.
3. Canada. Treaties, etc. 1992 Oct. 7.   4. United States—Foreign
economic relations—Latin America.   5. Latin America—Foreign
economic relations—United States.   6. Free ports and zones—
America.   I. Green, Roy E.
     HF1745.E57   1993
     382′.917—dc20   93–20299

British Library Cataloguing in Publication Data is available.

Library of Congress Catalog Card Number: 93–20299
ISBN: 0–275–94266–X

First published in 1993

Praeger Publishers, 88 Post Road West, Westport, CT 06881
An imprint of Greenwood Publishing Group, Inc.

Printed in the United States of America

The paper used in this book complies with the
Permanent Paper Standard issued by the National
Information Standards Organization (Z39.48–1984).

10 9 8 7 6 5 4 3 2

This volume is dedicated to my brother,

ROGER L. GREEN,

Pathfinder and Standard Setter,
Civic-Minded Citizen, Elected Public Servant, and Educator

Contents

Illustrations

FIGURES

TABLES

Acknowledgments

In a volume of this scope and dimension many individuals and institutions have contributed to bringing the project to a successful conclusion. I am especially indebted to Ramon Daubon and William Cartier of the Ford Foundation's Southern Cone Project, Santiago, Chile, for their encouragement and assistance in furthering our goals. Mr. Cartier in particular assisted me in identifying, recruiting, and coordinating the writing efforts of the volume's four South American contributors.

Demonstrating the true collaborative spirit of the venture, a number of authors performed double service by identifying other analysts whose expertise and timely research interests corresponded to the requirements of yet unassigned chapters. In this regard, I am particularly grateful for the counsel and efforts of Patrick Low and Arlene Wilson, and professors Randall Crane, Joseph Grunwald, and Ronald Wonnacott. While not contributors to this volume, professors Jeffrey Henig and Henry Nau of George Washington University, and Sylvia Saborio of the Overseas Development Council, were helpful to me in a similar manner.

More subtle was the research assistance provided by Carol Johnson and Jackie Berry, two friends who pointed me in the right informational direction at the very earliest stage of proposal development. Of course, the people who really make such a work come into being are the competent professionals at Praeger Publishers. Their wise counsel and editing helped to convert typed chapter drafts into a polished final manuscript. Nor can I forget to mention the important contribution made by my wife and companion, Patti, whose good humor and vast patience are keys to all my successful ventures. To all of the above, I wish to express my genuine gratitude.

Introduction

Much has been said and written in recent years about the risks and opportunities offered by the growing and increasingly competitive global economy. The fruits of unfettered domestic markets, and the benefits of internationally orchestrated freer trade arrangements, have long been espoused by Western leaders and financial institutions as necessary conditions for improving the material, if not necessarily the democratic, well-being of all nations and peoples.

The marked deterioration and sudden collapse of the Soviet system in Eurasia during the late 1980s and early 1990s served to expedite a worldwide search for endogenously appropriate and acceptable free market paradigms. However, the search was and is under way not only among the East European and former Soviet republics, but across the range of political economies in Asia, Africa, and Latin America. These investigations and transformations have emerged to financially stretch, competitively stress, and managerially challenge the resiliency and adaptability of long-established Western state economic structures and international arrangements. These nations in transition seek new models to follow as plans are being laid and implemented to pursue the long-admired and cherished benefits of freer markets. And while the calls for change may be a source of perplexity to some, and resistance for others, the search for new ways of doing business is now also being pursued full force within the traditional economic powerhouses of Western Europe, the United States, and Japan.

The Clinton-Bush-Perot presidential race of 1992 was a campaign characterized by each candidate's efforts to correlate in the electorate's mind an understanding of global trade and international competitiveness with domestic economic problems and dynamics. Unclear and unstable U.S. employment conditions, and a generally unsatisfying prioritization of domestic economic issues behind foreign policy exigencies by the Bush Administration, were the stuff that made rhetorical economics real for an increasingly anxious and hard-pressed citizenry. However, post-1992 election analyses seem to indicate that none of the candidates was particularly successful in describing for the U.S. electorate how their respective prescriptions for restructuring the national economy would or could be introduced to meet the challenges of stricter world competition—that is, without inflicting still further distress and dislocation here and abroad. This gap in public understanding remains, despite the fact that all three candidates published their individual plans for economic revitalization and spoke with great enthusiasm throughout the campaign about the necessity for making fundamental changes.

The election of Bill Clinton affords him the privilege and the opportunity that victory brings: the time, the motivation, and the responsibility to try to make his vision of economic prosperity a reality. However, this new U.S. president does not take office with a clean dance card, a blank check, or a balanced budget or trade account, nor with the ability to prioritize or control (for long) which events will demand his attention. And these presidential challenges come at a point when most industrialized nations—including the United States—have been operating at anemic economic levels.

By unseating an incumbent president, the Clinton Administration comes into office at a time and in a manner worthy of a simplifying analogy. It is a situation that seems similar to taking over the responsibilities for a major social event at the last minute. The guests have been invited, the menu and entertainment planned, the RSVPs received, and preparations made for how to dress and what to bring to the party. And while the table is being set, the scheduling hosts take ill, and a new and largely unknown couple from the neighborhood has suddenly been asked to take over for the evening. For the party's guests, and perhaps for the new hosts, the opportunity to alter events might well be tinged with some anxieties about their ability to change course so late in the process. On the other hand, the timing might well prove to be propitious.

On the table, of course, is the frayed but ongoing Uruguay Round of the General Agreement on Tariffs and Trade (GATT) negotiations; a growing uncertainty over plans that were previously thought to be solid for the next stage of greater European Community (EC) political and economic integration; a negotiated but unratified North American Free Trade Agreement (NAFTA); and a maze of agreements-in-principle for liberalizing trade in the Western Hemisphere. The latter developments have been stimulated by the Enterprise for the Americas Initiative (EAI).

HOW THE TRADE AGENDA EVOLVED

At a time when the United States was becoming increasingly mired in recession, or at least always seemed to be hovering near one, and was suffering from high budget and international trade deficits—which limited the options for cutting taxes or increasing governmental spending to stimulate a recovery—the Bush Administration targeted freer trade as its primary policy lever for pulling the American economy out of its malaise and for sustaining hope for future growth. Events had been proceeding at a rapid pace. There was to be a more tightly bound European Community, targeted for a symbolic unveiling in 1992. This momentous event was preceded on January 1, 1989 by the implementation of the Canada–U.S. Free Trade Agreement (FTA), based on a Canadian initiative that had anticipated the next steps toward greater EC integration.

Then came unexpectedly massive calls for financial assistance from the collapsing economic systems in Eastern Europe and the new states emerging from the former Soviet Union. As time marched on, inconclusive GATT negotiations (begun in 1986 during the Reagan Administration) began to complicate the situation, generating uncertainty among a growing number of nations (especially by those outside the EC and the Canada–U.S. FTA) about their future economic well-being within an increasingly unstable world trading system.

One important consequence of the European, Canada–U.S., and GATT developments was a renewal of Mexico's interest in trade negotiations with her northern neighbor. Many other Latin American countries also began to contemplate alternative trading arrangements and strategies, and to assess their prospects for participating in the just-announced Enterprise for the Americas Initiative. It was anticipated that the Mexican experience in negotiating and concluding an agreement with the United States and Canada, the NAFTA, would serve for many other Latin American nations as an important reference mode for possible future FTA deals.

As part of the call to arms for implementing this new, multifaceted U.S. economic strategy, President Bush's secretary of the treasury, Nicholas Brady, indicated that agencies such as the World Bank and the International Monetary Fund (IMF), and their regional affiliates, were to be the primary vehicles for the Administration's efforts to support market-oriented reforms in a credit-short world. The Canada–U.S. Free Trade Agreement was offered to the NAFTA and EAI negotiators as a benchmark for negotiating the conditions for equitable and mutually beneficial markets in North America and throughout the Western Hemisphere.

Although it remains unclear what the exact prioritization and correspondence of the NAFTA and EAI negotiations were to be with the Uruguay Round of the GATT negotiations, the multilateral (GATT) and the two regional (NAFTA and EAI) processes were obviously linked. Clearly some important issues were not resolved in NAFTA, pending the outcome of the Uruguay Round of GATT negotiations, and the success or failure of the Uruguay Round will have much broader implications for the evolution of NAFTA and the EAI within the Western Hemisphere. From the very beginning of the negotiations, it appeared that there was an informal consensus among the three negotiating NAFTA countries that it would be very convenient if some of the most difficult issues—agricultural subsidies and trade barriers, textiles trade restrictions, trade rules for subsidies and countervailing and antidumping duties, government procurement practices, and rules for intellectual property—were resolved through the multilateral process. Several contributors to this volume assess this linkage more closely.

A POLICY FEEDBACK RATIONALE FOR THE TIMING OF NAFTA AND THE EAI

Rather than seeing these regional initiatives as purely an attempt to leverage progress from the Uruguay Round of the GATT, the effort may also be viewed as a counterintuitive (some might say ironic) effort by the Bush Administration to secure some aspects of his legislatively stalled domestic economic agenda. Stepping back for a moment, the motivation for pursuing a North American Free Trade Agreement, and the inauguration of the Enterprise for the Americas Initiative, both during the extended GATT round of negotiations, might well be viewed as being more than a pragmatic response to temporal or strategic international necessities, or the beckoning of convenient geography. As a strategy, it may well have also been motivated from a deeply held and shared Reagan-Bush commitment to locking in their philosophy for freer commerce by connecting a domestic with an international economic agenda. This would represent a goal not all that different from the one articulated by President Salinas of Mexico in seeking the NAFTA.

One might well argue that there is a strategic policy feedback loop that has been compensating for an unfulfilled Reagan pledge to create a domestically expanding framework of freer enterprise zone policies. This policy loop might be viewed as connecting the Bush Administration's interesting decision to seek the NAFTA and to pursue the Enterprise for the Americas Initiative simultaneously with the GATT negotiations. All three sets of initiatives offer a similar freer market approach to stimulating economic recovery and growth.

The Reagan Administration, in originally promoting the enterprise zone concept, proposed a modest number of relatively small, targeted zones as an initial domestic experiment. Designated federal zones were to have focused primarily on distressed areas within larger urban (later extended to include some rural) markets. While never substantively enacted into law, this focus was likely intended as a first step toward broader application of the policy. For example, several Reagan-era proposals would have given each federal enterprise zone international duty-free port status. In its most expansive thinking, the Reagan Administration would have liked to have utilized the concept's basic principles nationally. However, internal arguments about the merits of creating such narrowly targeted areas within communities, as well as the Treasury Department's troubling estimates of lost federal revenues, complicated the legislative challenge for the Reagan Administration.

The common Reagan-Bush approach had been to reduce economic regulatory barriers and to move toward reliance on commercial forces for creating and sustaining new forms of wealth and opportunity. Both the Reagan domestic proposal for urban enterprise zones and his administration's successful negotiation of the Canadian–U.S. FTA, and the Bush initiatives to expand freer trade southward toward Latin America, were attempts to apply thematically comparable economic and political solutions for capital formation and for unleashing the marketplace. For President Bush, predilection may have discovered opportunity. But on the other hand, the Bush and Reagan initiatives faced comparable political and economic obstacles in promoting these objectives.

Given the much-maligned gridlock with Congress on most of his domestic proposals, Bush seems to have preferred international approaches to securing U.S. economic recovery. In the unceasing worldwide search for new solutions to long-entrenched social, economic, and political problems, it would appear to be more than mere coincidence that the prototype urban enterprise zone programs, upon which American state and federal legislators (and the Reagan and Bush administrations) drew for their proposals in the 1980s and 1990s, were located in Great Britain, and in the Four Tigers of Asia (South Korea, Taiwan, Hong Kong, and Singapore). An example closer to home has been an industrial sector enterprise zone program operating in Mexico since the mid-1960s. This is the Mexican Maquiladora program. And as we will examine later in this volume, the Maquiladora program has had a direct impact on U.S.–Mexican trade relations and negotiations.

In effect, the original Maquiladora program provided for a very large, but subnational, enterprise zone that permitted duty-free inbound imports of machinery, equipment, and components for processing or assembly within a 20-kilometer strip along the U.S. border, provided that the imported products were later reexported. As prospects for a successful NAFTA improved, the Mexican government has been modifying and extending the Maquiladora program further into the interior of the country—an application of enterprise zone principles that President Reagan might have anticipated for enterprise zones located in the United States.

WHAT'S IN A NAME: THE ENTERPRISE FOR THE AMERICAS INITIATIVE

On June 27, 1990, George Bush, fast approaching the zenith of his national and international prestige, in a ceremony held in the White House East Room, announced his new approach for conceptualizing and redressing the economic problems of Latin America. The approach was called the Enterprise for the Americas Initiative. Essentially the EAI called for the United States to negotiate a series of arrangements with selected Latin American and Caribbean countries: (1) to reduce their official debt to the United States; (2) to stimulate private investments in their economies; and (3) to take steps to promote trade liberalization among the nations of the Western Hemisphere—with the ultimate objective being to create a free trade zone throughout the hemisphere.

Under the debt component, the Bush Administration sought authority from the Congress to reduce and restructure existing U.S. concessional (that is, below market interest rate) loans for Latin American and Caribbean countries. The United States would reduce the principal of bilateral official debt when the countries met, as appropriate, three economic reform conditions. These were (1) the adoption of strong economic reform programs in conjunction with the International Monetary Fund and the World Bank; (2) the adoption of investment reform programs through the Inter-American Development Bank (IDB) or other multilateral institutions, or otherwise the implementation of an open investment regime; and (3) if appropriate, the completion of commercial bank debt reduction programs. The United States would accept interest payments on the restructured debt in local currency and place them in trusts to support environmental programs and projects agreed to by the participating governments.

The U.S. Congressional Research Service (CRS) reports that the 101st U.S. Congress authorized President Bush to negotiate official debt reduction agreements for the Food For Peace program (P.L. 480). The 102nd U.S. Congress authorized debt reduction for the Agency for International Development (AID), the Commodity Credit Corporation (CCC), and the Export-Import (Exim) Bank programs. But at the close of its second session (the last under President Bush), the 102nd U.S. Congress only appropriated $40 million to cover the costs of reducing P.L. 480 debt, and $50 million to cover the costs of other debt reduction under the Enterprise for the Americas Initiative. The Bush Administration had requested $310 million for AID debt reduction in FY1992 and $286 million for FY1993. The final continuing resolution for FY1992 foreign aid appropriations contained no funding for EAI purposes.

The second component to the EAI was that the United States was to encourage the establishment of a new multilateral investment fund (MIF), to be administered by the Inter-American Development Bank and to complement existing IDB and World Bank programs. The CRS reports that as of April 1992, pledged contributions from twenty-four countries resulted in an aggregated commitment of $1.3 billion (the publicly announced goal had been for $1.5 billion), to be provided over a five year span. These pledges included $500 million from the United States, $500 million from Japan, $50 million from Spain, $30.7 million from Canada, $30 million each from Germany and Italy, $20 million each from Argentina, Brazil, Mexico, and Venezuela, and lesser contributions from other Latin American countries. The 102nd U.S. Congress authorized and appropriated a single installment of $90 million toward the U.S. MIF pledge as part of the FY1993 foreign operations appropriations bill.

The third component of the Enterprise for the Americas Initiative pertained to trade liberalization and the creation of a hemisphere-wide free trade zone— which, if ever accomplished, would surely be the Initiative's most important achievement. The Bush Administration did not seek legislative authority for such a plan before Bush's leaving office. However, the United States did begin to negotiate bilateral trade framework agreements with Latin American and Caribbean nations to create special reciprocal trade arrangements, and to set up dispute resolution mechanisms to handle trade and investment issues.

As of mid-1992 the CRS reports that agreements had been signed with most countries in Latin America and the Caribbean. In Central America, these were Costa Rica, Guatemala, Honduras, Nicaragua, El Salvador, and Panama. In South America, bilateral agreements were signed with Bolivia, Chile, Colombia, Ecuador, Peru, and Venezuela. Multilateral framework agreements were signed with MERCOSUR (the South American common market composed of Argentina, Brazil, Paraguay, and Uruguay), and with the Caribbean common market (CARICOM) composed of twelve countries and a British colony. The Dominican Republic has also signed a framework agreement with the United States.

PRESIDENT CLINTON'S OPPORTUNITY TO REAPPRAISE THE REAGAN-BUSH FREE MARKET PARADIGM

Most observers seem to conclude that, given President Bush's general commitment to worldwide trade liberalization, NAFTA and the EAI's trade components appeared to be in line with previous Reagan and Bush administration policies. However, other analysts have suggested that alternative motivations lay behind the NAFTA and EAI proposals, viewing them as a means to secure leverage for greater change in the Uruguay Round of the GATT, and as a response to the emergence of a strong regional trading system in Europe. Still others have suggested that the emphasis placed by the Bush Administration on seeking regional agreements may have marked a significant shift away from dependence on the GATT as the primary vehicle for securing trade liberalization. The 1992 election has made the ultimate Bush motivation a moot question.

During his campaign for the presidency, Governor Clinton delivered a speech in Raleigh, North Carolina, just before the election and shortly after the draft NAFTA language had been published by the Bush Administration. During this October 4, 1992 address Clinton outlined his position on NAFTA and other trade policy issues. However, Clinton kept his own counsel that day and throughout the campaign and transition period about his views on the Enterprise for the Americas Initiative.

Clinton proposed five unilateral steps the United States should take in implementing the North American Free Trade Agreement. These steps were to be taken in addition to three supplemental agreements that he argued should be negotiated with Canada and Mexico before the agreement was implemented. The unilateral steps to be taken were (1) worker training and adjustment assistance beyond that promised by President Bush; (2) increased environmental cleanup and infrastructure investments; (3) assistance to farmers through strict application of American pesticide requirements and transition assistance;

(4) mechanisms for greater public participation in environmental disputes; and (5) assurance that foreign workers cannot be brought in as strikebreakers.

The first two supplemental agreements sought by Governor Clinton were to be for obtaining better enforcement of laws already on the books regarding environmental and worker standards. In his October 4 speech he argued that the negotiated NAFTA agreement "goes a long way to do this in protecting intellectual property rights and the right to invest in Mexico, but is silent with respect to labor laws and the environment." The third supplemental agreement sought was for greater protection for sectors of the U.S. economy that are threatened by a surge in imports.

At least while a candidate, ·Clinton felt he could take these steps, "without renegotiating the basic agreement." He summed up his overall views about trade policy by noting "the issue is not whether we should support free trade or open markets [but] whether or not we will have a national economic strategy to make sure we reap the benefits." Shortly after Clinton's election, Mexico's President Carlos Salinas indicated a willingness to participate in further discussions concerning mutually shared concerns for the environment. However, the Mexican president has opposed any reopening of the NAFTA negotiations. Since President Clinton's inauguration, these supplemental discussions have been opened.

THE CHOICES

Shortly after President Bush announced his new Enterprise for the Americas Initiative in June 1990, I began to develop a framework by which the Initiative's domestic, continental, hemispheric, and global linkages might be considered. Some time later, I was fortunate enough to assemble an extremely knowledgeable group of international analysts who were commissioned to monitor and assess the key trade issues and prospects associated with the Canada–U.S. FTA, NAFTA, and the EAI. Based on their individual chapter assignments, the analysts were asked to assess the diplomatic and domestic political priorities, rationales, and motivations of the negotiators who were charged with concluding one or more of the freer trade agreements.

The analyses commissioned for this volume have been chronologically ordered into the sequence by which specific trade negotiations were begun. First an analysis is presented from the perspective of the GATT negotiations. This global orientation session is followed by critical examinations of specific regional trade negotiations: the Canada–U.S. FTA and then the NAFTA. The volume concludes with a focus on the EAI's historical and political context, its component parts, and a survey of South American national reactions.

The Enterprise for the Americas Initiative: Issues and Prospects for a Free Trade Agreement in the Western Hemisphere is a collection of expert opinions organized into four parts: (I) Global Trade and Regional Economic Development, (II) The Canada–U.S. FTA and the Laboratory of the Mexican, U.S., and Canadian NAFTA Negotiations, (III) Keys to a Free Trade Zone in the Western Hemisphere: History, Opportunity, Motivation, and Timing, and (IV) The North American Free Trade Negotiating Track: Agenda Setting for the Enterprise for the Americas Initiative.

The first part, Global Trade and Regional Economic Development, is composed of two chapters that describe the diplomatic context of U.S.–Latin American trade negotiations as they have been framed by the Uruguay Round of negotiations on the General Agreement on Tariffs and Trade. These introductory chapters examine basic multilateral and plurilateral trade policy issues, time frames, and compatibility concerns coinciding with the emergence of the current wave of regional arrangements.

The first chapter, written by Patrick Low, considers a basic issue: Are regional trade agreements likely to complement or undermine efforts to revitalize the General Agreement on Tariffs and Trade? His assessment of how successful regional agreements like NAFTA and the EAI will be in opening up markets and extending the benefits of specialization through trade is broken up into a discussion of three fundamental questions: What do regional trade agreements offer that the multilateral system fails to deliver? How much does it matter, for the future of global trading arrangements, that these agreements contravene the most basic tenet of the GATT system, that of nondiscrimination? And, can they be characterized as stepping-stones toward a broader multilateral vision of international economic relations, toward a reborn GATT?

The second chapter in Part I is authored by Ronald J. Wonnacott. This chapter assesses alternative arrangements for developing trade in the Western Hemisphere. Notes Professor Wonnacott: "It is natural to interpret President George Bush's vision of liberalized trade from Alaska to Cape Horn as one all-encompassing plurilateral free trade area of equal partners. But from the beginning, there were other possibilities."

The second part of the collection, The Canada–U.S. FTA and the Laboratory of the Mexican, U.S., and Canadian NAFTA Negotiations, is composed of two sections. The first section considers the trilateral nature of the trade policy issues faced by the Mexican, U.S., and Canadian negotiators seeking a NAFTA. The first chapter (Chapter 3), crafted by Murray G. Smith, considers the Canadian perspective toward the NAFTA. The United States did not extensively study the potential effects of a free trade agreement with Canada on the United States before agreeing to enter into negotiations; however, Canada did evaluate potential effects on its economy for several years before requesting negotiations with the United States. This chapter provides a unique assessment of the Canada–U.S. FTA and a summary of Canadian expectations for NAFTA and beyond. The second chapter in this section (Chapter 4), authored by Arlene E. Wilson, evaluates the effect of the FTA on the United States in its first few years of existence, reviewing the United States' FTA negotiating goals and the FTA's initial effects on U.S. trade, investment, and the economy. The study ends with a discussion of the Canada–U.S. FTA's effect on NAFTA negotiations.

This section of Part II concludes with a Mexican assessment of Mexican–U.S.–Canadian NAFTA negotiations (Chapter 5). The analysis is provided by Carlos Alba Vega, and describes what led Mexico to seek an agreement. He provides a Mexican perspective on the NAFTA results, and evaluates the implications for different sectors within the Mexican economy. This chapter evaluates the Mexican economic imperatives and political and social impediments to market integration with the United States and Canada. Policy issues of trade, industry, the environment, energy, the economics and politics of debt and investment, the border areas, and migration are considered.

The second section of Part II provides two subnational pilot studies relevant to the NAFTA and the EAI. Chapter 6, written by Randall Crane, examines the Mexican maquiladora program as a regional economic development effort that has evolved over the years to set the stage for NAFTA and the EAI. The characteristics of the program, its historical development, and the associated problems are summarized. Looking ahead, the chapter also considers the impacts of a future lowering of trade barriers between the United States and Mexico.

The second study is a cross-border analysis of the U.S.–Canadian trading frontier, as it operates in a Pacific Northwest region known as Cascadia. In Chapter 7 Michael A. Goldberg and Maurice D. Levi offer their hypothesis that, with so much emphasis being placed today on international trading blocs among nations, it is typically overlooked that nations are ultimately comprised of functional and distinctive economic regions and that these regions often defy national boundaries. The framework that follows is offered as a prototype for analyzing these regions.

The third part of the volume, Keys to a Free Trade Zone in the Western Hemisphere, offers two chapters that assess the historical, economic, and political motivations that seem to be promoting, if not driving, the rapprochement of Latin America with the United States and vice versa. Joseph Grunwald in Chapter 8 examines why, in the Latin American context, unilateral trade liberalization and progress toward freer markets seem to be making regional integration more viable. Professor Grunwald explores the irony that finds Latin American countries, for many years limited by import-substituting industrialization and failed regional economic integration efforts and moving toward opening their economies to the world, now being tempted by the EAI to join a regional bloc. Joseph S. Tulchin follows in Chapter 9 with an essay evaluating how the EAI, from the vantage point of the United States, fits into U.S. policy toward the region and globally; how it fit into the policy apparatus of the Bush Administration; and how, if at all, it will affect U.S. relations with Latin America during the coming years.

The final part of the volume, The North American Free Trade Negotiating

Track, provides for an appraisal of the EAI from the perspective of three South American nations. The first perspective offered is from Argentina, and is authored by Roberto Bouzas (Chapter 10). Bouzas reviews the political and trade impacts of the EAI on Argentina, and then assesses its potential effects on the South American common market (MERCOSUR) from the standpoint of its two largest partners, Brazil and Argentina. The second South American EAI perspective offered is from the vantage point of Chile. In Chapter 11, Mladen Yopo H. analyzes why many consider Chile to be the next logical candidate— after Mexico—to sign a free trade agreement with the United States, or perhaps to join the broader NAFTA. He assesses what the political and economic costs and benefits of pursuing this course might be for both parties. The collection ends with Chapter 12, which is an analysis of Colombian reactions to the EAI, written by Mauricio Reina and Gladys Cristina Barrera. The analysis begins with a review of the development strategies and foreign trade policies pursued by Colombia over the last twenty-five years, and places the EAI within the context of Colombia's current foreign policy directives. Subsequent sections of the chapter evaluate the progress Colombia has made within the trade, investment, and foreign debt proposals contemplated by the EAI, and concludes with a consideration of the prospects for the EAI in the future.

While this collection will in all probability not produce a consensus on specific substantive issues, it does give the reader insights into the complex political, economic, social, and to some extent even the technical character of the efforts to expand world and regional trade. I hope this volume contributes to the dialogue on these important issues of freer trade, and increases the likelihood that we can move beyond dialogue to a fair and mutually beneficial set of agreements.

As a final word, I do wish to compliment my fellow collaborators in this project for their conscientious efforts to meet chapter purposes and timelines. I know all who read this volume will appreciate, as I do, their diligent and skillful efforts.

PART I

Global Trade and Regional Economic Development

1

The Free Trade Debate

Patrick Low

INTRODUCTION[1]

Little more than a decade ago, the General Agreement on Tariffs and Trade was unchallenged as the primary arbiter of trade relations among nations. It was not that GATT disciplines had been applied faultlessly in all circumstances for over thirty years,[2] nor that regional arrangements were nonexistent. But in those days there was no public debate as to whether regionalism and multilateralism were mutually destructive or reinforcing, nor any speculation that the GATT might be in terminal decline. Regionalism simply was not as important then as it has now become. And the GATT was not struggling then to bring home a multilateral trade negotiation—the Uruguay Round—whose extraordinary scope and ambition mean that a failure would be resounding, and plain for the world to see.

From its inception in 1947, the GATT had to deal with preferential trade, both in terms of tariff preferences and customs unions.[3] These were key exceptions to Article I of the GATT, which laid out the most favored nation (MFN) principle as the cornerstone of the GATT system. The MFN principle establishes that GATT contracting parties must extend the most favorable treatment accorded any country to all other GATT members. This, in short, is the rule of nondiscrimination.

In addition to the MFN exceptions that have been permitted over the years for tariff preferences (mostly in favor of developing countries), Article XXIV of GATT allows countries to establish customs unions and free trade areas, provided their purpose is to "facilitate trade between the constituent territories and not to raise barriers to the trade of other contracting parties with such territories."[4] The detailed rules of Article XXIV are designed to avoid the exclusionary manipulation of preferential arrangements at the expense of outsiders.

The GATT rules have only had limited influence on the shape of these arrangements and on the behavior of countries within them. This is partly because of imprecision in the provisions of Article XXIV, and also because there has been limited interest in granting the GATT full authority over regional arrangements. While the GATT rules have been geared to ensuring that the trade interests of outsiders are not unduly hurt by preferential regional agreements, the motivation of those inside them has often been political and strategic, and has therefore involved different priorities.

While there were relatively few regional arrangements in existence, and the European Community was the only one with a significant impact on the world trading scene, limited attention was given to the conflicts that might arise between regionalism and multilateralism. Moreover, until the 1980s, the United States was firmly committed to multilateralism, and pursued its trading interests with other countries accordingly. Forays into regional arrangements began with the Caribbean Basin Initiative in the early 1980s,[5] followed by a free trade agreement with Israel, the Canada–U.S. FTA, the North American Free Trade Agreement, and the Enterprise for the Americas Initiative. There are many other preferential arrangements in the region that are being initiated or reinforced, including the Central American common market, the Andean Pact, MERCOSUR, and an FTA between Chile and Mexico. Several other agreements among Latin American countries are in prospect. Globally, some 45 percent of world trade flows now take place under preferential arrangements of one sort or another.[6]

As prospective and actual regional arrangements continue to spring up with such frequency, one is bound to ask how successful these agreements will be in opening up markets and extending the benefits of specialization through trade. What do these kinds of agreements offer that the multilateral system fails to deliver? How much does it matter, for the future of global trading arrangements, that these agreements contravene the most basic tenet of the GATT system, that of nondiscrimination? Can they be characterized as stepping-stones toward a broader multilateral vision of international economic relations, toward a reborn GATT? These are among the questions explored in this chapter, and in the chapters that follow.

My next section discusses developments in the multilateral trading system, and examines why GATT disciplines have been increasingly called into question over the years, and why the Uruguay Round negotiations were not completed as planned. The section that follows then looks at regional trading arrangements in terms of what they have meant for international trade relations, where they stand in relation to the multilateral trading system, and what they may be expected to achieve by way of trade liberalization in the future. In the final section, there are some suggestions as to how policy makers might ensure that regional trade initiatives contribute to stable global economic relations.

MULTILATERALISM: NATURAL DECLINE OR MALIGN NEGLECT?

It is difficult in a short chapter to capture the complexity of circumstances leading to intensified pressure and a weakening of the GATT system. For these purposes, four factors that seem of particular relevance will be briefly mentioned.[7] First, broad economic and political changes have placed strains on existing institutions and challenged traditional assumptions underlying the way trade relations have been conducted among countries. A secular force at work is the relative decline of U.S. power and influence in global economic affairs. The authority and leadership of the United States underwrote the multilateral trading system for many years, but the commitment to do so appears to have waned. Whether by default or design, U.S. behavior has increasingly resembled that of the other major player in world trade, the EC, whose attitude toward GATT has always been equivocal. At the same time, relations between Japan and its major trading partners have come under considerable strain. This is in part because of the adjustment pressure that Japanese market penetration has caused in key sectors (such as autos and electronics), but also because of the belief that Japan somehow manages to benefit from open trading arrangements without offering adequate market access in return. A concern about some regional initiatives is that they may focus on finding ways of excluding Japan from the benefits of open trade.

With the end of the cold war, changed attitudes toward the trading system can also be explained by the diminution of strategic or geopolitical motivations for maintaining a coherent set of multilateral arrangements. Economic interests are now more prominent, and political arguments for supporting certain trading arrangements no longer carry much weight. In the GATT of the 1980s, this has been apparent in arguments over the rights and obligations of developing countries, and in numerous disputes between the United States and the European Community. Strains in the Japanese relationship have been played out mainly on a bilateral basis.

Second, unsatisfactory economic performance in different countries has undermined the commitment of some governments to open trading arrangements. The twin deficits (budget and trade) in the United States in the early 1980s led to a strong dollar and intense protectionist pressures. It was during this period that demands for reciprocity and an intense preoccupation with fair trade were at their height. Matters were not improved as economic recession took hold in many countries in the early 1990s. The direction of U.S. trade policy changed decisively in the 1980s, and spawned the "process protectionism" from which a growing number of countries may try to insulate themselves in future through safe-haven regional arrangements.

Third, the GATT system had been dogged for years by difficulties in certain sectors, notably agriculture, textiles and clothing, steel, autos, and electronics. GATT disciplines had either never really existed (as in agriculture, textiles, and clothing), or sectoral pressures were undermining basic GATT disciplines in such areas as safeguards, antidumping, and countervailing duties. New and innovative ways of frustrating trade were introduced that the GATT was ill-equipped to prevent. Two of the GATT's most important principles, nondiscrimination and the prohibition of quantitative restrictions, were looking increasingly tattered, as controlled exceptions to them became uncontrollable, or they were simply set aside.

Fourth, slippage in the observance of GATT disciplines was becoming acute precisely at the time that pressure was mounting for the GATT to assume responsibilities in the new areas of trade in services, intellectual property rights, and trade-related investment measures. There were deep divisions among GATT members on the appropriateness of including these matters on the GATT negotiating agenda, and the GATT was virtually paralyzed for three or four years from 1982 onwards as disagreements on these issues were played out in Geneva. The United States, with support from most industrial countries, eventually prevailed upon the GATT to take up these matters in the Uruguay Round.

The Uruguay Round Response

In a world of rapid change and uncertainty, protectionist pressure unprecedented since the Second World War, difficult economic circumstances, and diminishing faith in a multilateral approach to trade relations, governments of the major trading nations invested considerable effort in launching the Uruguay Round. The agenda for the round, which began in 1986, contained a negotiating mandate for virtually every old and new trade and nontrade issue that had been raised in GATT in the previous ten years.

How can the boldness of this endeavor be explained, in the light of the near-paralysis that plagued the GATT at this time? Some would say that talk was cheap, and that in accordance with the bicycle theory of policy management, the objective was to keep the machine upright, and not to worry about the direction in which it was pointed. Others would argue that the Uruguay Round was a far-sighted attempt to right all the wrongs of the system in one bold move.

In any event, the bicycle is wobbling a good deal, as the Uruguay Round was not completed on schedule at the end of 1990, and governments have continued to promise results but have failed to meet successive deadlines. Unsurprisingly, it has been the will of the EC and the United States that has determined the outcome. While ostensibly struggling to solve differences in agriculture, several other difficult issues have been left in abeyance. It is open to doubt that the political will exists to complete the negotiations, at least in terms of the agenda established when the Uruguay Round was launched.

Since the negotiations began, many developing countries have undertaken significant trade liberalization, heightening both their interest in stable international trading conditions and their frustration at the failure of the major trading powers to bring the negotiations to a successful conclusion. It is not the intention here to analyze potential Uruguay Round results, but rather to note that draft final texts on a multitude of issues offer some prospect of an improved trading environment, even though more could have been hoped for in several areas. Just as important, a successfully completed Uruguay Round would bring reductions of around 30 percent in existing tariff and nontariff barriers to trade.

To a degree, events overtook the Uruguay Round. The unexpected collapse of the Soviet Union seized the attention of policy makers, as did the Gulf War for a few brief months. At the same time, endogenous factors were also at work. In Europe, the EC had embarked on its 1992 program under the Single European Act, the Maastricht Treaty had been signed, the concept of the European Economic Area had been developed, and new accessions and association agreements were realized or in prospect. In North America, the Canada–U.S. FTA and NAFTA were negotiated, the EAI launched, and numerous framework agreements with Western Hemisphere countries signed. Were the major trading nations too preoccupied with these matters to attach the necessary priority to the Uruguay Round? Perhaps the temptation to downplay the Uruguay Round in all but words[8] was irresistible because no imminent crisis would follow from neglect of the multilateral process.

There is some irony in a situation where multilateral negotiations are delayed or set aside as regional initiatives attract attention, and then the regional results are held up as the consequence of failed multilateralism. Apart from the question of where an inconclusive Uruguay Round leaves the smaller members of the international trading community, it is important to consider the differences and similarities between prospective Uruguay Round results and the terms of regional agreements. Do regional arrangements fill in or compensate for the failings of the multilateral approach, or do they circumvent the problems? These issues are taken up next.

REGIONALISM: ANTIDOTE OR ILLUSION?

Regionalism and GATT

As already noted, the GATT allowed departures from the MFN principle at the outset for customs unions and free trade areas.[9] The exception was made in recognition of the fact that rigid strictures against these arrangements, which often responded to complex political and strategic imperatives as well as trade interests, would quickly create serious conflict between the GATT and its members. But from the GATT's perspective it was a risky compromise, because discrimination is inherent in regional arrangements.

There are three basic justifications underlying the GATT's insistence upon MFN treatment. First, the absence of discrimination makes for economic efficiency, in the sense that least-cost supply sources are generally accessible. Second, the MFN rule injects stability into trade relations. It avoids the inherent complexity and conflicts that are bound to arise where countries have to juggle a multiplicity of trade regimes in order to ensure that no parties feel cheated as the bargains they have struck are affected by later bargains struck with others. Third, the MFN rule makes it more costly for countries to reverse their liberal trade commitments, since they cannot pick and choose, and discriminate against those countries less able to defend their interests. The trouble with this last proposition, however, is that when the movement is in the opposite direction, toward trade liberalization, insistence on MFN treatment may have an inhibiting effect, and reduce the degree to which liberalization occurs.

Viner[10] showed a long time ago that geographically selective trade liberalization would have the combined effects of creating trade among participating countries and diverting trade from countries outside an arrangement. The degree of trade creation and trade diversion is an empirical matter, depending on preexisting trade patterns, the degree of differential competitive advantage in production among countries, the size of trade barriers selectively removed, and any effects on terms of trade from the liberalization. Countries within regional groupings benefit from trade creation, and also from trade diversion to the extent that diverted trade enters at lower prices following selective liberalization.

In this static analytical framework, however, the best that individual countries outside an arrangement can hope for is that they will not suffer from trade diversion. By definition, they cannot gain, they can only avoid losses. From a global perspective, "good" selective trade liberalization would mean that trade creation exceeds trade diversion in the aggregate. If third countries outside regional arrangements are to benefit at all when other countries enter into such agreements, it would have to be the result of the dynamic effects of trade liberalization, whereby growth and investment opportunities are created for the benefit of all. In practice, such benefits are difficult to measure, and to separate out from overall growth.

The relation between interregional and intraregional trade flows has, with the exception of the EC, been remarkably stable over the last thirty years, suggesting that regional arrangements have not had a large impact on the pattern of trade. This means that from an economic perspective, any important effects are dynamic in nature, and their magnitude and distribution remain uncertain.

There are three basic rules that regional arrangements are required to meet under GATT Article XXIV. First, upon formation of a customs union, barriers should not on the whole be higher or more restrictive than they were previously, and any duties increased above GATT-bound levels by a customs union member must be compensated for by other barrier reductions. Under a free trade agreement, it is assumed that there is no need for members to touch the trade regime facing third parties, since the constituent countries retain autonomy over external trade policies. The second GATT rule is that duties and other restrictive regulations should be removed on substantially all trade among the members of a customs union or free trade area. The third rule is that a time frame must be specified within which customs unions and free trade areas will pass from their interim, transitionary stage to full application.

The rule that the formation of customs unions should not introduce additional discrimination against third parties is not difficult to understand from a multilateral perspective, since increased external barriers would aggravate trade diversion. Perhaps an even better provision would be one that required the members of a regional agreement to compensate third parties for trade diversion, although there would doubtless be significant measurement problems and endless disputes about the appropriate level of compensation.

It is the rule about the complete elimination of trade barriers on substantially all trade that has created most difficulty in the many inconclusive examinations of regional trade agreements that have taken place in GATT over the years, and that is hard to justify in purely economic terms. As Johnson[11] noted some years ago, the theory of the second best tells us that there can be no presumption that more selective liberalization is better than less selective liberalization. Selective liberalization should only be pursued where it leads to trade creation, so why should the GATT insist on measures that are going to divert trade? The justification for this departure from economic logic is based on a political reality. Given the dynamics of regional agreements and the noneconomic objectives they generally serve, a rule that permitted selective trade liberalization would more likely be used to divert trade than to create it. This is identical to the political economy argument against made-to-measure interventions called for by the market imperfections modeled in the new international trade theories.[12]

Abstracting momentarily from political imperatives that might drive regional agreements, are there other justifications for preferring a regional to a multilateral approach? Considering the sacrifice of simplicity involved, the case would have to be made either in terms of procedural complications surrounding multilateralism, or in terms of the scope for more far-reaching agreements among a few like-minded countries. On the procedural front, it might be argued that GATT-type negotiations are cumbersome, time-consuming, and complex and carry high transactions costs, and that all this could be avoided at the regional level. The case is not convincing, since the reality in GATT is that negotiations always involve a handful of interested parties, and not the entire membership of over one hundred countries. The absence of timely agreement in the Uruguay Round reflects differences among the major players, and not the complications of seeking agreement among dozens of countries.

The validity of the more substantive point that a few like-minded countries might achieve higher levels of trade liberalization regionally than those attainable through the multilateral process, would have to be tested through a careful examination of regional agreements. There are two aspects to this question. First, if there are free riders and foot draggers at the multilateral level,[13] then a regional approach might yield better results. Second, to the extent that GATT does not cover issues that subgroups of countries wish to address, there is little alternative to a regional approach. It is just as possible, however, that instead of permitting countries to secure more liberal trade, the regional focus might indulge sectoral deals and market-sharing arrangements that would not pass muster in a multilateral setting.

Regionalism in the Western Hemisphere

The NAFTA is the most obvious benchmark against which to judge trends in regional integration in the Western Hemisphere.[14] Moreover, given the predominance of the United States in the region, it is the agreement to which all countries south of Mexico naturally look when they assess their interests in regional integration in general and the EAI in particular. Four questions to be considered in this connection are (1) how far does NAFTA liberalize trade; (2) to what degree are exclusionary, market-sharing deals to be found in the agreement; (3) has NAFTA solved problems bedeviling the Uruguay Round, or extended international cooperation to new areas; and (4) how far does a NAFTA-type arrangement correspond to the interests of countries under the EAI?

No attempt is made here to provide systematic answers to these questions, but a few brief comments will be made on each one. It appears that NAFTA makes significant strides in opening markets, although there are some exceptions and long phase-in periods before tariffs and other barriers reach zero. As far as tariffs are concerned, Mexico's reduction will be more significant on average, as they start from a higher base. The provisions on investment and trade in services represent advances on what was achieved in the Canada–U.S. FTA.

On the second question, exclusionary arrangements are mostly established through production-sharing arrangements embodied in NAFTA's rules of origin. Restrictive rules of origin in textiles and clothing and in the automobile sector require a high degree of domestic content before duty-free treatment can be accorded. There may be similar arrangements in other sectors, such as electronics. In addition, some agricultural products, including sugar, are subject to limited measures of liberalization. There is no mention of steel in NAFTA, but Mexico remains subject to antidumping complaints.

Several intractable problems in the Uruguay Round remain unresolved or have been avoided in NAFTA, such as the treatment of agriculture. As in the case of the Canada–U.S. FTA, it proved impossible to address antidumping, countervailing duties, or subsidy disciplines in any serious way. Mexico, like

Canada, secured a special dispute settlement mechanism for antidumping and countervailing duty cases, and Mexico was also required to change some of its antidumping provisions. It has been well documented how these policy instruments have been increasingly bent to protectionist ends, and used with growing frequency by several countries, including all three NAFTA signatories.[15] In this respect in particular, NAFTA has done less than what is promised should the Uruguay Round be completed.

Finally, the degree to which other Western Hemisphere countries will benefit from NAFTA-type arrangements with North America depends on their trade interests, the nature of the commitments that would be required, and various strategic and political considerations. As far as trade is concerned, smaller countries can expect to gain more than larger ones when they liberalize trade in each other's favor. But many Latin American countries do not trade as much with the United States as do Canada and Mexico, and most of what they trade is either free of duty (raw materials and primary products) or unlikely to receive better treatment under a regional agreement because of sensitivities in the United States (textiles and apparel, steel).[16] Moreover, to the extent that Latin American and Caribbean countries within the purview of the EAI would have to accommodate protectionist elements in an extended NAFTA in such sectors as agriculture, textiles and clothing, autos, energy, steel, and electronics, the benefits of closer association could be compromised, and the scope for extraregional investments narrowed.

The strategic and political arguments that might weigh with countries in the Western Hemisphere are, firstly, that if global trading arrangements look as though they are going to coalesce around a few large trading blocs, then small countries are going to want to guarantee a reasonable degree of access to one of the blocs. This is the safe-haven or "insurance policy" argument. Second, countries that have recently opened up to trade may see a benefit in using a regional agreement with North America as a means to pursue further trade liberalization. Or they may want to consolidate hard-won gains and make them more difficult to reverse. The first of these arguments rests on the failure of the multilateral system to protect the interests of small countries. The second objective could as easily be fulfilled under properly functioning multilateral arrangements as regional ones.

CONCLUSION

Regionalism is no substitute for multilateralism within the Western Hemisphere, especially for those countries with significant extraregional trade interests. The extent to which NAFTA-like arrangements offer a complement to more broadly based global arrangements depends on the content of such agreements. The more an FTA is bent to exclusionary ends by large countries within the region, the less its benefits to small countries. On the other hand, small countries will gain from arrangements that tie in their own liberalization efforts with secure access to large and diverse markets.

The assertion that regional agreements in the Western Hemisphere and elsewhere are a stepping-stone toward a rejuvenated global trading system, and not an obstacle to multilateralism, can be assessed with comparative ease. A progressive regional agreement that takes countries further and faster down the road of trade liberalization than they could go in GATT negotiations will be an open-ended agreement. There would be no reason to exclude newcomers from such an arrangement, nor to enter into complicated negotiations about sectoral deals and production sharing in order to specify the terms of accession. The conditions of accession would be predetermined, and all newcomers would have to do is meet the higher standards of open market access inside the agreement than those prevailing outside.

As discussed above, NAFTA, like other regional arrangements, embodies both extended trade liberalization and certain exclusionary features in sensitive sectors. In order to contain the latter, and work toward more liberal arrangements over time, it would seem essential to strengthen multilateral standards for regional arrangements, and maintain full accountability. Only in this way will regionalism genuinely complement multilateralism, rather than destabilize trade relations and reduce the gains from trade. Five steps are suggested.

First, work should be undertaken at the multilateral level to make the GATT criteria for regional agreements more operational. This requires a more precise definition, and where feasible quantification, of the standards that customs unions and free trade areas must meet. In particular, the concept of substantially all trade should be pinned down with greater precision, and a methodology established for ensuring that barriers are not raised against third parties, including through restrictive rules of origin. Consideration might also be given to the development of compensatory mechanisms that would apply beyond some threshold level of trade diversion.

Second, there should be a clause in all regional agreements that explicitly preserves the GATT rights of member countries. This is important where regional agreements do not cover all the ground covered by GATT, and would also help to guard against the dilution of GATT standards.

Third, there should be a commitment that where regional agreements go beyond the GATT in terms of establishing new fields of discipline, the parties will engage in multilateral consultation and negotiation to seek agreement on common approaches to the issues. This will make it easier in the future for regional agreements to mesh. At present, for example, there is nothing in the GATT about regional integration in the services sector, and the language on this in the draft Uruguay Round services agreement is vague on a number of key points. Similarly, innovations in such vital areas as antidumping law and practice should be held accountable, and fully applicable at the multilateral level.

Fourth, institutional mechanisms should be established to ensure the transparency and accountability of regional agreements at the multilateral level. This might mean that regional arrangements would be scrutinized on a systematic basis, much as the trade policies of GATT member countries are now under the Trade Policy Review Mechanism.

Finally, against a background of enforceable standards and rules for customs unions and free trade areas, the GATT's dispute settlement machinery should be available both to individual members of regional agreements and to third parties wishing to litigate against such agreements. Under NAFTA, for example, member countries retain the right to use the GATT's dispute settlement procedures.

NOTES

1. The views expressed here are those of the author and should not be attributed to the World Bank.

2. For example, the repeated failure of GATT to impose discipline in agriculture, or to prevent discrimination and the pervasive use of quantitative restrictions in textiles and clothing, have been well documented.

3. For a discussion of these original exceptions from the GATT's most favored nation principle, or the nondiscrimination rule, see Richard N. Gardner, *Sterling-Dollar Diplomacy in Current Perspective: The Origins and Prospects of Our International Economic Order* (New York: Columbia University Press, 1980).

4. Article XXIV, paragraph 4 of *The General Agreement on Tariffs and Trade* (Geneva: The General Agreement on Tariffs and Trade, 1986 edition).

5. Prior to this, in 1976, the United States had somewhat reluctantly introduced tariff preferences for developing countries under the Generalized System of Preferences. This was seen strictly as an exception to MFN arrangements.

6. Carlos Primo Braga and Alexander Yeats, "How Multilateral Trading Arrangements May Affect the Post-Uruguay Round World," Policy Research Working Paper No. 974 (Washington, D.C.: The World Bank, 1992).

7. A fuller discussion of these questions is to be found in a forthcoming book by the present author on U.S. trade policy and the future of GATT, commissioned by the Twentieth Century Fund of New York.

8. It will be recalled that the Uruguay Round was continually billed by the United States as its number one trade policy priority, even as enormous efforts went into completing the NAFTA negotiations in time for the Republican Party Convention in August 1992. Moreover, the heads of state of the Group of Seven (G-7) countries had singled out the Uruguay Round for special and urgent attention at the Houston, London, and Munich summits in 1990, 1991, and 1992.

9. When a customs union is established, its members agree to a common external tariff, while at the same time removing trade barriers among themselves. A free trade area, on the other hand, only involves the latter step, and each member country retains autonomy over its trade policies with respect to third parties. Rules of origin are, therefore, crucial in determining eligibility of goods for duty-free treatment in a free trade area.

10. Jacob Viner, *The Customs Union Issue* (New York: Carnegie Endowment for International Peace, 1950).

11. Harry G. Johnson, *Trade Negotiations and the New International Monetary System* (Leiden: A. W. Sijthoff, 1976).

12. Recent developments in the theory of international trade have shown that free trade may not be optimal in the presence of imperfectly competitive markets. Although there is nothing wrong with the theory, in practice it is often difficult to identify with precision the nature of the market imperfection and the appropriate response, leading to the political economy argument that interventions predicated on these arguments lend themselves to protectionist abuse. For a good brief discussion of these issues, see Paul Krugman, "Is Free Trade Passe?" *Journal of Economic Perspectives* 1, no. 2 (Fall 1987): 131–44.

13. For a discussion of the notions of free riders and foot draggers, see Gary Clyde Hufbauer and Jeffrey J. Schott, *Trading for Growth: The Next Round of Trade Negotiations*, Policy Analysis in International Economics No. 11 (Washington, D.C.: Institute for International Economics, 1985).

14. For discussions of NAFTA, see Gary Clyde Hufbauer and Jeffrey J. Schott, *North American Free Trade* (Washington, D.C.: Institute for International Economics, 1992); Carlos Primo Braga, "NAFTA and the Rest of the World," Nora Lustig, Barry P. Bosworth, and Robert Z. Lawrence, eds., *North American Free Trade: Assessing the Impact* (Washington, D.C.: The Brookings Institution, 1992); and Michael Hart, "North American Free Trade Agreement: The Elements Involved," *The World Economy* 14 (March 1991): 87.

15. Two excellent sources on antidumping are John H. Jackson and Edwin A. Vermulst, eds., *Antidumping Law and Practice: A Comparative Study* (Ann Arbor: University of Michigan Press, 1989), and Richard Boltuck and Robert Litan, eds., *Down in the Dumps: Administration of the Unfair Trade Laws* (Washington, D.C.: The Brookings Institution, 1991).

16. See John Whalley, "Expanding the North American Free Trade Agreement" (Paper prepared for the Institute for Policy Reform, Washington, D.C., August 1992).

2

Liberalizing Trade in the Western Hemisphere: Where Do We Want to Go, and How Do We Get There?

Ronald J. Wonnacott

INTRODUCTION

Set aside for now the detailed provisions that the United States has just nego-tiated in NAFTA with Canada and Mexico, and take a long look forward to where trade in the hemisphere is going. What sort of a trading system do we want in the Americas in ten to twenty years? And what broad negotiating prin-ciples do we need to get there? Is NAFTA consistent with these principles?

It is natural to interpret George Bush's vision of liberalized trade from Alaska to Cape Horn as one all-encompassing plurilateral free trade area of equal partners. But from the beginning, there were other possibilities. A second is a hub-and-spoke system that would develop if the United States, as the hub, were to sign separate bilateral free trade agreements with a sequence of spoke coun-tries. There are other possibilities, each representing some mixture of the first two. A clear appreciation of how the first two differ is essential to understanding any of the other more complex variations.

The August 1992 trilateral free trade agreement between Canada, Mexico, and the United States has apparently established a format very close to an expanding free trade area in which the United States and its partner countries will be trading freely, with the borders of each country open equally to trade with all of the others.

However, this agreement has not yet been ratified, and there is some risk—at least in Canada and the United States—that it will not be. If, say, Canada were to fail to ratify, leaving Mexico and the United States with a bilateral agreement, then in conjunction with the existing Canada–U.S. bilateral arrangement, a hub-and-spoke pattern would be established, with the U.S. hub having both a Canadian and Mexican spoke.[1] Thus, another reason for clearly understanding a hub-and-spoke system is to ensure that this is not erroneously viewed as an option that is roughly equivalent to an FTA. Finally, a hub-and-spoke system could develop if some new countries choose not to use the docking provision that would make them full partners in NAFTA, but are able somehow to liberalize some or all of their trade with the United States, or if the countries that now have gotten or are getting bilateral deals with Mexico choose not to dock into NAFTA.

OUTLINE OF THE CHAPTER

The next section describes existing trade flows among the nine largest trading countries in the hemisphere, and illustrates the broad differences between a plurilateral free trade area and a hub-and-spoke system, using Canada, Mexico, and the United States as the illustrative case.

Then there is a detailed comparison of the economics of a hub-and-spoke system versus an FTA. The economic effects of a plurilateral FTA are by now well known. In contrast, the economics of a hub-and-spoke system (sometimes called a system of overlapping free trade areas) is far more complex. One conclusion will be that, in comparison to a plurilateral FTA, a hub-and-spoke system can be expected to generate special benefits for the hub country, but even larger corresponding costs for the spokes, with the hub gaining at its partners' expense, and total collective income being reduced.

This comparison of a hub-and-spoke system to an FTA provides a preliminary answer to the question: Where should we be going? It also provides the foundation for addressing the other central question in this section on economics of a hub-and-spoke system: What happens to all countries involved if a hub-and-spoke system develops from scratch, that is, how does a hub-and-spoke system compare to the status quo? This would be the appropriate question if, for example, the United States were to fail to ratify NAFTA, and, after its demise, were eventually to return to negotiating bilateral agreements with other countries in the hemisphere.

The "Where Should We Be Going" section examines the specific interests in the trading regime that develops for each of the countries that have already embarked on liberalizing their trade—Canada, Mexico, and the United States. Of particular concern is the interest of the United States. Even though the analysis in this section indicates that the United States would be the apparent beneficiary of a hub-and-spoke system, the following section addresses a number of reasons for the United States to reject it. This section thus provides a more complete answer to our first broad question: Where do we want to go?

It addresses the other key question: How do we get there? The straightforward answer is to negotiate an expanding plurilateral free trade area by negotiating only the complete ascension into NAFTA of new applicant countries. However, there are certain important guidelines for even the simplest form of such a negotiation. As it stands, NAFTA is not sufficiently precise on this issue.

Finally, in examining the problems that arise in hub-and-spoke systems, we make no claim that this will be *the* issue in trade policy in the 1990s. It could be, especially in view of hub-and-spoke developments in Europe. However, there will be other important trade-related issues that will have to be dealt with as well, such as the development and international transfer of technology.

EXISTING TRADE AND ALTERNATIVE WAYS IT MAY BE LIBERALIZED

Figure 2.1 shows trade among Canada, Mexico, and the United States, and Table 2.1 extends this to include the six next largest trading countries in the hemisphere. Note how small two-way trade is between Mexico and Canada ($2.1 billion) even though both have a very large trading relationship with the United States. For example, Canada's trade with Mexico is only slightly more than 1 percent of its trade with the United States. Nonetheless, that small Canada-Mexico trade is still the Western Hemisphere's largest bilateral relationship, excluding those in which the United States participates.

These trade flows suggest that each country's primary interest in liberalizing its trade is to get free trade with the United States. This follows not only because the United States is its largest trading partner, but also because of the potential productivity gains from trading with a country with high income and advanced technology. When a country gets free trade with the United States, its percentage income gains can be very large, running well up into triple digits even if it closes only a small proportion of the present productivity gap between itself and the United States. (A small amount of closure should be easy, but further closure would become increasingly difficult.)

While no one would predict with assurance that growth in Mexico (and other countries in the hemisphere that similarly are able to move to an open, market-oriented economy and get free trade with the United States) will exceed the remarkable performance of the small dragons in Southeast Asia, it could happen. Like these dragons, Mexico has introduced trade- and market-oriented policies. But it has two advantages the dragons have not: free access to the huge U.S. market and geographical proximity to that market (so that gains from trade that might otherwise be dissipated in transportation costs can instead be translated into higher Mexican income).

Figure 2.1(b) shows the plurilateral FTA model, the one that has been closely—though not precisely—followed in the NAFTA negotiations. Note that this covers all the trade flows among the three countries. Figure 2.1(c) shows the hub-and-spoke system that would result if Canada fails to ratify the agreement, leaving Mexico and the United States with a bilateral agreement. The U.S. hub would trade freely with each spoke, but trade between the two spokes—Canada and Mexico—would not be free, as shown by the broken line. The

Figure 2.1
Trade Among Canada, Mexico, and the United States and Two Options for Liberalizing This Trade

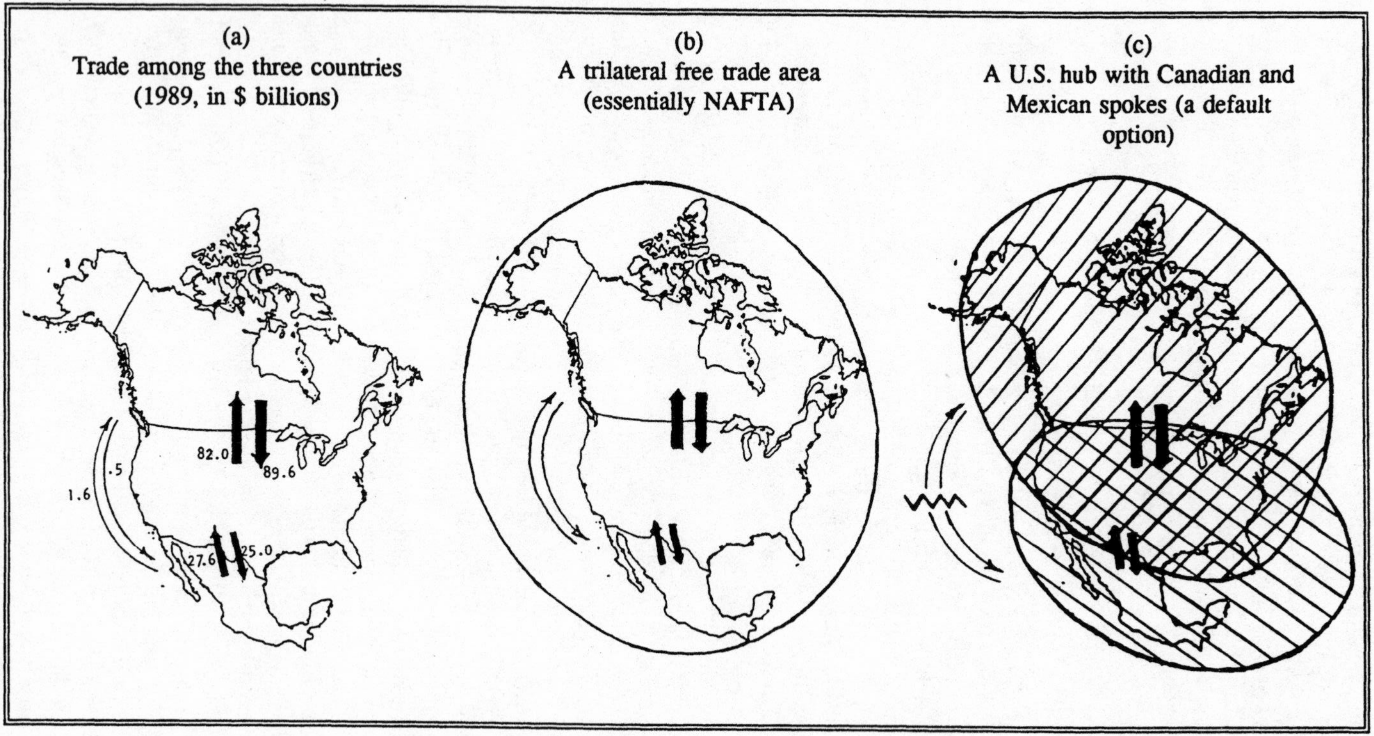

(a)
Trade among the three countries
(1989, in $ billions)

89.6
82.0
25.0
27.6
1.6
.5

(b)
A trilateral free trade area
(essentially NAFTA)

(c)
A U.S. hub with Canadian and
Mexican spokes (a default
option)

Table 2.1
Trade Among the Nine Largest Trading Countries in the Hemisphere, 1989, in Billions of U.S. Dollars

Exporting Country	Importing Country									Total (world)
	United States	Canada	Mexico	Brazil	Venezuela	Colombia	Argentina	Chile	Ecuador	
United States		82.0	25.0	4.8	3.0	1.9	1.0	1.4	0.6	369.0
Canada	89.6		0.5	0.5	0.1	0.2		0.1		121.0
Mexico	27.6	1.6		0.2	0.1	0.1			0.1	37.1
Brazil	9.0	1.1	0.4		0.3	0.2	0.7	0.7	0.2	33.0
Venezuela	7.2	0.6		0.2		0.3		0.2		12.0
Colombia	2.7	0.2			0.3		0.1	0.1	0.1	5.7
Argentina	1.5	0.1	0.2	1.1		0.1		0.4		10.0
Chile	1.5	0.2		0.4		0.1	0.2			8.2
Ecuador	1.6	0.2						0.1		2.4
Total (world)	493.0	129.0	33.7	20.0	7.6	5.0	4.2	6.5	1.9	

Note: All data are import figures except for the last column and U.S. and Canadian exports to Latin America. In a few cases, inconsistencies in the data—for example, between the export figure of one country and the corresponding import figure of its trading partner—have had to be arbitrarily resolved. Thus, beyond those for Canada and the United States, these data do not have a high degree of accuracy. Since the data have been rounded to the nearest $100 million, any trade flow of less than $50 million does not appear.

Source: International Monetary Fund, *Direction of Trade Statistics, 1991* (Washington, D.C., 1991).

small amount of Canada-Mexico trade has led many commentators to conclude that there would be little difference in the two regimes.

This is not in fact the case, for a number of reasons identified in this study.
But for now, one is obvious: The larger the number of countries that participate, the greater would be the difference, as shown in Figure 2.2(a), where
broken lines again show the rapidly multiplying trade barriers remaining between spokes as more are added—barriers that would not exist in a plurilateral
FTA. (Some barriers are not even shown, such as the tariff-ridden relationships
that would remain between Canada and Mexico and between Chile and Brazil.
With just six spokes, there would be no less than 15 tariff-ridden relationships.)
While the United States would see free trade as it looked out over the hemisphere, any of the spokes would see free trade as it looked toward the United
States, but a byzantine maze of remaining trade barriers as it looked toward the
other spokes. Compare this to a plurilateral free trade area covering all countries, in which all would see free trade in looking toward any of the others.

Figure 2.2(b) shows one of the many ways of combining the two regimes.
The United States has a spoke agreement with Canada, and another spoke
agreement with a full Latin American free trade area. Such combinations raise
a number of very special problems—especially, in this case, for Canada.

With this broadbrush comparison of the two regimes in hand, we now turn
to a detailed comparison of their economic effects.

THE ECONOMICS OF A HUB-AND-SPOKE SYSTEM VERSUS AN EXPANDING FTA

In this comparison of trading regimes, the U.S. hub and its trading partners
will take very different views.

For a U.S. Partner

Under an expanding FTA, each U.S. partner, such as Canada, would expect

1. the gains from free trade with the United States, *augmented by*
2. the later, additional gains from free trade with new countries like Mexico as each
   signs into the expanding FTA.

On the other hand, in a hub-and-spoke system, each U.S. partner would
acquire essentially the same gains from trade in (1) above when it signs its own
bilateral agreement with the United States; however, it would not get the full
gains in (2)—indeed, it could possibly even incur losses—as the United States
goes on to sign bilateral agreements with new spoke partners. Thus, U.S. trading partners will prefer an expanding FTA.

To illustrate: If the United States, with its Canadian bilateral agreement now
in place, goes on to sign a bilateral agreement with Mexico, Canada would not

Figure 2.2
How Complications Increase with the Number of Spokes

(a)

The U.S. hub with four spokes

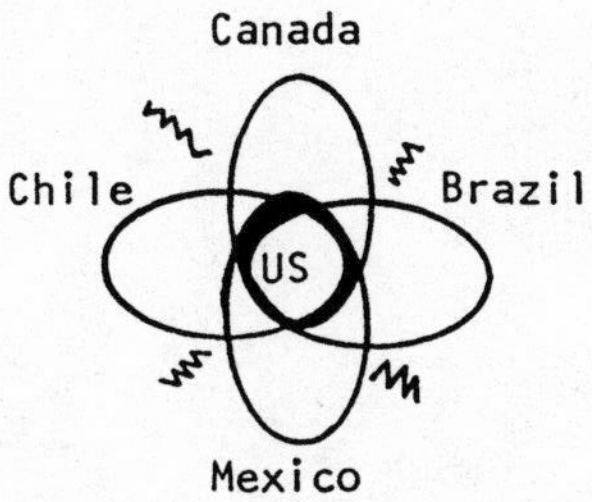

(b)

A U.S. hub with two spokes--Canada and a
Latin-American FTA

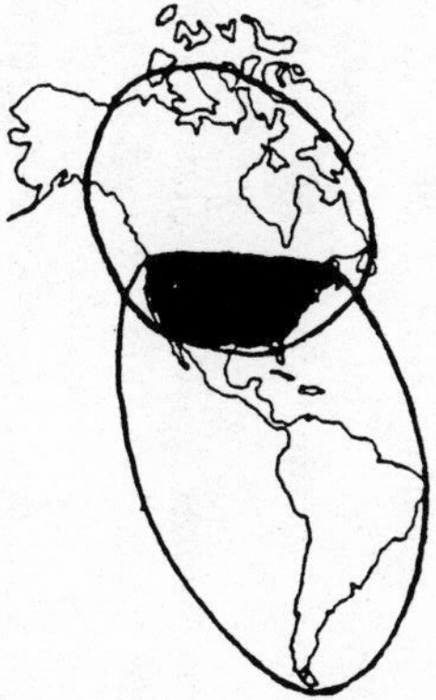

get the FTA benefits of free access to the Mexican market; instead Canada would get worse access because of the discrimination in the Mexican market it would have to face in competition with the United States. (Canadian exports to Mexico would still have to pay a Mexican tariff, whereas U.S. exports to Mexico would not.) Moreover, Canadian firms would have difficulty competing for another reason: They would not get the FTA benefits of less expensive duty-free Mexican inputs that would make them more competitive in world markets. Instead they would have to face stronger competition in North America and elsewhere from U.S. firms that would be able to acquire these low-cost inputs.

The more bilateral spokes the United States were to add, the wider the discrimination and the greater the consequent erosion of gains Canada would have to face. It is even conceivable that its initial gains from its own bilateral free trade agreement with the United States could be more than offset by second-stage costs down the road, leaving it worse off than before this process began. On the other hand, it is also possible that its second-stage costs could be more than offset if the analysis is broadened to take into account the indirect spillover benefits to Canada from exporting more to the new spokes, which might well be expanding rapidly due to their free trade with the United States. But whether an existing spoke such as Canada would benefit or lose overall once these second-stage effects are taken into account, the broad conclusion remains: It would benefit more from participating in an expanding FTA.

For the U.S. Hub

As it adds new spoke partners, the U.S. hub would acquire not only the benefits of an FTA—free access to the market of each—but also the benefit from getting preference in each spoke market in competition with all other spokes. Moreover, the U.S. hub would get another advantage not available in an FTA, because its producers alone would get duty-free inputs from all other participating countries. These special advantages for the United States—not available to its spoke partners—would make it a preferred location for investment, with the tax and other benefits this implies. This can be seen from another point of view: Any free trade agreement provides a location advantage for participating countries. In a hub-and-spoke system, the United States alone would fully realize this advantage because it alone would be participating in all the bilateral free trade agreements.

As an example of the special preference the United States would enjoy in each spoke market, a spoke bilateral with Mexico would give the United States preference in the Mexican market in competition with Canada. At the same time, its bilateral with Canada would give the United States preference in the Canadian market in competition with Mexico. As the United States adds more spoke bilaterals, it would benefit from more and more of these preferences. But in comparison with an FTA, any such U.S. gain would come at even greater expense to its spoke partner. This follows, under standard assumptions, from the lower level of efficiency and income in a hub-and-spoke system because it would have more remaining trade barriers. Thus, in comparing this system to an FTA, the gain to the hub-and-spoke winner (the U.S. hub) would be exceeded by the losses to the losers (the spokes). Moreover, this conflict in the interests of the U.S. hub and its spoke partners would be transparent, since the preferential advantages the United States would acquire in a hub-and-spoke system would be recognized by its spoke partners as the discrimination that they would have to face.

Why Would There Be Any New Applicants for Spoke Status?

As a hub-and-spoke system develops, why would new countries seek a spoke bilateral agreement with the United States? One answer is that a prospective new spoke country may, of course, be short-sighted, seeing only the immediate benefit of its own free trade with the United States, but not the subsequent buildup of costs as the United States adds new spokes. However, there is an even more fundamental reason that it might be willing to say yes, since it would have an incentive to do so even if it were to fully foresee the accumulating costs, and indeed even if it were able to foresee that costs down the road would exceed its initial free trade gains. The reason is that essentially all the new spoke's decision would do is give it benefits of free trade with the United States. If it says yes, it would get these benefits, which in the case of Latin American countries, may be very large; if it says no, it would not. It will have to face the costs of being discriminated against as the United States goes on to add new spokes—whether or not it decides to participate in this process.

Beyond this analysis, there may be a further incentive for a country to say yes if it is offered a spoke bilateral and views it as the only way of liberalizing its trade with a large and wealthy hub with which it already trades heavily. The prospective spoke may view such a bilateral as the only way to reduce the risks that its existing trade will be subjected to protective action by the hub. For example, Mexico has viewed a bilateral free trade agreement with the United States as a way of reducing the risk of being the target of 301 or some other form of U.S. unilateral action. Under Section 301 of the Trade Act, the U.S. government can impose penalties on imports from a country whose government is judged to be engaged in unfair trade practices. Thus, like Canada in the last decade, its objective is not just to get better access to the U.S. market, but also to reduce the risk of having its existing access damaged by unilateral U.S. action.

What Defense Do Spoke Countries Have?

A spoke country could eliminate one problem it would face—the continuing high cost of inputs from other spokes that would make it less competitive with the United States—by unilaterally removing its own tariff, thereby providing its industry with duty-free inputs from the other spokes. Why wouldn't it do this? It might, but this would not solve its other problem—the discrimination its exports would have to face in other spoke markets in competition with the United States.

If removing its own tariff is in the interests of each spoke country, why wouldn't they all do it? If they did, the discrimination each would face in other spoke markets would disappear. In effect, such unilateral action independently taken by all spokes acting in their own interest would transform a hub-and-spoke system into an FTA. Why wouldn't this just happen?

One reason is that, for some countries, unilateral tariff elimination may, in fact, not be in their economic interest; such a country might, for example, be thereby giving up tariffs that have been providing it with a terms of trade benefit. (By raising the domestic price of its imports, its tariff would have been reducing the quantity it has been purchasing, and a strong enough effect of this kind may have reduced the world price that it has been charged by foreign suppliers.) But even if it is in the individual interest of each, there is another reason: One cannot expect spoke countries to unilaterally cut their tariffs for the same reasons that countries have not unilaterally removed their tariffs in the past, even though it may have been in the individual interest of each to do so. These reasons include the political difficulties in selling any policy of "making concessions" (removing its own tariff) without requiring the same concessions from its trading partners, especially when the domestic producers hurt by this policy vote against it, while the consumers who benefit from it have a more diffuse interest and often vote on other issues. Finally, even if all countries were to embark on this unilateral policy, this would not completely succeed in transforming the system into an FTA for esoteric reasons that have to do with rules of origin.[2]

Another option for two spokes might be a bilateral FTA. For example, when the United States was initially considering a bilateral agreement with Mexico, it was suggested that Mexico and Canada could transform the resulting hub-and-spoke system into a trilateral FTA by negotiating their own bilateral agreement. Because each spoke would be getting a reduction in the other's tariffs as it reduced its own, this would be politically more feasible, and less likely to generate important terms of trade damage. However, the rule of origin problem would remain, along with the complications that would remain if the two spoke bilaterals with the U.S. hub were inconsistent (for example, no tariffs for Canadian goods entering the United States, but 2 percent tariffs on Mexican goods). Moreover, this "solution by adding bilaterals" becomes quickly impossible if the number of spokes increases. (Consider the large number of bilaterals that would be required in Figure 2.2(a), with each bilateral removing only one of the broken line sets of trade barriers, some of which are shown and some of which are not.) For all these reasons, the transformation of a hub-and-spoke system into one plurilateral FTA would require a plurilateral negotiation by all the spokes and the hub. And no matter how desirable they may view this, it may not happen because of its low placement on their list of negotiating priorities. Furthermore, the best, but far from guaranteed, possible outcome of such a negotiation would be the trilateral FTA they could have negotiated in the first place.

WHERE SHOULD WE BE GOING? THE INTERESTS OF CANADA, MEXICO, AND THE UNITED STATES

The Canadian Interest

There are several reasons why Canada should ratify the negotiated trilateral FTA, rather than failing to do so and thus allowing a hub-and-spoke system to develop. The first has already been explained in detail: It is preferable for Canadian firms to acquire lower-cost Mexican inputs and better access to the Mexican market under NAFTA, than to face worse access in a hub-and-spoke system. Second, failure to ratify, reducing NAFTA to a Mexico–U.S. bilateral, would mean that Canada would be sideswiped, insofar as Mexico's access to the U.S. market would be better than Canada's. An example is government procurement, where NAFTA gives Mexico and Canada better access to U.S. contracts than Canada has been receiving under the Canada–U.S. FTA. If Canada were to drop out of NAFTA, even if it remained in the FTA it could face discrimination in bidding on U.S. contracts in competition with Mexico.

Indeed, it can be argued that Canadians, whether they think NAFTA will benefit Canada or not, have had little choice but to participate. Once the United States and Mexico decided to go ahead, it became worse for Canada to stay away than to participate. In this respect, it has been like the Uruguay Round. It hasn't mattered whether Canadians liked it or not; it would have been worse to stay away. The reason is the same in both cases: the high cost of being an outsider when trading partners are liberalizing their trade.

There is another very special Canadian concern about a hub-and-spoke system. Suppose that Canada were to fail to ratify NAFTA, and a hub-and-spoke system were then to develop, not one country at a time, but instead in blocs. For example, suppose the United States then goes on to expand its remaining FTA with Mexico by including other Latin American countries, as in Figure 2.2(b). A similar outcome would occur if, following a collapse in NAFTA due to a U.S. failure to ratify, Mexico and other Latin American countries were to create an FTA that then negotiated a bilateral agreement with the United States. With Canada then left as an outsider to this new large spoke agreement, all the hub-and-spoke problems described so far would apply to Canada in spades.[3] The discrimination and competitive problems Canada would face would be far worse than those it would face even in a hub-and-spoke system in which each of these same Latin American countries were an individual spoke.[4] In my judgment, just preventing this outcome[5] has alone been a sufficient reason for Canada to participate in an expanding hemispheric FTA.

There is a further Canadian concern in maintaining trade and political balance. The addition of Mexico to an expanding free trade area—especially if it is augmented by the addition of other Latin American countries later—may be preferred by Canadians because it would provide some counterbalance to the weight and influence of the United States in the existing Canada–U.S. FTA. Compare this to a hub-and-spoke regime in which the United States, as the hub country, might be able to put a great deal of pressure on one spoke country at a time through threatened modification or reinterpretation of its bilateral agreement with that country, and thus be able to strengthen its already dominant position in the hemisphere.

U.S. dominance can occur at three levels. First, because of its size and wealth, the United States will dominate the Americas whatever the trade regime may be. Second, under a hub-and-spoke system, the United States would dominate further because it would acquire preferences where spoke countries would face discrimination—even if it does not use its hub position to exert pressure on its bilateral partners one at a time. Third, if, as a hub, it does exert this sort of pressure, it will be able to strengthen its dominant role even further.

The Mexican Interest

Mexico and other potential U.S. partners in the hemisphere have the same reasons for rejecting a hub-and-spoke development as Canada. For example, Mexico would find itself in exactly the same spoke situation as Canada, facing losses from discrimination in other spoke markets—an increasingly serious problem were the United States to continue to sign spoke bilaterals with other countries like Chile or Brazil. Moreover, Mexico should ask: If the United States continues to extend its free trade domain with a sequence of spoke bilaterals rather than within the disciplines and consistency imposed by the expansion of an FTA, what is to prevent Mexico from being sideswiped down the road by U.S. concessions to other Latin American countries of better access to its market than Mexico would be receiving? Because these problems for Mexicans would be similar to those already described for Canadians, they will not all be repeated here. But taken together, they make a strong case for Mexico to prefer an expanding FTA.

The U.S. Interest

There are also reasons why a hub-and-spoke arrangement is not in the interests of the United States, even though it would be the apparent beneficiary because of the special preferences it would receive. Offsetting these benefits, however, would be the costs to the United States—as well as to its spoke partners—because, compared to an FTA, a hub-and-spoke system would be a more complex trading network. Thus there would be a waste of extra time and effort that management, economists, lawyers, accountants, and so forth would have to devote to determining the least expensive trade and investment patterns throughout the maze of trade restrictions between spokes. As an example, it would become profitable to redirect some Mexican-Canadian trade into a duty-free routing through the U.S. hub. True, if a hub-and-spoke system were extended throughout South America, it is unlikely that Argentine-Brazilian trade would be similarly routed through the United States, since, in this case, higher transportation costs would almost certainly more than offset any tariff savings from the duty-free U.S. route. Nonetheless, there are many intermediate cases. For example, should some Brazil-Canada trade be redirected through the duty-free United States? While the extra time and effort that would go into answering such questions would provide a private payoff to lawyers, economists, accountants, and the trading firms hiring them, from a broader point of view it would be an unnecessary waste of these resources.

This waste of resources in extra administrative costs in a hub-and-spoke system would go hand-in-hand with a similar waste of resources due to the higher transportation costs that would be unnecessarily incurred, for example, from rerouting some Brazil-Canada trade through the United States. Such administrative and transport waste of resources would be above and beyond the waste and inefficiency already described in Section 3.

There would also be an unnecessary waste of resources in a hub-and-spoke system because of rent seeking. For example, as a hub-and-spoke system develops, the question will arise: Which country will be next? Rent-seeking firms in the hub may try to influence that decision in order to maximize the special preferential benefits they receive. The argument here is parallel to the traditional one in which rent-seeking firms seek to establish special benefits from the creation of, say, a monopoly position. Both preference in a foreign market and a domestic monopoly position are created by restricting entry of competitors; in the case described here of trade preference that U.S. firms are seeking in spoke markets, the restriction is on the entry of competitors from other spokes. In either case, rent seeking represents a social waste even though it may provide a benefit to the firms that engage in this activity.[6]

The waste described so far would occur even if the U.S. hub were to have consistent—indeed, identical—bilateral agreements with all of the spokes, for example, zero tariffs on its trade with all spokes, rather than, say, zero with some and 2 percent with others. However, in practice, independently negotiated spoke bilaterals may well be inconsistent; in this event, the maze would become even more complex, and the waste from rent seeking—along with excess administrative and transport cost—would be even greater.

Finally, managed trade may be easier to negotiate in a bilateral agreement than in a plurilateral FTA, and this will involve a cost insofar as managed trade deters specialization in response to comparative advantage and economies of scale.

Because a hub-and-spoke system would be more wasteful than an FTA, and accordingly would lead to a lower collective real income level, the assessment of a hub-and-spoke system by participating countries becomes even less favorable. This means that a hub-and-spoke system is likely to be even worse for spoke countries than implied earlier in the chapter. More important, it can no longer be convincingly argued that the hub—in this case, the United States— would prefer such a system to an FTA.

In addition, the United States has broader political economy reasons for avoiding a hub-and-spoke system. It would not be in the foreign policy interest of the United States to be seen as increasing its economic dominance in the hemisphere by participating in a hub-and-spoke trading structure that would leave markets in the Americas carved up into a patchwork of what the United States would rightly view as preferences but that its partner countries would correctly view as discrimination. Because the preferences built into such a system would benefit the United States at the expense of its partners in the hemisphere, a hub-and-spoke system would not be an equal opportunity partnership. The level playing field argument, so often abused in other contexts in the past, could then be used with considerable justification against the United States, because the rules of the trading regime itself would be biased in the United States' favor.

Another U.S. problem in a hub-and-spoke regime would arise if there were to be more applicants for U.S. bilateral agreements than U.S. negotiating resources could accommodate. The United States would then be forced to discriminate (in saying yes to some countries, no to others) in offering a negotiation that would itself be discriminatory.

A final disadvantage of a hub-and-spoke regime for the United States is that it could strengthen U.S. protectionism and thereby weaken the prospects for worldwide trade liberalization. The reason is that the U.S. administration, the major promoter and supporter of multilateral free trade (MFT) in the past, might encounter increased resistance from U.S. business interests because MFT would strip away the special preferential benefits they would be getting from a hub-and-spoke system. This raises the possibility that a hub-and-spoke configuration might encourage a new U.S. protectionism that would seek to protect U.S. firms against foreign competition, not just in the domestic U.S. market as always, but *also in the markets of spoke countries*, where U.S. exporters would be protected by preferential treatment. The problem with such a new U.S. "domestic-export protectionism" is that it might be able to masquerade as free trade because it would be the defense of a set of existing free trade agreements. But it would still be a damaging form of protectionism, insofar as it might be used to resist the two more appropriate objectives of U.S. trade policy—namely, an expanding hemispheric FTA and multilateral free trade in the GATT.[7]

HOW TO GET THERE? ARE WE ON THE RIGHT TRACK? OBSERVATIONS ON RATIFICATION AND FUTURE NEGOTIATIONS

Since NAFTA is essentially a plurilateral FTA, it has been the appropriate way to go. It is now important for all three countries to ratify it and to remain firm in their present commitment to plurilateral free trade. This means that key roles will now be played by Canada in ratifying NAFTA and thus preventing the present trilateral arrangement from degenerating into a hub-and-spoke system,[8] and by the United States in ensuring that such a system will not develop in the future. The United States can do so by rejecting any future bilateral overtures by other countries in the hemisphere and insisting that they join the existing plurilateral FTA instead. In that respect, NAFTA's ascension clause (its docking provision) is important, because it provides a relatively quick procedure for allowing new members to join, and this minimizes the problem of apparent discrimination that could arise if the entry of some countries has to be delayed in favor of others.

It is critical that the United States and its trading partners maintain their vision of an expanding, nondiscriminatory[9] FTA in the Americas. It has been that sort of vision of a freely trading world, rather than a cold calculation of what is in its own narrow economic interest, that has led the United States to promote and support multilateral free trade. That is the way the world should trade; it is in the collective interest of all countries. That vision of unrestricted trade is the one that the United States should continue to hold for the hemisphere.

Nonetheless, the conclusion of this chapter is that even if the United States *were* to reduce its decision to a narrow calculation of its own economic interest, this could still lead it, on balance, to prefer an expanding FTA. In assessing the alternative hub-and-spoke system, it is very difficult to argue that the preferential advantages it would provide the United States would offset the costs, both direct and indirect, from its trade-distorting inefficiencies and from its other offensive characteristics.

In my view, another negotiating guideline should be that the existing FTA not be substantially renegotiated every time a new applicant nation or group of nations is to be included. Not only might such a reopening seriously inflate negotiating costs; more importantly, a renegotiation of provisions might unnecessarily drag an FTA back into the political arena of the existing FTA partners. This point, now obvious in the Canadian case, seems particularly important for the present Mexican administration, which is apparently attempting to lock in trade and other reforms so that they cannot easily be reversed by future governments. Thus, it has a substantial interest in ensuring that NAFTA will not be substantially renegotiated in the future.

Why then did not Mexico just dock into the Canada–U.S. FTA without any of the renegotiation of that agreement that took place? There appear to have been two reasons, in addition to protectionist pressure from domestic U.S. sectors—in particular, autos and textiles, in which rules of origin were renegotiated. First, Mexico could not accept some of the energy provisions of the FTA; second, the United States required an agreement that would cover not only the existing developed partner (Canada) but also developing partners such as Mexico. With Mexico now included, substantial further renegotiation for prospective new developing members is no longer required. Indeed, NAFTA's docking-in provision to include further new applicants tacitly assumes that substantial renegotiation will not take place.

Nonetheless, some renegotiation will likely be requested by new applicants. What should the guidelines be? In my view, there are two. First, any change should further liberalize trade, rather than protect. Second, any change must be acceptable to all existing partners. In the NAFTA renegotiation of the original Canada–U.S. FTA neither of these guidelines was satisfied in the changes in rules of origin negotiated in autos and apparel, both of which increased protection against third countries and were opposed by Canada (although an eventual compromise agreement on these issues was achieved). On the other hand, both of these guidelines were satisfied in the greater access the United States provided to its partners in bidding on government procurement contracts. Since it is difficult for changes to satisfy both of these guidelines—and it will become more and more difficult in the future as the number of existing members that must be unanimous increases—such changes would be rare.[10] But on such rare occasions, these guidelines would allow the far from perfect NAFTA to be improved—an important objective in itself.

In a very important sense, the sequencing of trade liberalization in the hemisphere has been very fortunate: Canada–U.S. first, with an agreement covering by far the largest trading relationship; and Mexico, the next largest trading country in the hemisphere, included next. This has minimized the pressure at each stage to change the existing agreement. To see this from another point of view, suppose that the first hemispheric FTA had been an agreement negotiated by the United States with Brazil, or with Chile, or even with Mexico. Expanding such an agreement to include Canada might well have required a much more substantial set of changes to accommodate the requirements of Canada–U.S. trade, the largest trade flow in the world.

NOTES

1. The overlapping FTA or hub-and-spoke concept is the same as the two-sided triangle examined in Ronald J. Wonnacott, "Canada's Future in a World of Trade Blocs: A Proposal," *Canadian Public Policy* 1 (1975): 118–30; and Ronald J. Wonnacott, "Controlling Trade and Foreign Investment in the Canadian Economy: Some Proposals," Presidential Address to the Canadian Economics Association, *Canadian Journal of Economics* 15 (1982): 567–85. It is also essentially the same problem as the U.S. star with partner countries at the points described by Yung C. Park and Jung Ho

Yoo, "More Free Trade Areas: A Korean Perspective," in Jeffrey J. Schott, ed., *Free Trade Areas and U.S. Trade Policy* (Washington, D.C.: Institute for International Economics, 1989), 141–58. It was first called the hub-and-spoke problem by Richard G. Lipsey, *Canada and the U.S.–Mexico Free Trade Dance: Wallflower or Partner?* (Toronto: C. D. Howe Institute Commentary No. 20, 1990); Richard G. Lipsey, "The Case for Trilateralism," in Steven Globerman, *Continental Accord: North American Economic Integration* (Vancouver: The Fraser Institute, 1991), 89–124; and Ronald J. Wonnacott, *Canada and the U.S.–Mexico Free Trade Negotiations* (Toronto: C. D. Howe Institute Commentary No. 21, 1990). Ronald J. Wonnacott, *The Economics of Overlapping Free Trade Areas and the Mexican Challenge* (Toronto and Washington, D.C.: C. D. Howe Institute and National Planning Association, 1991) provided a detailed statement of some of the issues involved in a study that has been heavily drawn upon in this chapter. Finally, Carsten Kowalczyk and Ronald J. Wonnacott, in "Hubs and Spokes, and Free Trade in the Americas," University of Western Ontario, Department of Economics Research Report No. 9209, 1992, have developed a theoretical model to analyze such a system.

2. To illustrate, suppose there is a Canada–Mexico–U.S. FTA with a 50 percent rule of origin. A good with 25 percent U.S. content and 25 percent Mexican content would enter Canada from Mexico duty-free. But this good would not enter Canada from Mexico duty-free if there were instead a U.S. hub with Canadian and Mexican spokes, and Canada and Mexico were each to unilaterally eliminate its tariffs against the other, subject to the same 50 percent rule of origin; obviously this good could not enter Canada duty-free from Mexico since it would not have 50 percent Mexican content.

Moreover, this problem cannot be resolved by a unilateral redefinition of rules of origin by Canada, and by Mexico. To create an FTA in this way requires the U.S. hub to redefine its rules of origin as well. Furthermore, each unilateral removal by a spoke of its tariffs against other spokes would violate the GATT's MFN requirement in Article I.1 because this concession would be provided only to other spokes rather than to all countries.

But wouldn't these problems be avoided and the system transformed into an FTA if each spoke were to unilaterally eliminate its tariffs not just against other spokes, but against all countries, with no rules of origin required? Even in the unlikely circumstances that such a policy were politically feasible, it would not yield the same outcome as an FTA, since spokes would have removed their tariffs not only against each other, but also against all outside fourth countries. Moreover, the U.S. hub would likely object to this, since it would damage U.S. firms by removing the preference they would be getting in each spoke market not only against other spokes, but also against outside fourth countries. Thus, no matter which of these two unilateral routes the spokes might take, the U.S. hub would in some way become involved.

3. For example, Canada would not just face the discrimination described above in the Mexican market in competition with the United States; instead it would face discrimination in each Latin American market in competition with the United States and all other Latin American countries. Moreover, Canada would suffer in competition with the United States and all Latin American countries because they would all be getting inexpensive imports from each other.

4. If the whole Latin American FTA were to be one spoke, Canadian exporters would be discriminated against in each Latin American market, say Brazil, in compe-

tition with not only the United States, but with all other Latin American FTA members as well. Compare this to the situation in which *each* of these Latin American countries were to be an individual spoke; then the only discrimination Canada would face in any of these Latin American markets, say Brazil, would be in competition with the United States.

It has been suggested by Sidney Weintraub that a group of South American countries should form an FTA before approaching the United States about free trade. As the argument above implies, that could raise serious problems if their new FTA were to become a spoke to the U.S. hub. However, these problems would not arise if they were to dock into an expanding NAFTA.

5. Although this has been described as a nightmare outcome for Canada, there is another that would be even worse: withdrawal from its bilateral FTA with the United States as well. This would raise all the same problems described above, plus the problem of lack of access to the most important market and source of supply in the Americas: the United States.

6. There may also be rent seeking in an expanding FTA. But this is likely to be less wasteful, because an FTA is a less complex trading arrangement, with fewer trade constraints restricting the entry of competitors.

7. While it is important for the United States to view these two objectives as complementary, there is always the risk that it will view them as substitutes. But that is another story, as is indeed the possibility that even plurilateral free trade in the hemisphere may decrease efficiency because of the trade diversion it may cause.

8. NAFTA must also be ratified by Mexico (where there is little apparent risk) and by the United States (where there is greater risk). If the U.S. Congress fails to do so, then including Mexico in any way would seem to become a dead issue, at least in the short run, with the bilateral Canada–U.S. FTA being the only North American free trade relationship in which the United States would be participating.

9. Any form of regional trade agreement involves some discrimination against countries outside the hemisphere—but that cannot be avoided, short of removing world trade barriers or requiring that the countries in the agreement also unilaterally eliminate their trade barriers against the rest of the world.

10. Although NAFTA does not require that future changes should liberalize trade rather than protect, it does, in its ascension clause, require unanimous consent by existing partners. (While formally, unanimity is required to accept new members, the practise may be to accept new members along with the minimal concessions they require to join.) There is, however, an unfortunate oversight here. If and when smaller countries such as, say, a group of n Central American countries were to be included in the expanding FTA, the unanimity requirement might make further change essentially impossible. To prevent this, a change need not necessarily require the approval of all individual partner countries, but instead only the approval of the United States, Canada, Mexico, and this Central American bloc, with this bloc exercising only one vote rather than n.

PART II

The Canada–U.S. FTA and the Laboratory of the Mexican, U.S., and Canadian NAFTA Negotiations

3

The North American Free Trade Agreement: A Canadian Perspective

Murray G. Smith

INTRODUCTION

The prospect of a North American Free Trade Agreement has raised concerns that there will be a Fortress North America and that there will be significant trade and investment diversion. Many in the Caribbean, Latin American, and Asia-Pacific regions are concerned that their present trade links with North America will be weakened, while protectionist interests in the United States are concerned that investment from outside North America will use Mexico as a back-door export platform to the United States. Yet for others NAFTA is perceived as an opportunity, because it includes an accession clause. The validity of these concerns will depend upon the agreement's structure when it is ratified, assuming it is implemented on the basis of the text of the agreement initialled on October 7, 1992, the success or failure of the Uruguay Round of GATT negotiations and the timing of its conclusion, the subsequent behavior of the three NAFTA parties in subsequent multilateral and plurilateral negotiations, and the possible accession of other countries to the NAFTA.

This chapter first reviews some of the experience with the Canada–U.S. Free Trade Agreement. Second, the basic architecture of NAFTA is discussed and the relationship between NAFTA and the Canada–U.S. FTA is examined. Third, the chapter explores the linkage between the trilateral negotiations and the Uruguay Round of GATT negotiations. Fourth, some of the key elements of NAFTA are reviewed and a few observations are made about a very preliminary qualitative assessment of the trade creation and trade diversion effects.

Fifth, the broader repercussions for the global trading system and the potential issues raised by extension of NAFTA to other countries are discussed.

Assessment of the Canada–U.S. Free Trade Agreement

The implementation of the Canada–U.S. Free Trade Agreement was controversial in both countries. In the United States the high value of the U.S. dollar in the mid-1980s and the ensuing large trade deficit created protectionist pressures in the Congress that threatened to derail the free trade negotiations with Canada. These protectionist pressures made the negotiations difficult and they were concluded under the pressure of the deadline of expiration of the U.S. negotiating authority in October 1987. After the United States had passed implementing legislation, a passionate debate about the economic and political consequences of free trade became the central issue of the November 1988 federal election in Canada.

Before the Canada–U.S. FTA, the average Canadian tariff on dutiable imports from the United States was 9.2 percent, while the average U.S. tariff on dutiable imports from Canada was 3.3 percent. Since the tariffs were low and since the reductions are being phased in over ten years, it is difficult to measure the impact of changes in trade policy as compared with the impact of other economic policies.

The potential economic significance of the Canada–U.S. FTA is evident from the enormous volume of transactions between the two economies. Total two-way trade in goods and services between Canada and the United States exceeded $200 billion in 1991. When investment income is included, total bilateral commerce amounted to $210 billion. Canada purchased more than one-fifth of U.S. exports of goods, while the United States purchased about three-quarters of Canada's merchandise exports.

The FTA appears to have stimulated trade between the two economies, because the value of bilateral trade has expanded at an annual rate of 6 percent despite the fact that both economies have experienced recessions in 1990–91. Certainly bilateral direct investment flows have accelerated as U.S. firms increased investment in Canada and Canadian firms increased investment in the United States. Preliminary evidence from the pattern of trade indicates that specialization is occurring on an intraindustry basis—increased two-way trade flows within industries as firms specialize in product niches and exploit economies of scale. The pattern of trade specialization and industry rationalization so far is consistent with previous experience in reducing tariffs between Canada and the United States as a result of GATT negotiations. Similarly, the changing pattern of trade is broadly consistent with the analysis of economic models that predicted economic welfare gains to the Canadian economy of between 2 and 5 percent of Canadian GNP and between ½ and 1 percent of U.S. GNP.

One indicator of how firms are adjusting positively to increased international competition under the free trade agreement is that the two governments have agreed to accelerate the elimination of tariffs for about $6 billion in bilateral trade over two years. The decision to accelerate the elimination of these duties was made only after extensive consultations with firms and industry associations and no opposition to the quicker elimination of these tariffs was registered by any firm. Given that any firm could have vetoed the quicker elimination of duties, it is remarkable that such a large volume of trade was the subject of tariff acceleration.

One of the most innovative aspects of the free trade agreement, the replacement of judicial review of the agencies administering the antidumping and countervailing duty laws by appeal to binational panels, is working extremely well. Seventeen appeals have been heard by the binational panels. All have been processed within the strict time limits specified in the agreement and almost all the decisions by the panels, composed of American and Canadian trade specialists, have been unanimous. The binational panel process has drawn praise from legal commentators in both countries. The panels operate under the jurisdiction of the domestic trade laws of the importing country, but in about half of the appeals the panels have overturned or modified the findings of the regulatory agencies. Thus, the panels are providing effective and expeditious scrutiny of agencies that have often been perceived as arbitrary and protectionist in their administration of the trade laws.

Despite the fact that economic and legal specialists would give good grades to the FTA so far, popular perceptions of the agreement are negative in Canada, because of nationalist concerns about closer economic ties with the United States and because the implementation of the agreement has coincided with a recession in the two economies. Of course the recession could have generated protectionist concerns in the United States as well, but as the Canadian dollar appreciated about 20 percent against the U.S. dollar from the mid-1980s until 1991, protectionist pressures against Canada have abated somewhat in the United States while Canadian concerns about job losses in the manufacturing sector have intensified. In 1992 and into 1993, the anemic economic recovery and the depreciation of the Canadian dollar could stimulate increased U.S. protectionism against Canadian exports without ameliorating Canadian concerns about the perceived impact of the FTA, at least in the short term. For example, the U.S. steel industry has filed a large number of antidumping and countervailing duty cases against steel imports from Canada and other countries. However, as the economic recovery proceeds, the popular assessment in Canada of the impact of the free trade agreement may improve.

It is intriguing that some in the United States express some of the concerns about potential economic dislocation that could result from free trade with Mexico that many in Canada expressed in Canada's free trade debate. Thus, perceptions of the impact of the Canada–U.S. Free Trade Agreement may influence attitudes to the proposed North American Free Trade Agreement in the United States as well as in Canada.

THE NORTH AMERICAN FREE TRADE AGREEMENT:
THE EMERGING ARCHITECTURE

The overall architecture of the proposed NAFTA can be evaluated on the basis of the text of the Agreement as of October 7, 1992. Despite the fact that there was no explicit accession clause, Mexico might have acceded to the existing Canada–U.S. Free Trade Agreement with only minor adjustments to the existing agreement. The principal obstacles to this approach were that it was difficult to accommodate Mexican sensitivities in such areas as energy trade and investment without a full renegotiation of the Canada–U.S. FTA. However, it was an important goal to ensure that there is a common free trade area with common rules of origin for trade in goods among the three economies. Compliance with rules of origin is costly and the maintenance of two separate rules of origin for U.S.–Mexico and Canada–U.S. trade would inhibit the longer-term expansion of trade and investment within North America.[1] However, other issues such as agriculture were handled through three separate bilateral agreements. A different way of accommodating national sensitivities involves a generic free trade agreement, which provides common rules for trade in goods and services, investment, and protection of intellectual property, while each country has a protocol of exceptions and derogations.

NAFTA provides common rules of origin for the elimination of border measures according to an agreed schedule, common rules for trade in goods, services, investment, and intellectual property, and common dispute settlement procedures. However, energy trade and investment, trade in agricultural products, and cultural trade and investment are highly asymmetric or bilateral in their application. Although NAFTA will replace the Canada–U.S. FTA, residual elements of the Canada–U.S. FTA will continue to apply or be incorporated into NAFTA.

Some important issues were not resolved in NAFTA pending the outcome of the Uruguay Round of GATT negotiations, and the success or failure of the round will have much broader implications for the evolution of NAFTA within North America and its potential extension to other countries. Clearly the success or failure of the Uruguay Round will have important implications for the impact of NAFTA on offshore trading partners and the multilateral system. It is noteworthy that NAFTA goes beyond the Canada–U.S. Free Trade Agreement and anticipates the outcome of the Uruguay Round in incorporating an intellectual property chapter based on the Dunkel Text. The so-called Dunkel Text refers to the Draft Final Act for the Uruguay Round of GATT negotiations tabled by Arthur Dunkel, the director general of the GATT Secretariat in December 1991. In addition, NAFTA contains a number of new provisions about the environment. Environmental and human rights issues will attract considerable interest in the U.S. Congress as the NAFTA implementation process proceeds.

LINKAGES TO THE URUGUAY ROUND AND THE
MULTILATERAL TRADING SYSTEM

The uncertainties about the outcome of the Uruguay Round after the impasse at the Brussels Ministerial and the failure to break this impasse at the Munich Summit complicate the intra–North American arrangements and create potential problems for fourth countries in their trade and investment relations with NAFTA members. From the very beginning of the NAFTA negotiations it appeared that there was a vague consensus among the three countries that it would be very convenient if the most difficult issues—agricultural subsidies and trade barriers, textiles trade restrictions, trade rules for subsidies and countervailing and antidumping duties, government procurement practices, and rules for intellectual property—were resolved through the multilateral process. Of course the precise interaction between the NAFTA arrangement and the Uruguay Round agenda varies from issue to issue. Although an impasse in the multilateral negotiations reinforces interest in regional trading arrangements, the failure to deal with these more difficult issues as well as more prosaic issues such as multilateral tariff reductions, has made the substantive negotiations among the United States, Mexico, and Canada more difficult. And a continuing impasse will complicate the evolution of NAFTA and make its impact on the multilateral system more problematic.

Agricultural trade and subsidy issues illustrate some of the difficulties for the NAFTA negotiators arising from the impasse in the Uruguay Round. Many of Mexico's remaining import licenses and most of the quotas of Canada and the United States are concentrated in the agricultural sector. The delays in achieving a meaningful outcome to the Uruguay Round negotiations on agricultural subsidies and trade barriers have set the parameters for the trilateral negotiations. This is not a new problem. Neither the United States nor Canada was prepared to reduce domestic agricultural subsidies in the Canada–U.S. Free Trade negotiations because of concerns about the impact of EC and Japanese agricultural policies. For its part, Mexico was reluctant to dismantle its restrictions on imports of corn, grains, and lentils, because millions of small farmers depend upon these products, particularly while the United States and Canada retain substantial agricultural subsidies.

Closing the NAFTA deal before the conclusion of the Uruguay Round concluded posed a particularly serious problem for Canada on agriculture, because Canada remains politically committed to its Uruguay Round position (aligning it with other noted agricultural exporters such as Japan and Korea) of seeking to preserve and to extend import quotas for supply-managed products under Article XI of GATT. Thus, Canada was preoccupied with preserving the exceptions for these import quotas contained in the Canada–U.S. Free Trade Agreement. As a result, the agricultural arrangements in NAFTA consist of three bilateral agreements.

The Mexico–U.S. bilateral provides for replacement of import quotas and licenses with tariff rate quotas (TRQs), and the tariffs are eliminated over a ten or fifteen year time frame. Mexico has corn and dry beans and the United States has sugar and orange juice on a fifteen year phase-out. The Canada-Mexico chapter is analogous, except that dairy, poultry, and eggs are excluded. Thus, apart from Canada's idiosyncrasies, the market access elements of NAFTA on agricultural products are remarkably comprehensive. However, the obligations on domestic support and export subsidies appear to be merely hortatory except to incorporate the GATT obligations that are to be part of the conclusion of the Uruguay Round.

The situation on subsidies and countervailing duties in NAFTA is analogous to that on agricultural subsidies. NAFTA proposes to implement the Dunkel Text on subsidies and countervailing duties at the end of the Uruguay Round and abandons the effort to develop subsidy and countervailing duty rules, which was mandated in the Canada–U.S. Free Trade Agreement. Certainly the Dunkel Text on subsidies and countervailing duties offers a useful basis for introducing subsidy disciplines, in the form of prohibitions and/or giving some effect to the serious prejudice obligations under the GATT. Politically, a Uruguay Round deal involving Europe and Japan has the potential muscle to get changes in countervailing duty laws through the Congress, while NAFTA does not.

However, it is curious that the NAFTA countries do not contemplate the possibility that they might wish to improve or refine the rules for subsidies and countervailing duties among themselves either at the end of the Uruguay Round or subsequently. An unusual aspect of the Dunkel Text on subsidies is that it imposes tighter disciplines on the use of subsidies by subnational governments than it does on national governments. As three federal nations, the NAFTA countries might find it in their interest to modify this provision among themselves. Perhaps the NAFTA negotiators are being shrewd and anticipate that the provision of the Dunkel subsidies text that imposes greater discipline on subnational governments, which is in the text as a result of EC insistence, will be modified now that the Maastricht Treaty faces some hurdles. Government procurement is another example of where the Uruguay Round could go further than NAFTA, because of the attraction of the opening of the European and Japanese markets. It appears that there will be a substantial procurement package in NAFTA, however, that will go further than that under the Canada–U.S. FTA. In addition to coverage of the entities covered under the GATT procurement code, the United States appears willing to include the purchases of entities such as the Army Corps of Engineers, and Canada will include the purchases of departments such as Transportation and Fisheries. Mexico is including Pemex procurement as well as direct government purchases.

The interaction between NAFTA and the Uruguay Round with respect to intellectual property rules is intriguing. In essence the three countries have adopted the Dunkel Text on intellectual property, but the rights and obligations will apply only among the three countries unless the Uruguay Round is also implemented by January 1994.

A BRIEF REVIEW OF NAFTA: MANAGED TRADE OR FREE TRADE?

The *Wall Street Journal* has described NAFTA as managed trade, not free trade. This section reviews selected key elements of NAFTA and considers this broad question as well as the more conventional question, whether NAFTA is trade creating or trade diverting.

The outcome of the Uruguay Round will clearly be significant for the potential trade diversion consequences of NAFTA. It is evident that the potential for trade diversion in a free trade agreement involving Mexico, the United States, and Canada is significant because Mexico is a lower-wage, complementary economy. Of course, much of the potential for trade diversion derives from Canadian and U.S. trade barriers. For example, Mexico is not a major supplier of textiles and apparel products to Canada and Canada does not have bilateral restrictions on Mexican exports under the Multifiber Arrangement (MFA), but because Canada imposes high tariffs and bilateral restraints on low-cost suppliers under the MFA, Mexico might expand substantially exports of these products once it is exempted from Canadian tariffs. If, however, significant liberalization of tariff and nontariff barriers to textiles and apparel trade can be achieved in the Uruguay Round, then the potential for trade diversion will be reduced.

Rules of Origin and Border Measures

The proposed NAFTA will eventually eliminate tariffs and export duties among the three economies. In this respect the NAFTA would parallel the Canada–U.S. Free Trade Agreement, but the timetable for tariff reductions between Mexico and the United States and Mexico and Canada lags behind the present schedule of tariff reductions between Canada and the United States under the FTA. The rules of origin for NAFTA differ from the Canada–U.S. FTA most notably in the textiles and apparel sector, automotive products, and a few others.

Rules of origin are an essential element of any FTA. The pressure for restrictive rules of origin is greater in industries characterized by significant nontariff barriers to trade. Moreover, rules of origin in themselves can become significant nontariff barriers to trade. It is important that the trilateral NAFTA have clear and transparent rules of origin so that compliance costs and administrative discretion are minimized. The existing Canada–U.S. Free Trade Agreement utilizes primarily a change of tariff classification criteria to determine substantial transformation. However, assembly activities have a 50 percent direct cost of manufacturing requirement, which may be subject to some degree of ambiguity in measurement and administration. Restrictive rules of origin can frustrate the benefits of the removal of trade barriers.

Many misgivings by other countries about the NAFTA negotiations were prompted by U.S. proposals for more restrictive rules of origin in sectors such as textiles and apparel, automobiles, and computers. The valid purpose of rules of origin is to prevent trade and investment diversion when there are high and differentiated external trade barriers, but protectionist groups in the United States have sought to manipulate the rules of origin to claw-back benefits under the existing Canada–U.S. FTA and to limit the opening of trade under NAFTA. In the end, some of the more extreme proposals appear to have been discarded. In the case of computers, U.S. multinationals appear to have belatedly realized that the proposed restrictive and cumbersome rules would be damaging to their U.S. operations in a technologically dynamic and globalized industry. The neo-Stalinist mercantilists inside and outside the U.S. government lost this particular battle, but it appears there will be residual effects in the form of restrictive rules of origin for televisions and other electronic equipment.

The differences between the proposed NAFTA arrangements and the existing Canada–U.S. FTA can be illustrated by reference to a particular industrial sector that has been a central focus of concern during the trilateral negotiations, namely, the automotive sector. The United States pressed for a restrictive rule of origin for trade in automotive products under the trilateral free trade agreement. From a trade policy perspective it is puzzling why the United States, with a tariff of 2.5 percent on automotive products currently, and an MFN tariff that could be even lower after completion of the Uruguay Round, would care very much about the rules of origin for automotive products because the potential incentives for trade diversion or trade deflection are extremely limited with such a low MFN U.S. tariff. (Of course the situation is somewhat different with light trucks which have a 25 percent tariff as a result of the chicken war—a trade dispute in the early 1960s between the United States and the EC over the Common Agricultural Policy.) However, the economic impact and political clout of the automotive sector is such that the rules for this sector will receive great scrutiny in the Congress. Of course, the automotive sector is very important to the economies of Mexico and Canada.

The NAFTA negotiations over automotive rules of origin were influenced by trade disputes between Canada and the United States. Bilateral disputes over whether certain vehicle manufacturers are meeting the rules of origin under the FTA have important implications for the companies involved and will influence the perceptions of third country investors of the existing Canada–U.S. FTA and the proposed North American Free Trade Agreement involving Mexico, the United States, and Canada.

Complicated technical issues are involved in the current disputes over whether vehicles manufactured by the GM-Suzuki joint venture and the Honda subsidiary meet the rules of origin under the FTA. The key issue in each case is whether there is sufficient value-added occurring in Canada and the United States for the vehicles to qualify for duty-free trade under the FTA. Customs administration and legal interpretation of customs law are arcane issues, as was illustrated by a sudden ruling in the late 1970s that light trucks assembled in the United States were not transformed sufficiently to avoid paying the 25 percent U.S. duty.

The recent audit of Honda by the U.S. Treasury Department's Customs Service raises complicated issues. One of the issues involves the administration of "roll-up" or "roll-down." Under this approach, if major components such as the engine are deemed to meet the FTA rule of origin, then all of the value of the engine counts toward the required 50 percent direct cost of manufacturing—the engine is "rolled-up." On the other hand, if the engine is deemed not to meet the FTA rule of origin then it is "rolled-down," and only a small proportion of the value of the engine is counted toward the direct cost of manufacturing. The details of the Customs Service audit have been kept confidential at the request of Honda, but it is understood from press reports and industry sources that the administration of roll-up or roll-down is a key issue in the Honda dispute. Since engines machined and assembled by Honda in Ohio are not deemed to meet the FTA rules of origin, the Honda Civics assembled in Alliston, Ontario are not qualified for duty-free entry into the United States. As an illustration of the technical complexity, one of the issues is the legal relationship between the Honda subsidiaries in the United States and Canada. Apparently if the engines were manufactured by Honda in the same facility in Canada where the Civics are assembled using the same process and inputs used in Ohio, then the engines and the final product, the Civics, would qualify under the FTA.

Some of the technical issues involved in automotive rules of origin are the subject of an arbitration panel under the Canada–U.S. FTA. The binational panel under Chapter 18 ruled unanimously that Canada's interpretation permitting the deductibility of different types of interest charges was correct. Other technical aspects are being addressed in the NAFTA negotiations. For example, alternatives to the controversial roll-up process are proposed, which it is claimed would be more easily administered by the governments. In addition, the NAFTA arrangements propose a new mechanism to develop common interpretations of rules of origin, which is aimed at limiting the scope for unilateral interpretation of the rules of origin by the national customs authorities. This appears to be a useful innovation, but it remains to be seen whether this mechanism and the proposed new definitions of rules of origin can stand the rigors of legalistic deconstructionism that dominate the United States' conduct of trade relations at the present time.

Mexico and Canada resisted restrictive rules of origin in the automotive sector, in part because of concerns about the impact on existing Japanese assembly plants and upon new automotive investment by offshore firms. This issue and related issues about the Mexican automotive decree and duty drawback were among the most contentious issues in the negotiations. The Mexican automotive decree imposes a trade balance requirement upon certified vehicle manufacturers in Mexico if they sell imported vehicles on the domestic market. This so-called maquiladora is a duty-drawback or duty deferral arrangement for exports.

The clarification of rules of origin to a net cost basis apparently offsets a higher content number than the 50 percent direct cost of manufacturing in the Canada–U.S. FTA, but the equivalent percentage is debatable. Under NAFTA the content will stay at 50 percent for four years, rise to 56 percent for four years, and then be 62.5 percent. The latter number is more restrictive than the existing requirements under the Canada–U.S. FTA, notwithstanding the redefinition of rules of origin for automotive products. In order to cushion the impact on new investment, new automotive production facilities qualify for the 50 percent content level for five years.

It is customary in free trade areas to eliminate duty drawbacks for exports qualifying for preferred access to the markets of free trade partners. Thus, duty drawbacks were scheduled to be eliminated by January 1, 1994 in the Canada–U.S. Free Trade Agreement. For Canada, full duty drawback was extended for two years in NAFTA. Mexico obtained a seven-year transition period, before full duty drawback—known as maquiladora in Mexico—disappears in NAFTA. What is retained permanently is a device to eliminate double taxation—the lesser of the import duty and the drawback of the duty on imported inputs will be permitted to be remitted. Thus, goods not meeting the NAFTA rules of origin will continue to receive drawback.

In addition to the rules of origin for preferential tariff access, the other key issue for border measures under NAFTA will be the coverage of quotas and import licenses. In principle, all such quantitative restrictions should be eliminated, but there will be pressures to retain, at least for a considerable period, many of these quantitative restrictions.

The issue of restrictive rules of origin and the retention of quantitative restrictions on imports often are closely linked. Both Canada and the United States maintain extensive restraints on imports of textiles and clothing from low-cost countries. As a result of concerns, especially on the U.S. side, about the potential for trade diversion involving apparel made from offshore fabrics, special more restrictive rules of origin for apparel were included in the Canada–U.S. FTA. Under the Canada–U.S. FTA there was a double transformation test for apparel to qualify under the FTA—the fabric had to be woven and the garment manufactured in Canada or the United States to qualify for FTA treatment. Canadian apparel manufacturers who utilized fabrics from offshore sources complained and obtained substantial temporary TRQs for exports of garments to the United States manufactured with offshore fabric.

The situation in NAFTA is analogous, but even more complicated. Canada does not impose MFA restraints on Mexico, presumably because competitive pressures are not intense, but the United States does impose extensive restraints on Mexican apparel exports. Responding to intense political pressures from textile and apparel producers concerned about lower-wage competition from Mexico, the United States proposed and NAFTA contains triple transformation "yarn forward" and even quadruple transformation "fiber forward" rules of origin for textiles and apparel. (Recall that cotton is protected by Section 22 import restrictions in the United States, which helped trigger the Short-Term Arrangement for cotton textiles (STA) and the Long-Term Arrangement (LTA) for cotton textiles in the 1960s.)

These even more restrictive rules of origin for textiles and apparel in NAFTA created anxiety for Canadian textile and apparel manufacturers. Since the United States does not apply MFA restrictions to Canada, since the FTA rules of origin were less restrictive, and since Canada already had temporary TRQs for apparel manufactured with offshore fabric, the arrangement that was negotiated was a series of TRQs with growth factors for Canadian exports of textiles and apparel. The Canadian textile industry seems to be satisfied with this result but the apparel industry has claimed catastrophe, although the grounds for their claim seem dubious.

The highly restrictive rules of origin in textiles and apparel are motivated by protectionist pressures in the United States, but they may inadvertently serve the valid purpose of limiting trade diversions. Liberalization of textiles and apparel trade on a multilateral basis may increase short-term concerns about adjustment to import competition in the United States and Canada, but could also ease pressures for restrictive rules of origin for trilateral trade in this sector. Thus, these rules of origin in textiles and apparel ought to be revisited in the future, especially if the MFA is phased out as planned in the Uruguay Round.

Dispute Settlement

Under the Canada–U.S. FTA, Chapter 19 sets up a binational appeal mechanism, which can replace existing judicial review by the domestic courts of final decisions by the national administering agencies, as well as a review mechanism to monitor changes in antidumping and countervailing duty laws as they apply to the partner country. The objective of these dispute settlement procedures is to provide a more timely appeal mechanism than is available through the courts and to provide joint scrutiny of the decisions taken by the administrative authorities in both countries. Although the softwood lumber dispute influenced the free trade negotiations and the resulting agreement, the understanding on softwood lumber negotiated between Canada and the United States in late 1986 after the preliminary determination by the Department of Commerce was not affected by the FTA. Thus, the issue of stumpage subsidies remained to be resolved either through the future negotiations on subsidies or through the dispute settlement processes under the agreement. Now that Canada has terminated the softwood lumber memorandum of understanding and the United States has initiated a countervailing duty case against softwood lumber, the application of the dispute settlement processes to this difficult set of issues will be tested.

The free trade negotiations were, however, able to resolve some contentious subsidy issues in other sectors. In the automotive sector, the issue of Canada's export-based duty remission mechanism was resolved in a way that served both Canadian and U.S. objectives, while avoiding a potential U.S. countervailing action that would have been very disruptive to bilateral trade.[2]

The influence of U.S. protectionist pressures was evident in the softwood lumber dispute between Canada and the United States. Although various congressional bills directed against softwood lumber imports did not become law, a change in the interpretation of U.S. countervailing duty law by the U.S. Commerce Department in the 1986 *Softwood Lumber Case* resulted in a negotiated settlement where Canada imposed a 15 percent export tax on lumber shipped to the United States. The bitter conflict over softwood lumber shaped official attitudes on both sides during the free trade negotiations and influenced the agreement that emerged. In effect, the Canada–U.S. FTA seeks to prevent the recurrence of a softwood lumber situation where the administrative interpretation of the trade laws was perceived by Canadians as being altered in response to protectionist pressures. Just as the 1986 softwood lumber dispute shaped Canadian attitudes toward the Canada–U.S. free trade negotiations, the outcome of the 1991–92 softwood lumber countervailing duty case will influence both Canadian and U.S. attitudes to the dispute settlement processes for the trade laws in the NAFTA. Furthermore, the outcome of the 1991–92 case could influence the implementation of NAFTA.

There are difficulties in generalizing the binational judicial review mechanisms governing the trade laws under Chapter 19. Although there are technical differences, Canadian and U.S. trade laws and administrative procedures for the antidumping and countervailing duty laws are remarkably similar. It is more difficult to apply the Canada–U.S. agreement's review mechanism for decisions involving antidumping and countervailing duties to a third country like Mexico, whose domestic trade laws and administrative procedures differ substantially from those of the United States and Canada and which has a different legal system. To respond to this concern Mexico has agreed to implement trade laws and procedures similar to those of the United States and Canada. In addition, it is difficult to involve Mexico in this type of judicial review, because the Mexican legal system, which is derived from Roman law and the Napoleonic Code, does not have the same basic concepts of administrative law and judicial review that are common to the Canadian and U.S. legal systems. The proposed NAFTA arrangement does extend the Chapter 19 mechanism to Mexico, but it introduces a new Special Committee process, which can be triggered if a country fails to initiate a binational panel or to implement the panel results.

Internal Measures and the Trade Laws

The negotiation of import quotas and the trade laws is often linked to internal measures including subsidies, procurement preferences, and environmental regulations. Yet the asymmetries in the size and level of development of the three North American economies make it difficult to negotiate any restraints upon domestic policies. Mexicans and Canadians have often been extremely concerned about the threat to their sovereignty that could arise from U.S. dominance. For its part, the United States is likely to resist any restraints on its ability to take unilateral action.

Subsidies. It proved impossible to agree on disciplines on either agricultural or nonagricultural subsidies in the Canada–U.S. free trade negotiations, and it is evidently more difficult to develop effective rules limiting the use of domestic subsidies when an economy like Mexico, which has much lower income levels and greater infrastructure needs, is added to the negotiations. As a result, the subsidy issues, both agricultural and nonagricultural, are referred to the Uruguay Round for resolution. As noted above, it is curious that the NAFTA countries do not contemplate the possibility of refining these subsidy rules among themselves.

Antidumping Laws and Competition Policies. As with the countervailing duty laws, national antidumping laws are retained by each of the NAFTA partners. As was noted above, Mexico will amend its trade laws and procedures to make them similar to those of the United States and Canada. There is a chapter in NAFTA dealing with monopolies and restrictive business practices. A working group is proposed to examine the antidumping laws and competition policies, but no deadline is proposed. Although this proposal is virulently opposed in the United States today, the prospects could be much better five or ten years hence.

The lack of any substantial progress on the trade laws will be perceived as a shortcoming of NAFTA by many. However, this minimalist approach has one virtue. At least the three countries have avoided the route of common external antidumping and countervailing duty laws, such as is the case with the European Community. Common external trade laws would increase substantially the risk of managed trade.

Environmental Measures. Although at the outset the governments stated that environmental issues were being dealt with outside the trilateral free trade negotiations, the agreement contains a number of environmentally related provisions. The preamble makes an explicit reference to sustainable development. There are proposals to include environmental experts in panels and to make certain that environmental evidence is presented to panels. Responding to concerns about environmental issues, there is a proposed obligation that derogation of environmental standards should not be used as an investment inducement. Since the NAFTA retains the Canada–U.S. FTA provision permitting the parties to take bilateral disputes either to the GATT or, under the Agreement, and since NAFTA gives precedence to environmental agreements, there may be implications for GATT dispute settlement mechanisms, especially for cases involving environmental issues as environmental groups lobby for a NAFTA approach to environmental issues in the GATT.

Greater cooperation on environmental policies may be achieved through intergovernmental processes. Full harmonization of environmental regulations is almost certainly a futile objective, but it may be possible to agree on trilateral institutional arrangements that could monitor the effectiveness of environmental regulations and could propose standards to the three governments. In addition, the three governments may be able to agree, at least over time, on minimum standards for the most egregious pollutants.

Services and Investment

The NAFTA includes comprehensive chapters governing services and investment. The services chapter covers a broader range of services than the Canada–U.S. FTA, including specialty air transport services, land transportation, and for Canada-Mexico only, marine transportation. The investment chapter provides firms with recourse to an international arbitral mechanism to obtain financial compensation if discriminatory government policies or regulations violate the obligations of the investment chapter.

IMPACT ON THE GLOBAL TRADING SYSTEM

The NAFTA will create a large trading bloc and it cannot but have repercussions for the global trading system. Concluding NAFTA could stimulate trade liberalization either through creating pressure for progress in resolving the outstanding issues in the Uruguay Round, through competitive regionalism in Europe or Asia, or through more countries acceding to NAFTA. For the longer term, NAFTA raises some issues that clearly need to be addressed on the multilateral agenda.

Much depends on the structure of the trading arrangement. In particular, the key question is how the structure of the trilateral arrangement then influences the subsequent behavior of the partner countries. Will they become more preoccupied with internal negotiations and internal liberalization and less concerned about their trade and economic relations with the rest of the world? It can be argued that this is the case in a customs union and common market like the European Community. Or will the partners in the NAFTA take advantage of their greater independence in external commercial policies to seek to negotiate better access to nonmember markets either through bilateral or multilateral negotiations?

The complicated and customized structure of NAFTA means that fourth country accession will not necessarily be straightforward. It appears that each accession will have to be negotiated on a case by case basis. However, since any of the partners can proceed bilaterally, this may impose some limits on the more reluctant NAFTA members who might delay or obstruct the potential accession of other countries. Such an arrangement allows for greater openness in NAFTA, but on the other hand, it more clearly defines a concept of unequal treatment of countries outside the NAFTA. The danger of a fortress mentality in the Western Hemisphere can easily be overstated in a U.S. election year, and during an economic recovery of uncertain strength. But the political consequences in Asia can also be understated. Much depends on the confidence attached to mechanisms for reducing the potential for discrimination against Asian partners.

A very important, but difficult to assess, impact of NAFTA will be the implications of NAFTA implementation for the renewal of fast-track negotiating authority in the United States. If the passage of the NAFTA implementing legislation includes the renewal of fast-track authority, this will be very positive for the multilateral system. However, if the passage of NAFTA marks the last trade agreement implemented under fast-track procedures, the ensuing situation will be very damaging to the multilateral trading system.

CONCLUSION

The broad answer to the question of whether NAFTA is managed trade or free trade is that it is, on balance, freer trade. The NAFTA avoids any serious shift to managed trade because it reduces trade barriers among the partners without raising barriers against trade with other countries. According to conventional criteria under Article XXIV of GATT, such an arrangement is usually considered to be trade creating. But NAFTA is likely to receive rigorous scrutiny by GATT members and it could prompt tighter review of regional trade arrangements under GATT or the successor organization after the Uruguay Round. The most important reason that NAFTA avoids a drift to managed trade is that the three countries are not developing common external antidumping and countervailing duty laws. These laws are the motor of managed trade in the European Community and the United States.

Clearly the further liberalization of the Mexican economy, and the consolidation of recent economic reforms, are the most significant consequences of NAFTA. Some of the rules of origin are Byzantine in their complexity and some are clearly restrictive or discriminatory. The rules of origin in textiles and apparel are very restrictive, but this is more an issue among the NAFTA partners than for other countries. The restrictive rules of origin in this sector may serve to limit trade diversion. The complicated arrangements in the automotive sector do not lend themselves to a summary assessment, but the issue is more a matter of investment diversion or restriction than of trade diversion. Moreover, the automotive provisions are most problematic after 2002, when the 62.5 percent content rule is triggered. Much could happen before then. Indeed, since there have been some problems in interpretation of rules of origin under the Canada–U.S. FTA, the liberalization of trade and investment has been consolidated and extended. FTA disagreements apparently have been resolved in the automotive sector, since the procurement, investment, and services provisions have been extended in their coverage beyond the present.

A successful outcome to the Uruguay Round will enhance the prospects for achieving deeper liberalization of trade within NAFTA and reduce the potential for trade and investment diversion. It is in the interests of all three North American economies to avoid any tendency toward Fortress North America. An open and outward-looking NAFTA could serve to stimulate trade and investment flows across the Pacific and globally.

Other countries may accede to NAFTA in the future, but accession will have to be negotiated on a case by case basis. Hopefully, concluding the NAFTA deal and the prospect of more countries acceding to the arrangement will build pressure to break the impasse in the Uruguay Round. Beyond the Uruguay Round, NAFTA raises some important issues about the linkage of trade, environmental, investment, and competition policies that will need to be addressed on the multilateral agenda.

NOTES

1. This is the key point in Ron Wonnacott's incisive analysis of hub-and-spoke bilaterals. See R. J. Wonnacott, *Canada and the U.S.–Mexico Negotiations* (Toronto: C. D. Howe Institute Commentary No. 21, 1990).

2. For an analysis of the implications of the automotive provisions of the FTA, see Paul Wonnacott, "The Auto Sector," in Jeffrey J. Schott and Murray G. Smith, eds., *The Canada–United States Free Trade Agreement: The Global Impact* (Washington, D.C. and Halifax: Institute for International Economics, 1988), pp. 101–110.

4

A U.S. Perspective on the Canada–U.S. Free Trade Agreement

_____ *Arlene E. Wilson*

INTRODUCTION[1]

The U.S. and Canadian economies have been highly integrated for a long time. Bilateral merchandise trade flows are larger than for any other two countries in the world, partly reflecting intrafirm trade by companies that operate on both sides of the border. The vast majority of this trade flows smoothly. Although bilateral trade disputes are relatively rare, a few become contentious and attract considerable attention in the United States, as well as much concern in Canada, whose trade is heavily dependent on the U.S. market.

The Canada–U.S. Free Trade Agreement is the first bilateral trade agreement in recent history between the United States and a major trading partner.[2] In effect since January 1, 1989, the FTA liberalizes trade by phasing out all bilateral tariffs over a ten year period and eliminating a few nontariff barriers.[3] Many of the provisions, such as rules for investment, services, and energy trade, and dispute settlement procedures, provide a more secure environment for trade and investment in the future. The full benefits of these provisions will only be felt in the long run.

The main purpose of this chapter is to evaluate the effect of the Canada–U.S. FTA on the United States in the first few years, even though many of the economic benefits will occur over a period of years. This chapter begins with a review of U.S. goals in the negotiations. The FTA's effect on U.S. trade, investment, and the economy in the first three years is then examined. In order to give some indication of the potential long-run effects, the operation of the agreement's dispute settlement procedures since 1989 is evaluated. Finally, the FTA's effect on the North American Free Trade Agreement among the United States, Canada, and Mexico is discussed.

The principal finding is that the Canada–U.S. FTA has had a small, though positive, effect on U.S. trade, investment, and the U.S. economy so far. In the long run, the FTA is likely to have a larger effect, ultimately increasing U.S. productivity somewhat. Notably, the FTA's dispute settlement procedures have functioned quite well in the first few years of the agreement.

The success of the agreement with Canada was an important precedent for the NAFTA. Some of NAFTA's provisions (in the draft released September 7, 1992) are very similar to those of the Canada–U.S. agreement, some improve upon it, while others reflect specific bilateral concerns between two of the three countries.

The relatively small effect of the FTA on U.S. trade with Canada so far indicates that NAFTA is unlikely to increase U.S.–Mexican trade significantly in the near future. Like the agreement with Canada, the main economic benefits of NAFTA for the United States will probably occur over a period of years. Unlike the Canada–U.S. FTA, however, the North American agreement may lead to job losses in some industries if it stimulates U.S. firms to shift production to Mexico.

The FTA's role as a catalyst in changing the direction of U.S. trade policy may, in the long run, be more important than the agreement's effects on the U.S. economy. In retrospect, the free trade agreement with Canada may have been a turning point. U.S. willingness to consider bilateral agreements encouraged the Mexicans to request negotiations. Other Western Hemisphere countries responded with considerable interest to President Bush's Enterprise for the Americas Initiative. As the European Community's 1992 plan becomes a reality and de facto economic integration proceeds in the Far East, the U.S.–Canada agreement was the first U.S. step toward what may become worldwide regional trading arrangements.

WHAT DID THE UNITED STATES EXPECT
FROM THE FTA?

When negotiating the Canada–U.S. FTA, it appeared that the aggregate economic benefits to the United States in the near future would be relatively small. Since Canada's population is only one-tenth that of the United States, and Canada's gross national product (GNP) is only one-tenth the size of the U.S. economy, trade liberalization would likely have a much smaller effect on the United States than on Canada. And U.S. dependence on trade with Canada is far less than Canada's dependence on trade with the United States. In 1991, U.S. exports to Canada were $85 billion, or 20 percent of all U.S. exports, while Canadian exports to the United States of $96 billion were 75 percent of all Canadian exports.[4]

But in the long run an FTA held out the promise of a more efficient and competitive U.S. economy. If the Canada–U.S. agreement lowered trade and investment barriers, U.S. firms could restructure their production and reallocate resources to take advantage of economies of scale and a somewhat larger market, increasing U.S. productivity. The relative improvement in U.S. productivity would likely be much smaller than that for Canada, however, reflecting the disparity in size of the two countries.

Although the United States did not extensively evaluate the potential economic impact of an FTA before negotiating with Canada, the available studies indicated that the effect would usually be positive, but small. Drusilla Brown and Robert Stern, in a U.S. study, used a computable general equilibrium model to estimate the effect of tariff elimination on the United States. Assuming all bilateral tariffs were eliminated immediately, Brown and Stern estimated that U.S. income would increase by .03 percent—far less than 1 percent.[5] Two Canadian studies estimated that the U.S. gain would be 0.1 percent, while one Canadian study found a U.S. loss of .04 percent in real income.[6]

Nevertheless, some U.S. industries expected to reap significant benefits from a reduction in Canadian trade barriers. Of particular concern were Canadian subsidies, lack of protection for intellectual property rights, and a secure environment for U.S. investment, services, and energy trade. Elimination of tariffs was important both to multinationals that operate on both sides of the border and to some small businesses eager to export to Canada. Thus, most U.S. businesses strongly supported the negotiations.

In a broad sense, one U.S. goal was to stimulate multilateral negotiations through the General Agreement on Tariffs and Trade. Both the United States and Canada have, historically, preferred multilateral to bilateral trade liberalization. Although tariffs have been substantially reduced under previous GATT rounds, nontariff trade barriers, such as subsidies and restrictions on government procurement, are difficult to negotiate multilaterally. Important U.S. concerns, such as open markets in investment, services, and agriculture, are not covered by GATT rules. In the U.S. view, a successful U.S.–Canadian agreement would be a model for GATT negotiations. Furthermore, other countries, afraid of being left out, might be inclined to support multilateral negotiations. At the very least, if GATT negotiations proved impossible, an agreement with Canada would liberalize trade with the United States' major trading partner.

Finally, it would have been difficult for the United States to refuse Canada's request for negotiations, given the close relationship between the two countries over the years. Canada was eager to obtain secure access to the large U.S. market at a time when protectionist sentiment appeared to be rising in the United States. Additionally, an FTA would, Canada maintained, encourage their economy to become more competitive, a goal the United States wanted to support. U.S. unwillingness to negotiate might have adversely affected U.S.–Canadian cooperation in other important areas, such as defense and the environment.

DID THE FTA ACHIEVE THESE GOALS?

The United States achieved its goals of tariff elimination, a more open and secure environment for U.S. direct investment in Canada, secure access to energy resources, and rules for services trade. The FTA phases out all remaining bilateral tariffs over a ten year period and eliminates a few nontariff barriers. For example, the FTA liberalizes "buy national" government procurement restrictions, opens markets in wine and spirits, eases requirements for temporary border crossing for professionals, and provides safeguards for industries hurt by increased bilateral imports resulting from the FTA. More generally, the FTA provides nondiscriminatory rules for future trade and investment in a wide range of areas. These rules, along with the FTA's dispute settlement procedures, could make it more likely for business firms to trade with and invest in the partner country in the years ahead.

The United States fared less well over subsidies, by far the most controversial issue in the agreement. Historically, the Canadian government has taken a much larger role in the economy than the U.S. Government. U.S. business often views Canadian subsidies, which the United States claims are more extensive than U.S. subsidies, as unfair trade practices. U.S. countervailing duty (CVD) investigations may result in duties being applied to Canadian products to offset the alleged subsidy.[7] Canada argues that the U.S. CVD law is not always applied uniformly, is subject to political pressures, and consequently inhibits Canadian exports. The FTA's compromise was to establish a temporary dispute settlement procedure consisting of binational panels whose decisions are binding for countervailing duty cases, while a U.S.–Canadian working group developed rules for subsidies.

A few other U.S. goals remain unmet. The FTA contains no broad provisions on intellectual property rights and only moderately liberalizes trade in agriculture. Some sensitive sectors—notably transportation services, investment in Canadian energy, and the Canadian cultural sector (films, TV, books, and records)—were omitted from the agreement.

The FTA was intended to be the first step in an ongoing process of trade liberalization. Thus, the agreement establishes working groups to further liberalize trade in agriculture, automotive products, government procurement, services, subsidies, temporary entry for businesspersons, and harmonization of technical standards.[8]

ASSESSMENT OF THE FTA SINCE 1989

Effect on U.S. Trade, Investment, and the Economy

Merchandise Trade. In the first three years of the FTA, U.S. exports to Canada increased 19 percent, while U.S. imports from Canada increased 12

Figure 4.1
U.S. Exports to Canada and Canadian GNP

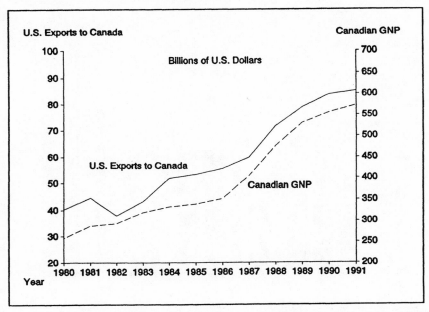

Sources: U.S. Department of Commerce, U.S. *Foreign Trade Highlights 1991*, p. 11, and U.S. *Foreign Trade Highlights 1988*, p. 82; International Monetary Fund, *International Financial Statistics Yearbook 1991*, pp. 271, 275, and *International Financial Statistics September 1992*, pp. 134, 138.

percent. All of this increase, however, cannot be attributed to trade liberalization resulting from the FTA. In fact, most of the increase probably reflects changes in economic activity in the United States and Canada.

As Figure 4.1 indicates, U.S. exports to Canada are closely associated with Canada's GNP. Over the 1980s, the growth in U.S. exports to Canada paralleled the growth in Canadian GNP fairly well, especially since 1987. It is likely that the level of economic activity (GNP) in Canada is the most important influence on U.S. exports to Canada. Although not shown here, U.S. imports from Canada are also closely correlated with U.S. GNP.

The appreciation of the Canadian dollar against the U.S. dollar made U.S. exports more competitive and contributed to the growth of U.S. exports to Canada. Most of the Canadian dollar's appreciation resulted from the Canadian government's attempt to fight inflation with a tight monetary policy. Interest rates rose, causing capital to flow to Canada, and the Canadian dollar appreciated. Indirectly, though, the FTA may have stimulated capital flows to Canada and contributed to the Canadian dollar appreciation. Capital flows into

Figure 4.2
U.S.–Canadian Merchandise Trade

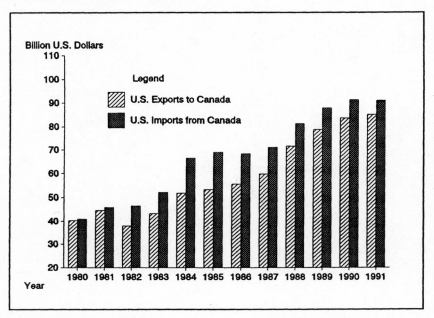

Sources: U.S. Department of Commerce, *U.S. Foreign Trade Highlights 1991*, pp. 11, 15, and
          U.S. Foreign Trade Highlights 1988, pp. 82, 87.

Canada from the United States and third countries increased around the time
the FTA was being negotiated, probably reflecting optimism about Canada's
more secure access to the U.S. market in the future.

Not enough time has elapsed to be able to separate out the FTA's effects on
bilateral trade from those of GNP and exchange rates. Nevertheless, the FTA's
effect is likely to be small, given the relatively small amount of trade that was
liberalized in the first few years of the agreement. About 80 percent of Canadian exports to the United States and 65 percent of U.S. exports to Canada
were duty-free before the FTA went into effect. Only about 10 percent of the
remaining tariffs were eliminated on January 1, 1989, with perhaps another 25
percent phased out by December 1991. Annual bilateral trade flows since 1980
are shown in Figure 4.2. U.S. exports to and imports from Canada increased
in all years except 1982 and 1986. From the perspective of the decade of the
1980s, increases in trade flows since 1989, while healthy, are not unusually
large. Thus, these data do not indicate any significant change in U.S. bilateral
trade flows arising from the FTA.

Although the FTA most likely was not the major influence on bilateral trade
flows since 1989, it may have increased trade of selected products. For example, lower Canadian tariffs from the FTA may have stimulated the large

increases in U.S. exports of fish products, furniture, paints and dyes, soaps and polishes, chemical products, plastics, paper products, apparel items, and electric machinery.[9]

Tariff elimination was popular with the U.S. and Canadian business communities. A little-known provision of the FTA provides for accelerated tariff removal, if requested and if both countries agree. The U.S. and Canadian governments, in 1989, 1990, and 1991, received a large number of requests for elimination of tariffs ahead of schedule. In the first two rounds of requests, tariffs were eliminated early on 650 tariff items, representing $8 billion in bilateral trade.[10] The final round of petitions (115 from the United States and 250 from Canada) is being considered in 1992 and is expected to be implemented in April 1993.[11]

Services. The services chapter is primarily a code of principles allowing no new restrictions in the future. In addition, attempts to roll back restrictions in three sectors—architecture, transportation, and telecommunications services—are included. Bilateral trade in services was already reasonably free of restrictions before the FTA went into effect. Moreover, few large bilateral disputes involved services. As a result, the overall impact of the services provisions was expected to be quite small.[12]

In general, bilateral trade in services, especially U.S. services exports, has grown significantly since 1989. U.S. receipts from travel and transportation, at $10.6 billion in 1991, almost doubled between 1988 and 1991, compared with Canadian receipts of $4.8 billion in 1991, which increased 15 percent over the same period.[13] Most likely the strong growth in U.S. receipts reflects the high Canadian dollar (not the FTA), which stimulated Canadian tourism in the United States.

U.S. exports of other private services (business, professional, technical, financial, telecommunications, education, and insurance services) to Canada also increased more rapidly than Canadian exports to the United States. Between 1989 and 1991, U.S. receipts grew 20 percent to reach $6 billion, while Canadian receipts grew 8 percent to $3 billion in 1991.[14]

Related to services, a large number of border crossings by professionals and businesspersons took place since the FTA went into effect. Spurred by the FTA's chapter making it easier for professionals to temporarily cross the border, the United States admitted 8,322 Canadians in 1991, up from 3,700 in 1989.[15]

Investment. Like services, the investment chapter establishes principles providing that no new restrictions be imposed in the future. It also liberalizes a few existing Canadian restrictions. Since Canada had restricted U.S. investment in the early 1980s, primarily through review procedures for new investments, this chapter was expected to stimulate U.S. investment in Canada by ensuring a more hospitable environment.

Bilateral direct investment flows since 1987 are given in Figure 4.3. The most striking observation is that, until 1991, Canadian direct investment flows to the United States were considerably greater than U.S. direct investment

Figure 4.3
U.S.–Canadian Direct Investment Flows

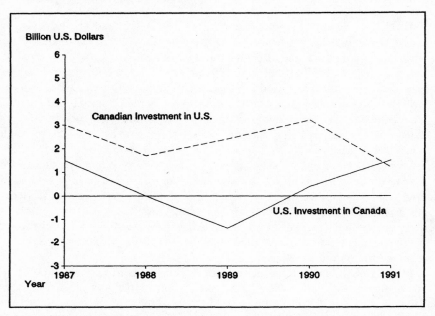

Note: Equity capital inflows and outflows are used as the closest measure of new direct investment,
        per discussion with Gregory Fouch at the U.S. Department of Commerce.

Sources: U.S. Department of Commerce, *Survey of Current Business, August 1992*, pp. 99–101,
          129–31, *Survey of Current Business, August 1991*, pp. 59–60, 92, and *Survey of Current
          Business, August 1990*, p. 73.

flows to Canada. Given that the U.S. economy is ten times the size of the
Canadian economy, the United States has benefitted much more than Canada
from bilateral investment flows over this period. Since the U.S. government's
policy was one of openness to foreign investment long before the FTA went
into effect, the agreement probably had a smaller influence on Canadian direct
investment in the United States than lower U.S. labor costs and the high Canadian dollar.

U.S. investment flows to Canada since 1987 were somewhat erratic, even
becoming negative in 1989. It is possible that 1987 investment flows were ex-
ceptionally high as the potential benefits of the FTA being negotiated were
anticipated by U.S. firms.

Impact on the U.S. Economy. One recent Canadian study attempted to iso-
late the effects of the FTA on the Canadian and U.S. economies using macroeconomic model simulations. According to Peter Pauly, in the first three
years of the agreement, "there are indications of minor gains in the U.S. as a

result of the FTA, but the orders of magnitude are insignificant relative to the variance of the business cycle over this period."[16]

The FTA may have contributed to the economic revival of some U.S. communities near the Canadian border. The Buffalo, New York area, in particular, appears to have benefitted. According to one report, eighty-seven Canadian companies moved to Buffalo between July 1987 and August 1991.[17] Lower U.S. wages, lower U.S. taxes, and less expensive U.S. real estate were probably the major factors, however, in the Canadian companies' decisions to move.

BILATERAL TRADE DISPUTES

Dispute Settlement Procedures

The FTA's two main dispute settlement procedures may be the most successful provisions of the FTA. One procedure, Chapter 18 of the FTA, which is modeled after the GATT, applies to most bilateral disputes other than CVD or antidumping (AD) cases. If bilateral consultations are unsuccessful, the Commission (the U.S. Trade Representative and the Canadian Minister of Trade) may refer the dispute to a five-member binational panel. The Commission has thirty days to resolve the dispute after receiving the panel's nonbinding report. If resolution is impossible, the United States or Canada may suspend equivalent trade benefits if its rights under the FTA are impaired.

As of August 1992, only three binational panels have been formed to resolve disputes. The first two panels involved disputes over lobster size and salmon landing requirements rights that predated the FTA. The third concerned the rules of origin in the automotive chapter of the FTA.

The relatively infrequent use of the Chapter 18 panel procedure may reflect the success of the FTA in preventing or resolving disputes at an early stage. Both the United States and Canada may have preferred to settle potential disputes through consultations. In fact, a number of issues were referred to consultation. Or fewer disputes may have occurred because the FTA reduced trade barriers and established nondiscriminatory rules for trade in many areas.

Another explanation for the infrequent use of binational panels is that Canada and the United States may prefer to refer disputes to the GATT. (The FTA gives them a choice of either procedure.) Although the FTA procedure was faster than the GATT in 1987, recent changes in GATT dispute procedures have reduced substantially the time limits within which decisions must be made. And, other things being equal, a complaining party in a bilateral dispute may prefer a GATT panel report because it has the moral force of all the GATT contracting parties behind it.[18]

Much attention has focused on the temporary dispute settlement procedures for CVD and AD cases, the Chapter 19 procedure. An innovative solution to a difficult problem, it has been used extensively and enjoys a reputation for being impartial, fair, and timely.[19]

Chapter 19 provides for a five-member binational panel to review, upon request, the final AD and CVD decisions to ensure that they are in accordance with domestic laws. It replaces review by domestic courts, but does not change each country's CVD and AD laws. The panel's decisions are by majority vote, and are binding. The FTA provides that this procedure is in effect for five years (with a possible extension of two years) while a working group develops rules and procedures for subsidies.

More than twenty binational panels have been formed to review CVD and AD decisions involving products as diverse as red raspberries, pork, and replacement parts for bituminous paving. Most panels have been requested by Canada, and refer to U.S. CVD, not AD, determinations.

The panels have worked quite well. The selection of panelists has been smooth, and considered fair. The FTA provides that each country appoints two panelists, in consultation with the other country, and the two countries agree on the selection of the fifth panelist from either country. In practice, the fifth panelist has been rotated between the United States and Canada; if the previous panel had three Canadians, the current panel has three Americans.

Despite fears that panel decisions might reflect the position of the country having the majority of panelists, this has not occurred. Some panels with a majority of Canadians have ruled against Canada, and some with a majority of Americans have ruled against the United States.[20] In fact, most panel decisions were unanimous. Furthermore, panel decisions have been much quicker than domestic judicial review likely would have been.

Chapter 19 provides for an extraordinary challenge committee in cases where a panel is alleged to have exceeded its authority, engaged in gross misconduct, or departed from a fundamental rule of procedure. Only one panel decision has been referred to an extraordinary challenge committee. Upholding the original panel decision in a case involving Canadian pork subsidies, the extraordinary challenge procedure may have improved confidence in the objectivity of the dispute settlement procedure.

Recent Trade Disputes

The dispute settlement procedures did not, of course, end all bilateral trade disputes. No highly contentious disputes occurred in the first few years of the agreement. Since 1991, however, disputes over beer, lumber subsidies, and the rule of origin for automobiles have attracted considerable attention. The FTA's dispute settlement mechanisms appear to have mitigated the severity of the disputes by providing a formal structure for clarifying and resolving them. The rule of origin dispute reflects to some extent the agreement's lack of clear guidelines.

Beer. Bilateral beer trade was $173 million in 1991, much less than 1 percent of total bilateral trade of $176 billion.[21] Nevertheless, U.S. firms have long complained that Canadian provincial restrictions on the licensing, pricing, sale, and distribution of beer, wine, and distilled spirits reduced their ability to sell in Canada. More recently, Canada claimed that both the U.S. states and the federal government discriminated against Canadian beer. The United States estimates, however, that Canadian provincial restrictions caused a loss of $80 million to U.S. firms, compared with a $5 million loss to Canadian firms as a result of U.S. beer restrictions.[22]

The FTA specifically exempts existing restrictions on beer from the FTA's provisions requiring national treatment.[23] The agreement with Canada does, however, require that no new restrictions be imposed. Thus, this dispute was addressed outside the FTA.[24]

Both countries appealed to the GATT, and GATT panels supported each country's charge of unfair trade practices by the other country. The United States, on the request of several U.S. beer companies, initiated a Section 301 investigation alleging unfair Canadian trade practices. In mid-1992, under this investigation, the United States imposed duties on beer imported from Ontario, which, according to the United States, imposed new restrictions on beer imports, in addition to maintaining old ones. Canada immediately retaliated with duties on some U.S. beer exported to Ontario.

In some ways, the beer case typifies bilateral trade disputes. Accounting for only a very small share of bilateral trade, yet important to a particular industry, it escalated rapidly and became contentious. As with some other disputes, it reflects concern by both U.S. business and the U.S. government with Canadian market-restrictive practices, especially those by provincial governments.

Softwood Lumber. This dispute, like beer, predated the FTA, and has received a great deal of attention. Although softwood lumber accounts for a small share (3 percent) of U.S. imports, it is an important industry in the province of British Columbia and in the Pacific Northwest states. Consequently, each country responds quickly to any threat to its share of the U.S. market.

The main issue is that the Canadian provincial governments' stumpage fees (charges for the right to cut trees) are alleged to be lower than those in the United States, in effect providing a subsidy to Canadian producers. The United States initiated CVD investigations in 1982, 1986, and 1991. The 1986 determination calculated provincial subsidies at 15 percent, reversing the 1982 decision that found Canadian subsidies too small to provide an unfair advantage. To avoid U.S. duties, the Canadian government signed a Memorandum of Understanding (MOU) with the U.S. government in 1986. Canada agreed to impose a 15 percent tax on Canadian exports of lumber, which would be reduced or eliminated as provinces increased their stumpage fees.

The FTA recognizes and supports the Memorandum of Understanding. Both countries agree that the FTA "does not impair or prejudice the exercise of any rights or enforcement measures" arising out of the MOU.[25]

The United States initiated the third CVD investigation when Canada announced in 1991 that the Memorandum of Understanding would be terminated because many provinces had increased their stumpage fees. In 1992, this investigation resulted in a final subsidy determination of 6.51 percent, which was found to be injuring the U.S. industry.

The softwood lumber dispute illustrates the difficulties involved in subsidy determinations. Defining and measuring subsidies is not an easy, clear-cut task. Since interpretations vary, the CVD process is subject to charges of political influence.

An FTA Chapter 19 binational panel is currently reviewing the 1992 U.S. CVD determination to see if it is consistent with U.S. law. A decision is expected in 1993. If the panel decision in this highly visible dispute is perceived to be fair and objective, and is respected by both Canada and the United States, it will further strengthen the credibility of the binational panel process.

Rule of Origin for Automobiles. Beginning in 1991, the U.S. Customs Service audited several automotive firms located in Canada to determine if they met the FTA's criteria for duty-free treatment. According to the FTA's rules of origin, at least 50 percent of the direct cost of production (materials, labor, energy, and factory overhead) for automobiles with third country content must take place in Canada or the United States to qualify for duty-free treatment.

But the FTA does not spell out how the 50 percent requirement should be calculated. According to John P. Simpson, deputy assistant secretary of the U.S. Treasury Department, "the guidelines used to make those determinations in that agreement (the FTA) are too vague and allow for misinterpretation and inconsistencies in calculations."[26]

The most publicized case involved Honda's Ontario plant, which claimed to have 75 percent U.S. or Canadian content. Honda and the Customs Service differed in their interpretation of the methodology to be used in calculating content. The Customs Service ruled in 1992 that Honda Civics assembled in Ontario from January 1, 1989 to March 30, 1990, did not contain 50 percent U.S. or Canadian content, and thus were subject to duties and penalties.

Another automotive rule of origin case concerned whether or not nonmortgage interest costs could be included in direct costs. An FTA Chapter 18 dispute settlement panel ruled in favor of Canada that the interest costs could be included in direct costs. The panel report suggested that the two countries adopt regulations and administrative procedures to reduce misinterpretations in the future.[27]

THE FTA AS A MODEL FOR THE NORTH AMERICAN FREE TRADE AGREEMENT

Mexico's goals in seeking a free trade agreement with the United States were similar to those of Canada in many ways. Like Canada, Mexico wanted secure access to the large U.S. market, which might stimulate foreign investment into

Mexico. A free trade agreement with the United States might make a reversal of Mexico's 1980s economic reforms by a future government less likely.

It would have been difficult for the United States to refuse Mexico's request for negotiations, which provided an opportunity to improve relations with an important neighbor. Growth in the Mexican economy, which might be reinforced by a free trade agreement would benefit the United States. Among other things, an agreement might stimulate U.S. exports and might reduce the amount of illegal immigration to the United States.

Successful implementation of the Canada–U.S. FTA and the relatively few problems in the first few years provided an impetus to the North American agreement. Although many chapters in the Canada–U.S. FTA reflect specific U.S.–Canadian bilateral issues, the NAFTA negotiators began with the Canadian agreement as a starting point. Indeed, some NAFTA provisions, such as tariff elimination, temporary entry for business persons, and energy trade, are quite similar to those in the FTA. The North American agreement goes further than the Canadian agreement in some respects, and improves upon it in others. The NAFTA includes chapters on intellectual property and land transportation, issues where agreement was not reached in the Canadian agreement. Experience with the FTA's inadequately defined rules of origin led to clearer, more specific rules in NAFTA.

The successful operation of the Chapter 19 dispute settlement procedure in the first few years of the FTA led to its being included in the North American agreement, with some modifications. Notably, the NAFTA procedure is permanent, not temporary, as in the agreement with Canada.

The NAFTA addresses potential import competition in the same way as the agreement with Canada. The phasing out of tariffs over a period of years provides time for adjustment in sensitive industries in both agreements. The procedures for temporarily reimposing tariffs if an industry faces increased import competition are similar.

The North American agreement does not, however, include provisions to mitigate adjustment problems that might occur if U.S. firms shift production to Mexico in response to the agreement. This issue, not a concern in the FTA, arose because labor costs are considerably lower in Mexico than in the United States and Canada. Moreover, Mexican labor, health, and safety standards are lower, and are sometimes inadequately enforced.

To allay fears that U.S. environmental standards might be challenged as trade barriers, NAFTA specifically provides that the United States may retain its standards even if they are higher than those of Mexico. NAFTA's investment chapter provides that firms from Mexico and the United States may not lower standards to attract investment.

The experience with the U.S.–Canadian agreement since 1989 indicates that NAFTA's effect on U.S. trade with Mexico will be fairly small in the short run. U.S. exports to Mexico, 7 percent of all U.S. exports, are much lower than U.S. exports to Canada. Since Mexican tariffs were reduced before the

North American agreement was negotiated, most Mexican tariffs are not excessively high now. Furthermore, the majority of studies evaluating the North American agreement predict that trade liberalization from the agreement will have a small effect on U.S. trade with Mexico.

The Canadian agreement provides few guidelines for estimating potential U.S. plant relocation to Mexico resulting from a NAFTA. Slightly lower U.S. labor costs may have influenced some Canadian decisions to produce in the United States. The U.S.–Mexican differentials in labor costs, however, are much greater. It is not possible to accurately project the magnitude of future production shifts to Mexico based on the experience with the Canadian agreement.

CONCLUSION

The Canada–U.S. Free Trade Agreement had a small, though positive, effect on bilateral trade and investment since 1989. Most of the growth in bilateral trade probably reflected the increase in GNP in both countries. The high Canadian dollar relative to the U.S. dollar also likely stimulated U.S. exports to Canada. Since some of the FTA's provisions concern rules for future trade and investment, the full benefits of the FTA will only be realized over a period of years.

The FTA's dispute settlement procedures appeared to improve the bilateral environment for trade. Although bilateral trade disputes still occurred, the dispute settlement procedures provided a formal structure for clarifying and resolving them. In particular, the temporary dispute settlement procedures for countervailing duty and antidumping cases were used frequently, and enjoy a reputation for being impartial, fair, and timely.

The relatively small effect of the FTA on U.S. trade with Canada since 1989 suggests that NAFTA will also have a minor effect on U.S. trade with Mexico in the near future. The question of large investment shifts (and potential U.S. job losses) from the United States, however, was not an issue in the negotiations with Canada, since labor costs in both countries are similar. Thus, the experience of the FTA since 1989 provides no guidelines for estimating the magnitude of potential production shifts induced by NAFTA from the United States to Mexico.

In retrospect, U.S. willingness to negotiate bilaterally with Canada, despite its historical preference for multilateral agreements, may have been a turning point in U.S. trade policy. The experience of negotiating with Canada and implementing the FTA provided an important precedent for NAFTA and future trade agreements in the Western Hemisphere.

NOTES

1. This chapter reflects the viewpoint of the author and not necessarily that of the Congressional Research Service or the Library of Congress.

2. The United States also has a free trade agreement with Israel, in effect since 1985, but U.S. trade with Israel is only about 1 percent of total U.S. trade.

3. The text of the Canada–U.S. Free Trade Agreement can be found in U.S. Congress, House of Representatives, *United States–Canada Free-Trade Agreement*, Communication from the President of the United States, 100th Congress, 2nd sess., July 26, 1988, House Document 100-216.

4. International Monetary Fund, *Direction of Trade Statistics Yearbook 1992* (Washington, D.C.: IMF, 1992), 123, 402.

5. Drusilla K. Brown and Robert M. Stern, "Computable General Equilibrium Estimates of the Gains from US–Canadian Trade Liberalisation," in David Greenaway, Thomas Hyclak, and Robert J. Thornton, eds., *Economic Aspects of Regional Trading Arrangements* (New York: New York University Press, 1989), p. 76.

6. Ibid.

7. According to current U.S. law, a countervailing duty is imposed if the U.S. Department of Commerce determines that a subsidy exists and the U.S. International Trade Commission finds that a U.S. industry is materially injured or threatened with material injury by such imports.

8. For a more complete discussion of these provisions, see Arlene Wilson and Wayne Morrison, *United States–Canada Free Trade Agreement: Implementation and Elaboration* (Washington, D.C.: U.S. Library of Congress, Congressional Research Service, CRS Report 89-484 E, August 8, 1989).

9. Jeffrey Hawkins, "The Canada–U.S. Free Trade Agreement: An Interim Assessment," *Business America* 113, no. 8 (Washington, D.C., U.S. Department of Commerce, April 20, 1992), 3.

10. Peter E. Johnson, "Implementation of the Free Trade Agreement on Track," *Business America* 113, no. 8 (Washington, D.C., U.S. Department of Commerce, April 20, 1992), 6.

11. Ibid.

12. Jeffrey J. Schott, "United States-Canada Free Trade: An Evaluation of the Agreement," *Policy Analysis in International Economics* 24 (Washington, D.C., Institute for International Economics, April 1988), 32.

13. Based on data in U.S. Department of Commerce, *Survey of Current Business* 71, no. 9 (September 1991): 71, 72; no. 6 (June 1992): 108.

14. Based on data in U.S. Department of Commerce, *Survey of Current Business* 72, no. 6 (June 1992): 108.

15. Hawkins, "The Canada–U.S. Free Trade Agreement," 5.

16. Peter Pauly, *Macroeconomic Effects of the Canada–U.S. Free Trade Agreement: An Interim Assessment*, Studies on the Economic Future of North America (Toronto: Center for International Studies, University of Toronto and The Fraser Institute, n.d.), 9.

17. Clyde H. Farnsworth, "Free-Trade Accord Is Enticing Canadian Companies to U.S.," *New York Times*, August 9, 1991, A1.

18. Gary N. Horlick, "The US–Canada FTA and GATT Disputes Settlement Procedures: The Litigant's View," *Journal of World Trade Law* 26, no. 2 (April 1992): 9.

19. U.S. Congress, House Committee on Small Business, *What is Next for the United States–Canada Free Trade Agreement?* Hearings, Testimony of Charles F. Doran, 102nd Cong., 1st sess., September 4 and October 1, 1991, p. 54.

20. Joseph A. McKinney, "Dispute Settlement Under the U.S.–Canada Free Trade Agreement," *Journal of World Trade* 25 (December 1991): 125.

21. U.S. Department of Commerce, Trade Net Data Retrieval System.

22. "U.S. Hits Back at Canadian Beer," *Financial Times*, July 25/26, 1992, 2.

23. Article 1204 of the FTA. Chapter 8 of the FTA, however, eliminates most Canadian discriminatory practices involving wine and spirits.

24. In another bilateral beer dispute, two FTA Chapter 19 panels reviewed a Canadian dumping determination against U.S. firms. In August 1992, the panel reports affirmed in part and remanded in part the determinations of dumping and injury.

25. Article 2009 of the FTA.

26. "US Offers Two Options on Auto Origin Rules," *The Journal of Commerce*, January 21, 1992, 2A.

27. "U.S., Canada Report Progress on Plywood, Other Trade Issues," *International Trade Reporter* 9, no. 24 (Washington, D.C.: The Bureau of International Affairs, June 10, 1992), p. 1007.

5

A Mexican Assessment of the North American Free Trade Agreement Negotiations: Issues and Prospects

Carlos Alba Vega

THE FORMALIZATION OF A GROWING TRADE RELATIONSHIP

What led Mexico to seek a free trade agreement with the United States and Canada? What possible impact will this have on Mexico's future development and its relations with other nations, especially the rest of Latin America?

The rapprochement between Mexico with the United States is taking place within a context of recent profound changes in the international economic system.[1] The main reasons behind the Mexican government's present bid to seek the establishment of a free trade zone with the United States and Canada are as follows:

1. There has been recognition of a marked interaction between the Mexican and U.S. economies, which has grown steadily over the last hundred years.

2. The neoliberal development model, which has taken on a dominant global role since the 1980s, gave rise to the reform of the state, as well as the economic liberalization of most industrialized and developing countries.

3. The new Europe envisioned for the 1990s may have a decreasing need for close economic ties with Latin America.

4. Economic and political upheavals have occurred in the former Soviet Union and Eastern Europe. In the economic sphere it is believed that these zones will be the future competitors with the developing countries in the field of foreign trade, and especially in matters relating to the attraction of foreign investment.

5. The free trade agreement was signed by the United States and Canada in 1988,[2] which threatened to have a negative impact on the introduction of Mexican goods and services into the North American free trade zone that was created largely as a response to the formation of the European bloc.

For the last hundred years or more, relations between Mexico and the United States have been growing closer,[3] despite the historic divergence in their political positions[4] and despite, or perhaps because of, the enormous economic gulf between the two, and due to reasons of geographic destiny. Some of the main elements involved in this relationship are as follows:

1. The accumulated direct U.S. investment in Mexico increased almost threefold over the last ten years, rising from $7.3 billion in 1982 to $9.0 billion in 1990.[5]

2. Almost 1,500 export Maquiladora companies (in-bond assembly plants)—most of which are U.S. owned—were set up over the last twenty years along Mexico's northern border. Nevertheless, most of the companies arrived after 1982, attracted by the steep devaluations of the Mexican peso and the fall in Mexican wages. The number of firms has risen 15 percent annually since 1982; they now represent 15 percent of the manufacturing industry work force (450,000 workers) and 8 percent of the foreign currency earnings.

3. The United States accounts for 87 percent of the almost 7 million tourists who visit Mexico each year. Between 1965 and 1985 the tourist sector grew at an annual rate of 7.1 percent, and even during the crisis of the 1980s (a crisis of the external debt, the fiscal deficit, the fall in petroleum prices, and the effect of the national policy of economic adjustment), jobs in tourism rose from 3.7 to 4.6 million between 1982 and 1986.[6]

4. There is a significant migratory flow of young Mexicans who cross the border without documents for seasonal work in the United States. Until ten years ago the vast majority were men from rural areas; however, the urban and female population percentage has now increased. It is impossible to give an exact figure, but the number is calculated in the hundreds of thousands. In 1984 it was estimated that there were 1.4 million permanent Mexican illegal aliens in the United States (without counting dependent family members), apart from those who were working legally. Furthermore, close to 100,000 Mexican residents cross the border daily to work in the United States for wages seven times higher than in Mexico. The population born in Mexico and living in the United States increased from 2.5 million in 1980 to 4.1 million in 1988. During the same period, the proportion of Mexicans within the alien population in the U.S. rose from 18 percent to 24 percent.[7]

5. The amount of dollars sent back by Mexican workers is of vital importance in the regions where the migrants come from. This factor helps offset the impact of the crisis on the precarious local economies. There is no precise figure for the amount repatriated. A 1984 study calculated the amount as being $1.8 billion, which was only exceeded by earnings from oil and manufacturing exports and tourism.[8] A recent study based on Banco de México's data shows the increasing importance in volume of workers' remittances during the 1980s, to the extent that in 1990 they

amounted to almost $2 billion, not including remittances through informal channels.[9]

6. The smuggling of goods from the United States—on a small or large scale—has been a common practice in Mexico for many decades. There are probably very few Mexicans who have not, at some time of their lives, bought *fayuca*, that is, a product smuggled into Mexico without taxes being paid.

7. The capital flight from Mexico to the United States worsened after the 1960s. There is no agreement on the amount of capital involved; however, according to the average of six studies, it is estimated that the amount between 1976 and 1984 rose to $21.5 billion for Argentina, $13.3 billion for Brazil, $3.8 billion for South Korea, $21.1 billion for the Philippines, $25.2 billion for Venezuela, and an average of $43 billion for Mexico.[10]

8. The illegal trafficking in drugs produced in Mexico or that pass through the country in transit to the U.S. market is a major issue. According to a statement made by President Salinas de Gortari in his 1991 annual address to the nation, the value of drugs confiscated in Mexico in 1990 exceeded the total amount of Mexico's foreign debt.

9. The foreign debt is another extremely important issue between the two countries. At the beginning of the 1970s, when former president Echeverría took office, the foreign debt totaled $4 billion dollars; by the end of his administration the debt had risen to $20 billion. During the presidency of his successor, López-Portillo, the debt rose to $100 billion.[11] The renegotiation of the foreign debt was one of the Salinas Administration's most outstanding international achievements.

10. The Mexican market's plunge as a result of the economic crisis and adjustment policies drove some companies to begin exporting to the United States while others increased and concentrated their exports in that market. However, the relative fall in productivity in the United States in comparison with the European Economic Community and the newly industrialized countries, especially in Southeast Asia, the trade deficit, and finally the recession led to increasingly protectionist measures that affected Mexican exporters. Phyto-sanitary and hygiene standards were utilized to stop Mexican products like foodstuffs and fruits (avocados), ostensibly voluntary export restraints were imposed on some goods, such as textiles (Multifiber Agreement), iron, and steel; questions about hygiene were raised on some foodstuffs; ecological reasons were raised in the case of some seafoods, such as tuna; and unilateral antidumping practices were applied (beer, glass, cement, and plastic).

Within this context, and with the proposed North American Free Trade Agreement, the Mexican state seeks to achieve the greatest tariff cuts possible on Mexican exports, while recognizing the economic differences of the three countries; eliminate the nontariff barriers facing Mexican exports within a framework of clear reciprocity; ensure secure and increased access to the U.S. and Canadian markets that will lead to long-term certainty; accomplish fairness in the solution of controversies and prevent the application of unilateral measures by the U.S.; and obtain full complementarity of the three economies. For the Mexican state, the NAFTA is seen as part of an overall strategy to support the economic modernization process. The strategy seeks, at the same time, to satisfy the internal development demands and the new conditions imposed by the globalization process. With the end of the cold war and ideological confrontation, there is a fierce struggle to obtain capital, acquire technology, and penetrate new markets.

THE RESULTS OF THE NEGOTIATIONS

Some of the most sensitive issues in the NAFTA negotiations from the Mexican point of view are related to energy resources, especially oil; foreign investment; agriculture; textiles; and the automobile industry.

Oil

With respect to oil, the five basic premises of the Mexican negotiators are preserved: The Mexican state shall maintain sovereignty over, and direct ownership of the petroleum; only the Mexican state may be involved in the direct trade of petroleum, natural gas, and refined and basic petrochemical products; Pemex may not enter into risk contracts; there shall be no undertaking to guarantee the supply of petroleum; and foreign gas stations will not be permitted in Mexico.

However, prior to starting the negotiations, the Mexican government changed the classification of many products that were registered as part of the basic petrochemical group. Nevertheless, the transfer of these products to secondary petrochemicals meant profound changes in the industry without a formal modification of the constitution.

Foreign Investment

Only the Mexican government may invest in satellite systems and ground stations, telegraphs, and radio-telegraphs, provide postal services, and engage in the operation and administration of the railroads and the issuance of legal tender. Furthermore, only Mexicans by birth may acquire ownership of land and waters along the Mexican coasts and borders.

Until the possibility of a NAFTA, there had been no modifications to the Foreign Investment Law. However, the Regulation of Foreign Investment Law was created (published in May 1989), which allowed 100 percent foreign investment in more than 80 percent of cases. (Previously, the maximum allowed without prior authorization was 49 percent.)

In 1982, the accumulated direct foreign investment totaled $12.9 billion; in 1986 it had risen to $17.1 billion; in 1988 the figure was $24.1 billion; and by 1990 it had reached $30.3 billion. Foreign investment from 1986 to 1990 ranged between $2.4 and $3.8 billion per year.[12]

Agriculture

In agriculture the negotiation was complicated by Mexico's interest in achieving self-sufficiency in agricultural production of basic foodstuffs, and expanding control of production and distribution networks. Another obstacle was the low level of Mexican productivity in some important products, due not only to the climatic and natural conditions but also to important social and sector-based policies.

This implies reducing Mexico's dependence on imported foodstuffs. Since the mid-1970s, the subsistence agricultural sector, which concentrates on the production of basic foodstuffs, has been in a state of chronic crisis; a large part of staples have to be imported. For example, maize imports from 1980 to 1990 totaled $3.9 billion, soya imports amounted to $2.7 billion, and sorghum, $2.8 billion. Apart from this, the integration of Mexican agriculture into NAFTA will be subject to well-defined limits imposed by nature and society. According to many farmers and analysts,[13] this sector will not be able to compete with the United States and Canada in the short and medium term. Vegetables and fruit, such as tomatoes (northwest), cucumbers (northwest and west), zucchini and avocados (Michoacan), mangoes (northwest, west, and Gulf), pineapples (Gulf and south Pacific), citrus (northeast, Colima, and Gulf), coffee (Veracruz), and other goods such as flowers, are competitive in the North American market due to certain climatic, seasonal, or socioeconomic advantages because of the high labor requirements. Consequently, the producers of fruits and vegetables, who in recent years have penetrated the European and Japanese markets, believe that NAFTA is indispensable in solving the nontariff barrier problem.

Nevertheless, when it comes to products with a low labor requirement and a high degree of mechanization due to the type and size of the arable area, as in the case of grains, cereals, and oil-seeds for human consumption, the productivity levels in the United States and Canada are much higher than in Mexico. With the exception of wheat grown under highly favorable conditions in the Mexican northwest where production per hectare is 1.7 times higher (4 tons against 2.9 in the United States), the U.S. productivity in cereals and grains far outstrips Mexico's. For example, the crop yield for maize is 1.68 tons per hectare in Mexico against 5.31 in the United States; rice is 3.5 against 6.17; barley, 1.72 against 2.07; and oats, 1 against 1.40. In the case of soy beans, the production in both countries is similar, although Mexico only produces 500,000 tons while the United States produces more than 41 million.[14] According to agricultural sector analysts, it is not only possible to boost productivity in Mexico, such productivity increases cannot be delayed. However, in Canada and the United States there is a set of factors that enable them to compete highly advantageously: the availability of large tracts of arable land, the quality of the seasonal lands and the natural irrigation systems, and the climatic and soil fertility conditions that make it possible to reduce the risk of disease and fertilizer expenses. Besides these advantages provided by nature, in the United States, as in the European Economic Community and Japan, there are well-defined agriculture support policies because of interest group pressures. This is illustrated by the financial and other resources channeled toward research, infrastructure, and other direct and indirect supports for producers, which include price guarantees, subsidies on loans, production insurance, purchase and storage guarantees, pest-fighting programs, and financing for the construction of housing. Within this context, Mexican agriculture, undercapitalized and subordinated to urban-industrial growth for several decades, now has to face the serious problem of the withdrawal of the support of many government institutions, such as Anagsa (insurance), Banrural (loans), Conasupo (purchase, storage, and supply of staples) and Fertimex (fertilizers). In light of these conditions, according to the proponents of this argument, the Mexican agricultural sector that produces grains and cereals will not be in a position to compete in an open North American market for long unless it receives similar supports. For many agricultural specialists, this means giving up national sovereignty to ensure the availability of basic foodstuffs for the population. From this point of view, and in parallel with the NAFTA negotiations, various vital points have been discussed and analyzed: defining what is meant by food sovereignty and the products in which Mexico needs to be self-sufficient; the real possibilities of competing, product by product; and the producers' organizations' degree of negotiating room to ensure that the NAFTA does not go beyond national interests and the needs of several million rural producers.[15]

As a result of the negotiations, the agricultural sector (including livestock) obtained the longest tariff reduction term. In the case of maize, beans, and powdered milk, the period is fifteen years. The initial Mexican tariff on maize is 215 percent. It is expected that 40,000 tons of powdered milk will be imported annually, which is slightly lower than the average over the last few years.[16]

In 1992, the government modified Article 27 of the Constitution, with a resulting change in the tenure of the *ejido* (commonly held land). The *ejidatario* lands may now be sold after these highly controversial changes. From the government's point of view, these modifications were made to give the *campesinos* full ownership of the lands and promote various forms of organization, production, and investment in farming.

Textiles

The textile industry is one of the sectors most affected by Mexico's freer trade policies. Both the garment and textile industries are going through a profound crisis related to the collapse of the market and the free imports of the 1980s and the sociotechnical changes imposed by industrial restructuring. Personnel layoffs and the efforts made by the companies to obtain more flexible labor relations—until now guaranteed by a Collective Contract, which is negotiated by the entire textile sector, and not by each industry and its employees individually—gave rise to lengthy strikes in most of the sector in 1992. Furthermore, the U.S. Multifiber Agreement sets restrictions on imports from Mexico. In this respect, with the signing of NAFTA, all quotas on Mexican textiles and garments that meet the rules of origin regulations will be immediately eliminated. The basis to determine origin under the regulation will be the origin of the thread, which must be produced in any of the three countries. According to the talks, the "tariff peaks" will also be immediately removed in the United States for Mexican exports; the maximum start-up tariff will be 20 percent. Forty-five percent of Mexico's exports to the United States will soon be tariff-free. Mexico will only immediately eliminate taxes on 20 percent of the U.S. exports and will keep the present restrictions on used clothes.

The Automobile Industry [17]

The manufacture of vehicles and automobile parts has been at the forefront of the industrial integration of the three countries, and it has also been the driving force behind Mexico's export dynamism in the last decade. The industry directly or indirectly employs 450,000 workers and its exports account for a quarter of the industry whole. The proposal is for United States and Canada to immediately eliminate tariffs on automobiles; taxes on light trucks will be cut from 25 percent to 10 percent immediately and eliminated in five years; and the tariffs on heavy trucks, tractor trailers and buses will be eliminated in ten years. Likewise, Mexico will reduce tariffs on cars from 20 percent to 10 percent immediately and on light trucks in five years. The tax on heavy trucks, tractor trailers, and buses will be eliminated in ten years.

Under NAFTA, the United States will immediately eliminate the tariffs on 81 percent of Mexican automobile parts exports; on 18 percent of the exports in five years; and the remaining 1 percent in ten years. In recognition of the economic asymmetry, Mexico's future policy for lifting taxes will be different. Tariffs will be removed immediately from 5 percent of the imports from the United States; 70 percent in five years; and the final 25 percent in ten years.

In relation to the elimination of non tariff barriers, Mexico proposes keeping restrictions on the free import of cars and light trucks for ten years, while the period for buses will be five years.

The free import of used vehicles that meet the current pollution and safety norms will come into effect in the sixteenth year of the agreement and will culminate at the end of the twenty-fifth year.

The rule of origin for a vehicle to benefit from the customs preference is as follows: The net regional cost must be more than 50 percent of the net manufacturing cost during the first four years of the agreement when ratified. This limit will be raised to 56 percent during the following four years; after the ninth year, it will be set at 62.5 percent. This percentage has been considered as being highly protectionist by various European and Asian countries, and by some economic analysts.[18]

In order to further a gradual integration of the regional automobile sector, NAFTA envisages a progressive deregulation of the current provisions in the three countries: the Automobile Decree in Mexico, the Fuel Efficiency Laws in the United States, and the Bilateral Sector Agreement between Canada and the United States.

Tariff Elimination

Various terms were established in the talks for the elimination of tariffs so that each sector may have a period of transition. These groups, or sectors, were chosen by the negotiators to classify which business activities would be eligible for phased out tariffs over specific periods of time.

First Group: Immediate Elimination of Tariffs. The United States will eliminate 84 percent, and Canada 79 percent, of the taxes on Mexican nonoil exports. Mexico will remove tariffs on 43 percent of U.S. merchandise and 41 percent of goods from Canada. Capital goods account for 80 percent of these imports (machinery, electronic instruments and equipment, nonautomobile transport, and chemical products).

Second Group: Gradual Elimination over Five Years. The United States and Canada will eliminate taxes on about 1,200 products (including a large number of automobile and textile products), which in 1991 accounted for 8 percent of Mexico's nonoil exports. Mexico will remove tariffs on 2,500 products (18 percent and 19 percent of the imports from the U.S. and Canada).

Third Group: The Progressive Elimination of Duties Until the Tenth Year of NAFTA. Canada and the United States will eliminate tariffs on 7 percent to 12 percent of Mexico's nonoil exports. Mexico will eliminate taxes on 38 percent of imports from her partners.

Fourth Group: Elimination of Tariffs in the Fifteenth Year. Each country will eliminate the remaining 1 percent on imports. This group includes Mexico's most sensitive products, such as beans, maize, and powdered milk.

From the Mexican government's point of view, the structure of these phasing-out periods means three things. First, there is certainty for the producers about the tariff profile, which enables them to make rational business decisions. Secondly, the imbalance in development by the United States and Canada is recognized. Indeed, Mexican exports, according to the NAFTA agreement text, will have quicker access to the United States and Canada, especially with the consolidation of the 4,000 items that come under the United States Generalized System of Preferences. Finally, it means that the Mexican economy will, on average, have more time in which to modernize and adapt to the new market.

The elimination of nontrade barriers is of equal importance to the lifting of tariffs. NAFTA envisages the suppression of permits, quotas, and other quantitative restrictions on exports and imports in the three countries. Furthermore, Mexican exports cannot be discriminated against by local, state, or provincial laws in the United States or Canada.

The elimination of tariffs will be applied to goods wholly produced in the region, goods that come under a different tariff category than those of foreign materials, and goods that meet the regional content requirements.

Customs Issues

A common certificate of origin will be established; customs processing rights will be eliminated in July 1999; and early rulings will be given on the fulfillment of the rules of origin to provide legal security for importers and exporters.

Duty Drawbacks

The rebate on taxes paid for the importing of goods from outside the region will be eliminated in 2001 for products that meet the rules of origin. After a grace period of seven years, the rebate on products that do not meet the rules of origin will be limited to a sum determined in accordance with preestablished criteria.

Safeguards

A system of safeguards for products that meet the rules of origin was agreed upon by NAFTA negotiators. If imports seriously damage a domestic industry, the tariff in force prior to the agreement may be reestablished once, for no more than three years.

THE BUSINESS COMMUNITY AND THE NAFTA

Although the Mexican business community is a very mixed group, there is a favorable consensus regarding the future Agreement among medium- and large-scale enterprises.

The Transnational Companies

These companies redirected their sales toward the external market after the collapse of the domestic market and the devaluations of the peso. These companies are now largely responsible for the export drive, accounting for almost half the sales of manufactured goods.[19] Transnational companies—the most outstanding example being those in the automobile industry—naturally side with the Mexican government in the NAFTA negotiations, because they have boosted exports to their country of origin and the resurgence of protectionism in the United States is a threat to the circulation of their products. However, some of these companies may insist on preventing new transnational companies—especially Asian and European—from setting up operations in Mexico with the sole intention of assembling parts manufactured in other countries and to use Mexico as a springboard for exports to the north. Consequently, a group of transnational companies is pressing for the establishment of stiff origin regulations, that is, for requirements of a high percentage of domestic integration for a product to be considered as Mexican.

Large Mexican Enterprises

Mostly located in the Mexico City conurbation and Monterrey, these companies generally produce intermediate consumer goods for both the domestic and export markets. These companies began the so-called industrial reconversion at the beginning of the 1980s, and many of them joined up with transnational companies to gain access to technology and to be able to compete in the export market. During recent years, there has been a convergence of the government's economic policies and the interests of these companies that represent the principal private participants in the NAFTA negotiations, since they are interested in having free access to the U.S. market.

Small and Medium-Sized Companies

These companies arose under the protection of an import-substitution policy that later became a transnationalized model. These firms are mainly involved in the traditional consumer goods industries (foodstuffs, beverages, footwear, leather products, textiles, and clothing) and in the manufacture of some metal products. These businesses are principally located in the center and west of Mexico, and they have always opposed Mexico's entry to the GATT. The crisis of 1982 affected them to a lesser extent than those producing intermediate consumer and capital goods. However, in 1987 and 1988 the freer trade measures dealt them a severe blow because of the stiff competition from Asia, in such products as clothing, footwear, leather goods, furniture, toys, and some metal goods. According to this business sector, NAFTA could offer some market niches and comparative advantages in North America over their Asian competitors.

The Small and Medium-Sized Businesses That Arose in the North of Mexico in Recent Decades

Unlike others in this category, these businesses have depended less on government concessions and protectionism in their foreign trade. These enterprises and a large sector of the middle class that arose as a business community during Mexico's economic boom were not organized in a corporate association with the state. Thanks to this independence, they were able to exercise privileged action in the electoral field, frequently for the benefit of the National Action Party (PAN), a right-wing, middle-class, business-oriented party with close ties to the Catholic Church, which has broken the ruling party's (PRI) traditional hold on some local and gubernatorial elections. This is one of the reasons behind PAN's victory in the gubernatorial elections in two northern states: Baja California (Ruffo, 1991) and Chihuahua (Barrio, 1992).

The Micro and Small Industries

This business sector,[20] which is largely informal, proliferated in the 1970s and 1980s. These producers have been completely marginalized in the political representation of their interests. The leaders of the micro-industries fear and distrust the NAFTA negotiations. They are skeptical about the possible benefits that a free trade zone may have for their small businesses, which generally produce low-quality articles for the low-income market in Mexico. The future of the small-scale producers depends on the domestic market, investment, and wages.

The Agricultural Producers

The producers of fruits and vegetables, which include some of Mexico's most powerful agribusinesses, are impatiently waiting for NAFTA to open the door to the vast U.S. market for several of their products on which there are no tariff barriers. The producers of grains, cereals, and oil-seeds, including the poorest and least organized *campesinos* who cultivate mostly nonirrigated land, believe that they do not have the natural advantages or the necessary economic policy support to compete with the U.S. and Canadian producers. According to many analysts, this agricultural sector is the most vulnerable to free trade.

CONCLUSION

There is an obvious question in relation to the cost and benefits of NAFTA for each one of the three countries. Who has most to gain and who has most to lose?

Some analysts consider that Mexico might gain most in the short and medium term because the market the United States and Canada offer Mexico is much bigger than the market Mexico offers the other countries. This would offer greater opportunities to Mexican producers, while in the short term the United States and Canada face a depressed and segmented Mexican market and a population with little purchasing power. Nevertheless, the low wages of Mexicans represent an advantage for certain types of Canadian and U.S. enterprises in Mexico, especially assembly plants.

If Mexican salaries were to rise toward the levels of those in the partner countries, as some people believe will happen, this advantage would diminish, but in this case the expansion of the Mexican market would offer new opportunities to U.S. and Canadian enterprises.

On the other hand, the risks seem to be higher for Mexico than for the other partners. Two-thirds of Mexico's trade is with the United States, while less than 5 percent of U.S. trade is directed toward Mexico. From this point of view the U.S. stake is less than the Mexican one.

Although the North American Free Trade Agreement talks do not imply a customs union (there will not be a common external tariff for third countries) and even less a common market (there will be no free circulation of people or capital, only goods and services), the agreement, if implemented, will have social, economic, political, and cultural implications and consequences for Mexico which, in many cases, are still unforeseeable.

In the social sphere, the main consequences will be seen in employment patterns. It is quite possible that the present internal migratory trends will become more acute, in that there will be a greater rural exodus to the urban centers and the new industrialization zones, principally along the northern border. Stopping the migration of illegal aliens to the United States is an important issue for the U.S. government in signing the agreement, since it is argued that new jobs will be created in Mexico. The great challenge facing Mexico, not only with this agreement, but also with the adoption of the new development model, is to ensure that the benefits are reasonably fairly distributed throughout the population. So far, increased exports of manufactured goods, increased foreign investment, the return of capital, the notable drop in inflation, the 4 percent economic growth in 1991, and the other achievements of the macroeconomic policy have not benefited most Mexicans. The severe drop in the standard of living for the majority as a result of the economic crisis and the adjustment policies adopted in the 1980s are still present. Will NAFTA lead to higher real wages for Mexicans in the long run—as the negotiators in the three countries claim[21]—or is Mexico's role to be based historically on a complementary economic function on the basis of low wages and a passive, subordinate integration, as the opposition argues?[22]

In the economic sphere, the signing of the agreement will affect the direction of accumulation: on what, how, when, and where to produce. But will the Mexican economic system have the capacity productively to integrate highly mixed agricultural, industrial, and service regions and sectors?[23] Is the fact that most of the economic dynamism is backed by foreign capital important for Mexico? Will NAFTA lead to greater diversification of Mexico's trade relations, in which the United States now accounts for two-thirds of the volume, while trade with Latin America represents less than 4 percent of the total? Will the small- and medium-sized industries be able to face international competition in their own country and somehow form part of the export model, as has happened in some parts of Italy and some Southeast Asian countries? In short, with this new model will Mexico be able to counteract the internal division between the modernized, export-oriented sectors and the vast marginalized sectors?

From a political perspective, it is important to ask whether the state can redirect the development of society; whether it will have room to maneuver to preserve natural resources—especially oil—and protect the environment; and whether it will have the freedom and independence to participate in strategic and military alliances at an international level.

In the cultural sphere, the agreement poses a challenge for the transformation of local, regional, and national identities.

In conclusion, by changing the development model and seeking free trade with the United States and Canada, Mexico will face a growing challenge: making economic growth compatible with social integration within a framework of democratic expansion and in the context of the preservation of national values regarding sovereignty and independence.

NOTES

1. Mario Ojeda, "El cambiante contexto internacional a finales del segundo milenio," in Mario Ojeda, José Sarukhán, Jorge Hernández Campos et al., *Hacia un tratado de libre comercio en América del Norte.* Presentación por Jaime Serra Puche. (México: Grupo Editorial Miguel Angel Porrúa, 1991), 320.

2. Sidney Weintraub, *México frente al Acuerdo de Libre Comercio Canadá–Estados Unidos* (México: Editorial Diana-Centro de Investigación para el Desarrollo, A.C., 1991).

3. Blanca Torres, ed., *Interdependencia. ¿Un enfoque útil para el análisis de las relaciones México–Estados Unidos?* (México: El Colegio de México, 1990); Gustavo Vega Cánovas, ed., *México ante el libre comercio con América del Norte* (México: El Colegio de México-Universidad Tecnológica de México, 1991); *Informe de la Comisión sobre el Futuro de las Relaciones México–Estados Unidos, El desafío de la interdependencia: México y Estados Unidos* (México: Fondo de Cultura Económica, 1988).

4. Lorenzo Meyer and Josefina Z. Vázquez, *México frente a Estados Unidos. Un ensayo histórico, 1776–1980* (México: El Colegio de México, 1982); Lorenzo Meyer, "La crisis de la élite mexicana y su relación con Estados Unidos. Raíces históricas del Tratado de Libre Comercio," in Gustavo Vega Cánovas, Comp., *México–Estados Unidos, 1990* (México: El Colegio de México, 1992), 73–93; Carlos Alvear Acevedo and Alberto Ortega Venzor, *TLC Marco Histórico para una negociación* (México, Ed. Jus, 1991), 326.

5. Jorge Amigo Castañeda, "Regulación y proyectos de inversión extranjera en México," *El mercado de valores* 51, no. 7, Nacional Financiera (April 1, 1991): 3–7.

6. Norman A. Bailey (with the help of Susan Aaronson), "La inversión extranjera en México," in Riordan Roett, comp., *México y Estados Unidos: El manejo de la relación.* (México: Siglo XXI, 1989), 45–62.

7. Fernando Lozano Ascencio, "Las remesas enviadas por los trabajadores mexicanos en Estados Unidos en 1990: reflexiones sobre su monto y significado económico y social," in Gustavo Vega, *México Estados Unidos, 1990*, 55–72. Based on Karen A. Woodrow and Jeffrey S. Passel, "Post-IRCA Undocumented Immigration to the United

States: An Assessment Based on the June 1988 CPS," in F. D. Bean, B. Edmonston, and J. S. Passel, *Undocumented Migration to the United States: IRCA and the Experience of the 1980s* (Rand Corporation and The Urban Institute, 1990).

8. Manuel García y Griego, "La oferta de emigrantes mexicanos a Estados Unidos, 1990–2010," in Jorge A. Bustamante and Wayne A. Cornelius, eds., *Flujos migratorios mexicanos hacia Estados Unidos* (México: Fondo de Cultura Económica, 1989), 67–114; Juan Luis Orozco, *El negocio de los ilegales: Ganancias para quién* (México: Instituto Libre de Filosofía, 1992).

9. Fernando Lozano Ascencio, "Las remesas enviadas por los trabajadores mexicanos en Estados Unidos en 1990: reflexiones sobre su monto y significado económico y social," in Gustavo Vega, *México Estados Unidos*, 1990, 61. The figures are based on information given by Banco de México, *Informe anual 1990*, 23, 264.

10. Robert Cumby and Richard Levich, "On the Definition and Magnitude of Recent Capital Flight," in Donald R. Lessard and John Williamson, *Capital Flight and Third World Debt* (Washington, D.C., Institute for Economics, 1987), 38–43, tables 3.1–3.6.

11. Thomas J. Trebat, "La deuda exterior de México: viejas lecciones, nuevas posibilidades," in Roett, *México y Estados Unidos*, 106.

12. Castañeda, "Regulación y proyectos," 3–7.

13. José Luis Calva, *Probables efectos de un tratado de libre comercio en el campo mexicano* (México: Fontamara, 1991); see also Hubert Carton de Grammont, *Los empresarios agrícolas y el Estado: Sinaloa, 1893–1984* (México, Instituto de Investigaciones Sociales, UNAM, 1990), 277.

14. Demetrio Sodi de la Tijera, "TLC-soberanía alimentaria," *La Jornada*, 2 March 1991, 27.

15. Ibid.

16. José Díaz Moll, Founder and member of *Union General Obrero Campesina Popular (UGOCP)*, "El campo mexicano y la apertura comercial," *La jornada*, September 1, 1992.

17. See Jorge Carrillo, coord., *La nueva era de la industria automotriz en México: Cambio tecnológico, organizacional y en las estructuras de control* (Tijuana, Baja California: El Colegio de la Frontera Norte, 1990), 364.

18. Sidney Weintraub, "Las perspectivas del TLC en el Congreso Estadounidense y ante el posible triunfo de Bill Clinton," Seminar in El Colegio de México, Mexico City, September 8, 1992.

19. Héctor Hernández Cervantes, "Apertura comercial y proteccionismo: fomento industrial e inversiones extranjeras," in *El mercado de valores* 48, no. 10, Nacional Financiera (May 15, 1988); Carlos A. Rozo, "El Acuerdo de Libre Comercio en la disputa por la hegemonía mundial," in *La integración comercial de México a Estados Unidos y Canadá: ¿Alternativa o destino?* (México: Siglo Veintiuno Editores, 1990), 127–46; Kurt Unger and Luz Consuelo Saldaña, "Las economías de escala y de alcance en las exportaciones mexicanas más dinámicas," *El Trimestre Económico* 46(2), no. 222 (April–June 1989), 471–95.

20. Carlos Alba Vega, "La microindustria mexicana ante la liberalización económica y el Tratado de Libre Comercio de Norteamérica," in *Foro Internacional* (México: El Colegio de México, forthcoming.

21. Jaime Serra Puche, Secretary for Commerce and Industrial Promotion, "Las negociaciones sobre el tratado trilateral de libre comercio," Conference organized by

the Asociación Nacional de Universidades e Instituciones de Enseñanza Superior (ANUIES) and El Colegio de México, México, September 10, 1992. Jaime Serra Puche, *Reunión de Información sobre la Negociación del Tratado de Libre Comercio entre México, Canadá y Estados Unidos de América, ante la Comisión de Comercio del Senado de la República*, August 14, 1992.

22. José Angel Conchello, *El TLC: un callejón sin salida* (México: Grijalbo, 1992), 289; John Saxe-Fernández, "Aspectos estratégico-militares inmersos en el proyecto de integración de América del Norte," in *La integración comercial de México a Estados Unidos y Canadá*, 84–103.

23. For the economic and sectoral impacts see Adalberto García Rocha, Timothy Kehoe, José Romero, and Horacio Sobarzo, "Efectos de un Tratado de Libre Comercio sobre la economía mexicana," in Ojeda, Sarukhán, Hernández Campos et al., *Hacia un tratado de libre comercio en América del Norte*, Preface by Jaime Serra Puche, 199–240; Eduardo Andere and Georgina Kessel, comps., *México y el tratado trilateral de libre comercio: Impacto sectorial* (México: ITAM McGraw Hill/Interamericana de México, S.A.de C.V., 1992), 384.

6

Trade Liberalization and the Lessons of the Mexican Maquiladora Program

Randall Crane

INTRODUCTION[1]

Any comparison of the pros and cons of free trade depends critically on the perspective taken. Even then, forecasting the impacts of changes in trade policy is an inexact and speculative science. In the case of the United States and Mexico, however, we have the advantage of observing the progress of a continuing experiment in the loosening of trade barriers. The maquiladora program, an export processing zone for foreign-owned assembly operations, has been in operation for over twenty-five years. This Mexican government program allows foreign firms, most of which have been U.S.-owned, to manufacture goods in Mexico with Mexican labor and with foreign materials imported nearly duty-free. The U.S. government's part of the arrangement allows these firms to export the completed goods back to the United States with import tariffs paid only on the value added to the product in Mexico.

The program has benefited U.S. firms directly by providing an alternative to distant and more costly Asian labor markets. On the Mexican side, maquiladoras have generated a level of foreign exchange second only to petroleum. From a handful of companies and an employment base of a few hundred workers in 1965, the sector has now grown to over 2,000 firms and nearly 500,000 employees. By any reasonable growth standard, the program has been a success for investors and consumers in the United States and many workers in Mexico.

There are other affected groups, however, and growth is not the only relevant standard. Opportunities have been missed on all sides, and growing pains are more pronounced with each passing day. The sector has had only minor stimulative impact on the industrial and technological development of the larger Mexican economy, for example, even in those regions where the operations are concentrated. In this respect especially, the maquiladora assembly operations have disappointed observers and participants alike by remaining an economic and geographic enclave within Mexico. Export processing zones in other developing countries, particularly in the recently industrialized nations of Asia, have served as a springboard for industrial and technological advances, through the strategic development of forward and backward linkages with other home industries. In contrast, the maquiladora industry has not moved much beyond assembly. The learning curve for export-oriented Mexican industry has been less steep than hoped for, even while the size of the sector, and the dependence of the Mexican export economy on the sector, continues to grow. The labor force has experienced only moderate transformation, and the technological capacity of the nation has not increased in step with employment growth.

In addition, the Mexican economy has in many ways paid dearly for the rapid development of the maquiladora industry. Rapid urbanization in the border areas where most maquiladora activity is concentrated has strained public and private infrastructure beyond capacity and, in some areas, led to declining living and health conditions of tragic proportions. Enforcement of environmental standards is uneven at best, which has had an impact on the health of workers and of the residents living near industrial centers. The success of individual maquiladora plants has been irregular as well, raising concerns about the level of dependence of the Mexican economy on foreign markets and foreign capital, particularly in border regions.[2] Some observers have argued that if the maquiladora industry were to close up shop tomorrow, perhaps due to rapid wage growth in the border labor markets, the nation would have little to show for the experience other than border communities that have grown too fast and haphazardly to accommodate their populations.

These concerns are real and legitimate, and they bear tidings for additional trade liberalization initiatives such as the NAFTA and EAI efforts, even while the benefits of such efforts have more to offer Mexico in the short run than any other participant. Given the many opportunities presented by the opening of the Mexican economy, it is clear that the benefits promised by free trade should amount to more than semi-skilled job growth and poor residential living standards. Compounding the process of the integration of the Mexican economy with its NAFTA partners are two additional factors: the gap in wealth and wages between the United States and Mexico is larger than any two adjacent nations in the world, and the Mexican economy suffered its worst downturn of the century in the mid-1980s, from which it has yet to recover. A fear of dominance and exploitation by the United States overlays this contrast. Based on experience, this perception of the United States as a threat to both its sovereignty and its economic integrity has long influenced Mexican attitudes toward a more integrated U.S.–Mexican economic structure. At the same time, the capital required to take advantage of more open borders and to finance industrial renovation cannot come from within Mexico in the near term.

Against this backdrop is the almost certain prospect of lowering trade barriers. What are the implications for the maquilas, and how can the maquiladora experience inform our judgment regarding the impacts of further trade liberalization on Mexico? The future of Mexican industrial development is a thorny issue, and has been addressed sector by sector in Carlos Alba's chapter in this volume. The present chapter will accept the narrower charge of viewing the maquiladora program as a regional economic development effort that has evolved over the years to set the stage for a NAFTA and an EAI. The characteristics of the program, its historical development, and the associated problems will be summarized. Looking ahead, the chapter will also consider the impacts of a future lowering of trade barriers between the United States and Mexico.

BACKGROUND CHARACTERISTICS AND TRENDS

The increasingly competitive trade relations of the developed nations are, in many ways, reflected in the division of production and labor across the developing countries. One such example is the development of export processing zones in several developing countries, where relatively inexpensive labor mainly assembles finished goods for export from imported materials.[3] These zones have offered many countries a viable avenue for participation in foreign markets, by means of international subcontracting. In Mexico, the example is the "In-Bond Industry" or maquiladora program. Located for a time exclusively along the border with the United States, the plants in the program are still largely concentrated in the North. The participating firms may import materials and machinery duty-free for additional processing or assembly of goods for exportation. In compensation for foregone tariff revenue, there are many potential advantages to Mexico. They include the economic development of the base regions, the transfer of technology from the developed nations sponsoring and supervising local operations, and the infusion of foreign exchange in the form of local wages and purchases of local materials and services.

The close of the Bracero program in the mid-1960s provoked the creation of the industry. Before that time, up to 200,000 workers were allowed to enter the United States from Mexico for agricultural employment each year.[4] In part to deal directly with the resulting unemployment in the border area, and to promote border area development, the Border Industrialization Program (BIP) began in 1964. It designated a 12.4 mile (20 kilometer) strip along the U.S./Mexico border as an export processing zone, where no taxes or customs duties were imposed on the materials imported as manufacturing inputs—unless the final product was sold within Mexico. On the U.S. side, lower import duties were levied on goods assembled or processed in the border zone for export to the United States. This special treatment occurred when goods entered under either U.S. tariff items 806.30 and 807.00 (before 1989), under the Harmonized Tariff Schedule item 9802 (since 1989), or, if eligible, duty-free under the Generalized System of Preferences (GSP).[5]

The legal environment of the industry has evolved over time, with a trend toward more flexibility with respect to permitted locations, foreign ownership rules, and the share of maquiladora output that could be sold domestically. In 1971 new regulations allowed maquiladora firms to be completely owned by foreigners in all industries except textiles and apparel. They also allowed maquiladora firms to operate in a limited number of areas outside the border region. These were revised the following year to allow for the location of maquila operations in any area targeted for industrial development—mainly areas outside the major metropolitan areas of Monterrey, Guadalajara, and the Valley of Mexico (Mexico City)—such that the industry is today officially called the In-Bond Industry program. By 1983, certain industries were allowed to sell as much as 20 percent of their output in domestic markets, with the requirement that the product had at least 15 percent Mexican content and did not compete directly with any domestic production. Those products sold domestically were then liable for import duties.

Long-term leases and related limited rights of land possession within fifty miles of the border or thirty miles of the coastline, which may not be foreign-owned, has been permitted since 1971. The government is apparently planning to adopt more lenient land ownership rules for border and coastal land in the near future, perhaps in the form of longer leases or direct foreign ownership.[6] The hope is that foreign investors will be more willing to invest in property improvements in the border areas, including infrastructure that would support other development. Restrictions on foreign investment in other sectors were relaxed further in May 1989. Limited foreign ownership in secondary petrochemicals, telecommunications, automobile parts, and others was permitted for the first time since the revolution. In other sectors, such as tourism, complete foreign ownership was allowed. The most recent decree governing the industry was published in December 1989, removing several restrictions on the operation of maquiladora firms and simplifying the administrative process for obtaining government approval for operation.[7] A maquiladora plant may receive permission to sell an amount of output on domestic markets equal to up to half as much as it exports, with some restrictions and with import tariffs levied only on foreign content. The next step in the legal status of the industry may be a move in status from rule by presidential decree to one based on legislation.

Table 6.1 illustrates how the number of maquiladoras, their employment, and the value-added in Mexico has increased during this period of institutional change. Between 1983 and December 1991, the number of maquiladora plants grew by more than threefold, from 600 to just over 2,000. Employment in the industry grew by roughly the same proportion. Of the total number, 1,444 border maquila plants were located within the border zone, or 72 percent, and

Table 6.1
Employment and Value-Added in the Maquiladora Industry, 1970–1991

Year	Number of Maquiladoras	Total Employment	Value Added In Mexico ($millions)
1970	120	20,327	83
1980	578	119,546	772
1981	605	130,973	976
1982	585	127,048	851
1983	600	150,867	818
1984	722	199,684	1,155
1985	789	211,968	1,268
1986	844	249,833	1,295
1987	1,432	305,253	1,598
1988	1,441	369,489	2,337
1989	1,699	429,725	3,047
1990	1,924	472,000	3,635
1991	2,013	486,723	4,010

Sources: Gary Hufbauer and Jeffrey J. Scott, *North American Free Trade: Issues and Recommendations* (Washington, D.C.: Institute for International Economics, 1992); Instituto Nacional de Estadística Geografia e Informatica (INEGI), *Estadística de la Industria Maquiladora de Exportación 1978–1988* (Aquascalientes, Mexico: INEGI, 1989), and unpublished INEGI data provided to the author by the Mexican commerce ministry (SECOFI, 1992).

569 firms were located in the interior.[8] The border firms also employed 73 percent of the maquiladora labor force, amounting to over 16 percent of the nation's total manufacturing employment.[9] By September 1992, the Mexican commerce ministry (SECOFI), which administers the maquiladora program, reported that the maquiladora dollar income represented 8.1 percent of the balance of payments.[10] Most of this growth has occurred since the devaluations of the peso in the early 1980s, when relative wages in Mexico fell to less than one-half their prior level. Still, the mix of Mexican and foreign content of maquiladora output has been relatively steady over the last decade, with imported materials accounting for 77 percent of the value of maquiladora output and Mexican goods and services contributing 23 percent.[11]

These patterns naturally vary by industry and by location. The sectors with the largest number of firms have historically been electrical and electronic goods, textiles and apparel, and furniture manufacturing, as shown in Table 6.2. Automobile parts and equipment does not have a large number of plants, but employs 23 percent of the national maquiladora work force. Services is a growing but small employer, representing less than 5 percent of maquiladora employees.

The regional impact of the border area maquiladoras is substantial in those areas where the firms mainly locate, as shown in Table 6.3. Maquila firms now account for about 26 percent of total manufacturing employment in Mex-

Table 6.2
Employment and Value-Added by Selected Industries, 1991

Industry	Number of Maquiladoras	Total Employment	Percent of Maquila Employment	Value Added In Mexico ($millions)
Electronics & Electrical Equip.	496	161,807	33.2	1,463
Automobile Parts & Equip.	158	111,956	23.0	1,088
Other Manufacturing	365	64,120	13.2	56
Textiles	308	45,726	9.4	25
Furniture	254	26,528	5.5	24
Services	90	22,334	4.6	12

Source: Unpublished INEGI data provided to the author by the Mexican commerce ministry (SECOFI, 1992).

ico's six northern border states. These activities are further concentrated in the major cities, with Tijuana having 24 percent of the plants and nearly 13 percent of the employment of the maquiladora sector. Ciudad Juárez has over one-quarter of all maquiladora employment, with about half the number of firms as Tijuana. Together with Mexicali and Matamoros, these cities contain

Table 6.3
Employment by Selected Cities, 1991

City	Number of Maquiladoras	Total Employment	Percent of Maquiladora Employment	Value Added In Mexico ($millions)
Tijuana	492	62,632	12.7	57
Ciudad Juárez	260	125,383	25.8	103
Mexicali	133	20,151	4.1	20
Matamoros	96	38,051	7.8	64
Tecate	80	4,738	0.9	4
Nuevo Laredo	60	16,915	3.5	16
Chihuahua	57	31,915	6.5	268
Mexico City	26	2,994	0.6	42
Guadalajara	24	5,097	1.0	84
Monterrey	16	1,858	0.4	33

Source: Unpublished INEGI data provided to the author by the Mexican commerce ministry (SECOFI, 1992).

plants that employ over half the sector's workers. There have been a number of in-bond firms locating in the interior industrial cities of Guadalajara, Monterrey, and Mexico City, but only on a very modest scale. These cities are the largest in Mexico, with more than 30 percent of the nation's population, yet they represent only 3 percent of the maquiladora employment base.

To summarize, the industry experienced dramatic growth through the 1980s and into the 1990s in employment and foreign exchange. This growth is just beginning to expand into the vast interior of Mexico, but remains most visible in concentrations in a relatively few cities along the border. There is some evidence that the dominance of light assembly operations is giving way to manufacturing activities requiring more skilled labor and greater local service and material inputs, but the pace of this change is slow. The next section reviews the collateral problems most commonly associated with the sector's growth.

PROBLEMS

While the maquiladora phenomenon has clearly been beneficial in many respects, such as job creation in the northern border regions of Mexico, it has had its share of difficulties. This chapter has already described, in part, the direct benefits of the industry's development, in terms of the employment and foreign exchange generated over the past twenty-five years. Foreign manufacturers, mostly based in the United States, have also benefited in the form of reduced labor and other production costs. Some of these savings have no doubt been passed on to the consumers of these goods through increased production and lower prices. Since most production is exported, most of these consumers are in the United States, but Mexican consumers have increasing access to these goods as well. Many of the other chapters in this book identify and discuss these generic benefits of opening markets in considerable detail.

There are also costs, both real and imagined, which may be loosely grouped under five headings: (1) the weak forward and backward linkages of industrial maquiladora activity to the larger Mexican economy; (2) the migration of U.S. jobs to Mexico; (3) Mexican overdependence on foreign markets and economic dominance by the United States; (4) the environmental impacts of industrial development and population growth, including workplace health issues; and (5) the lack of investment in support infrastructure necessary for future economic development. There are other cost and equity issues associated with the regional development of the border and the economic status of the industry, to be sure, but this list touches on the concerns mentioned most frequently.

The Mexican economy has suffered through a severe economic slump over the past ten years, caused in part by protectionist trade policies and the enormous debt taken on during the boom years of high oil prices. While the maquiladora program has generated impressive levels of employment and foreign exchange in the interim, it has made only a minor dent in the estimated 800,000 jobs needed each year to accommodate new entrants into the work force.[12]

This record could be improved if the industry played the role of providing the mechanisms for technology transfer, worker training, and industrial integration that export processing operations have played in other countries, such as Korea. Rather, the maquiladoras represent in too many ways a physical and economic enclave, removed from the industrial heart of the nation. In part, this is due to geography. The industrial centers of the nation are found in its major cities, as in any country, and export-assembly operations have not been encouraged in those areas. One-third of the economic activity of Mexico takes place in the Mexico City area, which is home to less than 1 percent of the maquiladora operations.

Opportunities do exist for forward and backward linkages with other Mexican industries, but the pace of this change is slow. Some evidence of this trend is represented by the so-called "new maquiladoras."[13] These firms train workers and produce more sophisticated products with a higher share of locally produced components (an increase from 1.7 percent to 6 percent over the past ten years). This pattern is expected to continue over time, particularly as the benefits of free trade and the pressures of competition are extended to other sectors of the economy. As the economy of Mexico improves, the government may be capable of providing more start-up support for suppliers, and promotion of industrial linkages through investment in training and credit programs. The maquiladoras may never become wholly integrated into the Mexican economy, but it is clear they will play an important role in the industrial development of Mexico, which will in turn promote the integration of Mexico into the international economy.

With this increased industrial integration, an increase in the Mexican content of maquiladora exports may well come at the expense of U.S. component suppliers. U.S. workers therefore fear this will expedite the migration of industries, and jobs, to Mexico. While labor costs remain an important consideration for many products, their share of production costs continues to fall. The overall employment impacts of the maquiladora sector, and freer trade generally, remain difficult to forecast with precision, given the enormous uncertainty over the domestic and foreign responses to changes in market structure, changes in market demand, and changes in production costs. Nonetheless, a good deal of effort has been devoted to measuring these impacts. Most studies suggest that the shift of production to Mexico, and increases in maquiladora imports, would have relatively modest net effects on total U.S. employment levels.[14] Recent U.S. Department of Labor studies, for example, have found that the most dramatic changes would be in the distribution of U.S. employment among industries rather than the aggregate net gain or loss of jobs.[15] A study of the likely impacts on California of a NAFTA also emphasized the differential impacts on industries by sector.[16] A free trade agreement will limit the ability of the United States to maintain the wages of its low-skilled workers through import protection, given the comparatively low level of Mexican wages. Many of the affected industries disproportionately employ low-skilled workers, many of whom are in turn recent Mexican immigrants. In each case these assessments of employment impacts account for the reality that U.S. jobs already face competition from low-wage countries, whether from Mexico or Malaysia or elsewhere. It is in this sense that some rationalize job flight to Mexico as the least bitter pill among the available alternatives.

The U.S. employment impacts of increased trade are not all negative. With the growth and development of the Mexican economy will come rising Mexican demand for U.S. products by consumers, and growing demand for U.S. materials and technology by Mexican industry. In the maquiladora case, these multiplier effects have been most noticeable in the border regions. Studies of border state economies have measured a strong interdependency and a stimulative effect of maquiladora growth on employment and firm starts on the U.S. side of the border.[17]

There has long been concern within Mexico that the success of the maquiladora sector has made the country excessively dependent on external markets and foreign investors.[18] The corollary is that the employment gains may be transitory, depending as they do on international wage differences that may fade with time. As relative wages increase, so will the comparative advantages of the Mexican assembly labor market decrease, and the firms may leave. Moreover, the popular debate has included concerns regarding the growing potential for foreign exploitation of both labor and land. These firms have prospered at a time when Mexican wages were extremely low, and able workers had few options. This sense that foreign employers took advantage of the Mexican labor force at a time of unexpected and severe vulnerability was heightened by the high proportion of women maquila workers, especially during the early years of the industry.[19] Recent years have seen the proportion of male workers gradually rise from less than 20 percent ten years ago to about 35 percent today. The number is as high as 50 percent in some sectors, such as transportation equipment.

Questions have also been raised as to whether the impacts of differences in environmental laws and regulatory enforcement practices have encouraged foreign firms to treat Mexico as a potential site for "dirty" industries. Regarding firm behavior, these concerns take two forms: those related to environmental standards governing industrial production, and those related to occupational health standards. Environmental groups on both sides of the border have long complained about the lack of attention and resources provided by either the Mexican government or by maquiladora operators to deal with the pollution and other environmental impacts of industrial development in the border region.[20] It has been reported that some foreign industries establish themselves in Mexico because environmental controls there are less strict, or are less well enforced, than in the United States and elsewhere.

Health standards for workers in the workplace represent another area of contention. Observers argue that economic growth in Mexico may well come at the cost of decreased health of the labor force when foreign firms apply different safety and health standards to Mexican workers than for those in their home countries. Perhaps the most common public health risk is due to lax enforcement of the regulations governing the storage of hazardous materials within the maquiladora buildings. Most of the data on the occupational hazards associated with these materials are anecdotal, however, owing to the lack of data on industry practices and employee health generally.[21]

The prospect of NAFTA has stimulated new interest in border area conditions, and there is hope that recent official initiatives addressing these issues reflect more genuine enthusiasm than in the past, but environmental programs of one sort or another have been in place for years. Under Mexican legislation and Annex 3 of the 1983 U.S.–Mexico Binational Agreement for the Protection of the Border Environment (the La Paz Agreement), waste generated by U.S. maquiladoras must be transported back to the United States.[22] However, this requirement has been avoided, due to loopholes and lax enforcement and driven by the reality that the cost of disposing of hazardous waste in Mexico is about one-tenth the cost in the United States. The U.S. Environmental Protection Agency reported in 1987 that only around twenty of the 1,200 border zone maquiladora enterprises in place in 1987 had kept to this agreement.[23] Illegal dumping of waste may also occur, possibly on a widespread basis. Enforcement efforts have been hindered by the underfunding of the Mexican environmental regulatory agency, the Secretaría de Desarrollo Urbano y Ecología (SEDUE) that, until early 1992, had enforcement responsibilities.

Other environmental issues include health risks to residents of neighborhoods where firms locate and where, due to rapid urban immigration, people live in close quarters with inadequate water and sewage systems.[24] This is an indirect consequence of the maquiladora growth, and no doubt of future economic development in the border region and interior cities. Untreated sewage and water supply problems are major concerns in nearly every border community. In some instances, such as Tijuana and Nogales, binational water treatment and financing arrangements are in place. Air quality is also an issue. Population growth in the region, as in all the major cities of Mexico, has been at levels well beyond the capabilities of even a middle-income nation to prepare for.

A final set of problems with the maquiladora industry does not represent costs induced by the development of the sector so much as obstacles to its continued success, however one measures that success. Bottlenecks have become evident in several sectors, including labor, transportation, and public infrastructure. There is evidence that labor markets in border cities have tightened, which may limit the rate of expansion of manufacturing activity if wages lag below the level required to maintain low turnover rates.[25] This could dampen productivity growth. The increasingly poor living conditions in many of the urban areas in border cities may also contribute to lower rates of growth in labor supply.

The transportation and shipping network in Mexico is a prime example of the potentially critical role of public infrastructure in economic development. The combination of poor roads, an undersized railroad system, labor restrictions in trucking (only Mexican trucks and drivers may transport goods by truck within Mexico), a thinly spread air network on the Mexican side of the border, and increased concern about drug smuggling on both sides, has led to a painfully inadequate transportation infrastructure, particularly for movement across the border. More than 4,000 trucks cross the border every day, many of which require the assistance of professional intermediaries, or "brokers," who facilitate the completion of the customs paperwork and provide guidance through the sizable regulatory apparatus governing transborder shipments. All shipments are subject to customs inspections on both sides of the border. U.S. customs officials have stated that they are prepared to deal with the future increases in traffic, but staffing and facility size have not kept pace with current traffic flows.

These problems are, for the most part, massive in scale. They reflect structural changes in the U.S. economy, on the one side, and the growing pains faced by an industrializing nation, on the other. As such, they are not entirely avoidable. Both countries have considerable flexibility in the manner in which they choose to manage and accommodate these changes, however. Environmental and infrastructure problems require a combination of resources and political will. By their nature, the private sector will not solve these problems without financial assistance, economic incentives, and strong regulatory guidance by the governments having jurisdiction.

In 1992 the U.S. and Mexican governments announced the creation of clean up funds of $600 million to address environmental conditions in the border region. Though only a beginning, the amount is clearly inadequate to the task, particularly given the expectation of continuing rapid industrial development and population growth in these areas. Another sign of activity on the Mexico side is the reshuffling of environmental and development responsibilities within the federal cabinet, resulting in the creation in early 1992 of a new environmental and development ministry, Secretaría de Desarrollo Social (SEDESOL), replacing SEDUE and consolidating some functions of other ministries. The exact role of the new ministry is not yet clear, but it may signal the kind of commitment needed from the federal government for further progress.

The major concern, however, is the commitment of Mexican regulatory authorities to enforcing the laws already on the books. A significant obstacle to progress is the insufficient funding for enforcement efforts combined with the character of the administrative framework, which reflects the heavily centralized nature of many Mexican institutions. Sufficient discretionary enforcement authority is often not extended to the ranks of the officials in the field, with the result that regulations are applied unevenly and with hesitation. The problem, therefore, is not simply one of funding or the political will of the nation's leaders, but administrative reform in the lower ranks as well. The oft-stated promise of these trade negotiations is that this domestic strength, as well as overall regional growth, will be supported and financed by the gains from more

open trade. The more subtle issue of the overdependence of the Mexican economy on export assembly operations and U.S.-based firms can only be addressed by strenuous efforts to diversify and to promote domestic industrial growth.

LESSONS AND IMPACTS

Trade liberalization efforts typically attempt to increase the joint competitiveness of all negotiating parties. The intent is to offer protection against third
parties and trading blocs, on the one hand, and to promote trade among participating countries, on the other. Some of the main goals of the NAFTA
negotiations, for example, include expanding trade relationships within North
America along the lines of the maquiladora industry.[26] The draft NAFTA
agreement signed in December 1992 will ease restrictions on foreign investment in exporting firms and encourages increased technology transfer from
exporters to local firms, while promoting each participating country's exports.
It also aims to facilitate the transport of supplies, parts, and components from
one country to another for export production.[27] In addition, the negotiations
concerned administrative matters, such as customer support, fiscal burdens,
supporting local services, and access to domestic markets. Other components
of NAFTA are discussed elsewhere in this volume. As it happens, these tend
to mirror the areas where the maquiladora regulations have been moving over
the past twenty years.

How will trade liberalization affect the maquiladora firms that are in place,
and the growth of the sector in the future? In many respects, increased trade
throughout the Americas will provide additional opportunities for the maquiladora industry. Existing U.S. and Canadian maquiladoras should benefit from
NAFTA by reducing plant operating costs and facilitating the incorporation of
new technologies and manufacturing processes. Any new agreement will also
stimulate growth in new export enterprises by increasing the demand for imported goods previously excluded from more favorable trade terms. The latter
include chemical, paper, plastic, and other industries, which should complement existing maquiladoras. Other companies will benefit from the reduction
of shipping and telecommunications barriers.

The main attraction of maquiladoras from the U.S. perspective has been the
ample supply of low-wage labor to perform labor-intensive assembly activities,
along with duty-free reentry of U.S. materials contained in the final product.
Under NAFTA, U.S.-owned maquiladora operations would realize a further
cost saving if the product meets the rules of origin—that is, complete import
duty relief on the value added in Mexico—similar to GSP, but without a value-
added condition. From the standpoint of other foreign investors in maquiladoras, guaranteed access of Mexican goods to the U.S. market is more likely
to be the primary benefit. Continuation of the maquiladora program would
permit duty-free entry into Mexico of home-country sourced parts and components, with the eventual possibility of duty-free entry into the U.S. market.

This raises a potential U.S. concern about how the rules of origin will operate under NAFTA, which are more important in certain import-sensitive sectors that are also important maquiladora sectors. These include apparel, electronics, and motor vehicles and parts.

Various other problems with the continuing process of trade liberalization can be predicted based on the maquiladora experience over the years. The lack of transparency of Mexican rules and regulations has been an obstacle over the history of the maquila industry. Initially, informal concessions were given to specific firms in the form of exceptions. Over time these were more widely applied, and eventually they became presidential decrees.[28] In the past, foreign investments in the domestic Mexican economy faced obstacles by way of performance requirements or absolute barriers in some critical sectors. Simplification of Mexican government regulations and easing of some of the restrictions on foreign investment and foreign ownership have led to a rapid acceleration in investment in the maquiladora sector. This suggests that foreign investment in other sectors throughout the economy may be responsive to a similar effort in deregulation and liberalization of investment rules. As the Mexican economy becomes more open and rules on foreign investment become more liberal, the incentives offered to export-oriented enterprises may not significantly differ from those available to firms that produce primarily for the domestic market.[29]

CONCLUSION

In response to concerns that NAFTA will lead to U.S. job losses and other problems on both sides of the border, it is useful to realize that Mexico will continue to relax domestic trade restrictions with or without a treaty. Along with the reduction in import tariffs and the number of controlled items, the most visible example of this dramatic and largely unilateral change in Mexican policy is the maquiladora program. On the one hand, every indication is that Mexican participants in the NAFTA negotiations have sought to preserve the characteristics of the maquiladoras, by extending to them the benefits of trade liberalization. More than 95 percent of the products in the maquiladora industry have no problems complying with the rules of origin of trade. Most products that cannot be considered products of North America will continue to receive the benefits of current maquila regulations until the duty drawbacks eventually cease.

At the same time, Mexican businesses will face new competition in domestic markets, so there will be losers as well as winners for non-maquila industry. The trade advantages the in-bond industry has enjoyed compared to the rest of the private sector in Mexico will most likely diminish as foreign investment in other industries becomes less restricted and non-maquila production gains access to foreign markets. In the short to medium run, the border maquilas will maintain considerable transportation advantages over interior industries, particularly if NAFTA reduces the paperwork and bureaucracy attached to transborder travel. This advantage will diminish with time, however, as customs and port administration continue to reform. It is also the case that, despite considerable infrastructure problems in the border region, some industries have international trade infrastructure in place that industries elsewhere in Mexico must still develop. The net effect is difficult to anticipate, but it is likely that existing maquiladora activity will benefit from trade reform, while the growth rate of the industry as a whole will slow. Whatever comparative advantages there are at present to investing in a maquiladora industry in Mexico will appear smaller in a post-NAFTA world. This does not mean that the maquiladora firms will suffer under a free trade agreement, only that the benefits of trade liberalization, along with its costs, will be distributed more equally across the country.

NOTES

1. I am grateful to several officials in the Mexican Secretariat of Commerce and Industrial Development (SECOFI) for their generosity with data, to Luis Suarez-Villa for a helpful discussion and to Glenn Jenkins and Sidney Weintraub for comments on an earlier version.

2. In a page 1 article, the August 16, 1992, Orange County edition of the *Los Angeles Times* reports that nearly one-quarter of the maquiladora firms with roots in Orange County had gone out of business in the previous eighteen months.

3. For a survey of export processing zones elsewhere, see The World Bank, *Export Processing Zones* (Washington, D.C.: The World Bank, 1992).

4. This treatment follows Gregory Schoepfle, "Implications for U.S. Employment of the Recent Growth in Mexican Maquiladoras," *Frontera Norte* 3 (1991), 25–54.

5. Gregory K. Schoepfle, *U.S.–Mexico Free Trade Agreement: The Maquiladorization of Mexico?* (Washington, D.C.: Bureau of International Affairs, U.S. Department of Labor, April 1990).

6. *Los Angeles Times*, Orange County edition, August 3, 1992.

7. Secretaría de Comercio y Fomento Industrial (SECOFI), *La Industria Maquiladora de Exportaciao y el Tratado de Libre Comercio* (Mexico City: SECOFI, 1991).

8. Unpublished data from Instituto Nacional de Estadística Geografia e Informatica (INEGI) provided to the author by SECOFI (Mexico City, 1992).

9. Ibid.

10. Reported by Ricardo Castillo in *The News* (an English language daily in Mexico City), October 3, 1992.

11. Schoepfle, "U.S.–Mexico Free Trade Agreement."

12. These issues have been stressed by many analysts, including Joseph Grunwald, "Assembly Industries, Technology Transfer and Enterprise Zones," in Roy Green, ed., *Enterprise Zones: New Directions in Economic Development* (Newbury Park, Calif.: Sage Publications, 1991), and Sidney Weintraub, "The Maquiladora Industry in Mexico: Its Transitional Role," in Sergio Díaz-Briquets and Sidney Weintraub, eds., *Regional and Sectoral Development in Mexico as Alternatives to Migration* (Boulder, Colo.: Westview Press, 1991), 155–67.

13. See Patricia A. Wilson, *Exports and Local Development: Mexico's New Maquiladoras* (Austin: University of Texas Press, 1992).

14. See the assessments summarized in Gary Hufbauer and Jeffrey J. Scott, *North*

American Free Trade: Issues and Recommendations (Washington, D.C.: Institute for International Economics, 1992); and Nora Lustig, Barry Bosworth, and Robert Lawrence, eds., *North American Free Trade: Assessing the Impact* (Washington, D.C.: The Brookings Institution, 1992).

15. See Schoepfle, "Implications for U.S. Employment," and Gregory K. Schoepfle and Jorge F. Perez-Lopez, "The Impact of Maquiladoras on U.S. National Employment and Employment in Selected Industrial Sectors," in Khosrow Fatemi, ed., *The Maquiladora Industry: Economic Solution or Problem?* (New York: Praeger, 1990), 37–56.

16. Raúl Hinojosa-Ojeda, Sherman Robinson, and Goetz Wolff, "The Impact of a North American Free Trade Agreement on California: A Summary of Key Research Findings," Working Paper No. 3, The Lewis Center for Regional Policy Studies, University of California, Los Angeles (September 1992).

17. See the U.S. International Trade Commission report, "The Impact of Increased United States–Mexico Trade on Southwest Border Development," USITC, Washington, D.C. (November 1986) and the studies summarized in J. Michael Patrick, "The Employment Impact of Maquiladoras Along the U.S. Border," in Fatemi, *The Maquiladora Industry*.

18. See the discussion in Weintraub, "The Maquiladora Industry in Mexico."

19. The role of women in the maquiladora labor force, by sector, is summarized and explored in Susan Tiano, "Women Workers in the Electronics and Garment Industries: Who Assembles in Mexicali Maquilas?" *Latin American Studies* 3 (1990): 63–82.

20. See Roberto A. Sánchez, "Environment: Mexican Perspective," and C. Richard Bath, "Environment: U.S. Perspective," both in Sidney Weintraub, ed. *U.S.–Mexican Industrial Integration: The Road to Free Trade* (Boulder, Colo.: Westview Press, 1991), 303–17 and 318–35; and Mary E. Kelly and Dick Kamp, "Mexico–U.S. Free Trade Negotiations and the Environment: Exploring the Issues," Border Ecology Project Discussion Paper, Texas Center for Policy Studies, Austin, Texas (January 1991).

21. Roberto A. Sánchez, "Health and Environmental Risks of the Maquiladora in Mexicali," *Natural Resources Journal* 30 (Winter 1990): 163–86.

22. Ibid.

23. Sánchez, "Environment."

24. Journalistic accounts of living conditions among maquiladora employees in border cities are found in William Langewiesche, "The Border," *Atlantic Monthly*, June 1992, 91–108, and Sonia Nazario, "Boom and Despair: Mexican Border Towns are a Magnet for Foreign Factories, Workers and Abysmal Living Conditions," *Wall Street Journal*, September 22, 1989, p. 1.

25. Patrick, "The Employment Impact."

26. Bernardo González-Aréchiga, *Estrategias de negociacion del tratado de libre comercio para la industria maquiladora de exportacion,"* (Tijuana: El Colegio de la Frontera Norte, June 1991).

27. Ibid.

28. Schoepfle, "U.S.–Mexico Free Trade Agreement."

29. Ibid.

7

The Evolving Experience Along the Pacific Northwest Corridor Called Cascadia

_____ *Michael A. Goldberg and Maurice D. Levi*

INTRODUCTION

The historical accidents that shaped the division of the Hudson's Bay Company's Oregon Territory and that resulted in the purchase of Alaska, detached from the "Lower Forty-Eight" by a sovereign state in between, have no bearing on the economic realities of the region, which has become known as Cascadia.[1] The national and state borders that cross the land between the Arctic Ocean and Oregon's southern border are simply political artifacts, hiding a harmony of interests and opportunities that makes Cascadia as meaningful an economic entity as California. Indeed, as we shall argue, it has much that is the envy of California, including untapped water, bountiful power, and room to breathe. What we intend to show is that as borders come down with free trade, the prospects for Cascadia are as endless as its magnificent shorelines on the Arctic and Pacific oceans, and its mountains stretching from the Pacific to the plains. With so much emphasis being placed today on international trading blocs among nations, it is typically overlooked that nations are ultimately comprised of functional and distinctive economic regions and that these regions often defy national boundaries. Cascadia, as we seek to demonstrate, is such a transnational region. The framework that follows should be seen as a prototype for analyzing these regions.

For our purpose here, Cascadia consists of Alaska, British Columbia, Washington, and Oregon. The common Asia-Pacific focus of these four units is the reason we exclude Idaho and Alberta, which are sometimes also included in Cascadia.[2] We shall examine the region's growth, the economic interdepen-

Figure 7.1
Cascadia Population: As Part of Total Canada–United States

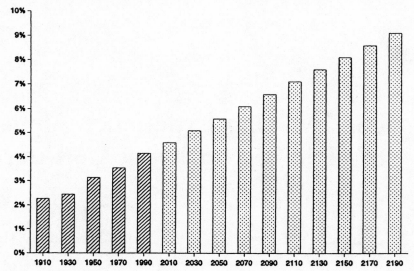

Note: Linear extrapolation.

Sources: Statistics Canada, *Postcensal Annual Estimates of Population by Marital Status, Age,*
Sex and Components of Growth for Canada, Provinces and Territories, June 1991, pp.
34–35; U.S. Department of Commerce, Economics and Statistics Administration, Bureau of the Census, *Statistical Abstract of the United States,* 1962–1991 issues.

dencies that have already emerged, and the potential for further integration
during the ten year phase-in of the 1989 Canada–U.S. Free Trade Agreement.
Since the experience with free trade is so short, and since conventional Hecksher-
Ohlin trade theory can be problematic at the subnational level, much of what
we say involves projections based on insights of the new trade theory of Krugman[3]
and others, and on developments in dynamic industries that are yet to become
part of the economic statistics—in software, hardware, biotechnology, aerospace, silviculture, aquaculture, and so on.

SIZE AND GROWTH OF CASCADIA

As Figure 7.1 shows, Cascadia's population is still only a little over 4 percent
of that of the United States plus Canada. However, this is almost double the
importance of Cascadia's population at the beginning of the century. Furthermore, as the projections in the figure show, if the populations of Cascadia and
the remainder of the United States plus Canada continue to grow at the average
rates of the last eight decades, by 2190 Cascadia will have almost 10 percent
of U.S. and Canadian population.

Figure 7.2
Population Changes: Canada and British Columbia

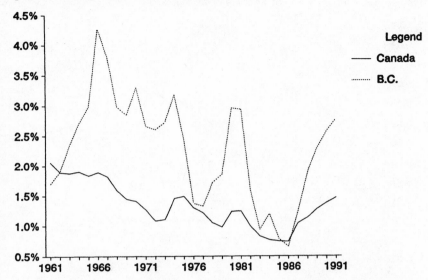

Source: Statistics Canada, *Postcensal Annual Estimates of Population by Marital Status, Age, Sex and Components of Growth for Canada, Provinces and Territories,* June 1991, pp. 34–35.

The rapidity of population growth in the components of Cascadia vis-à-vis Canada and the United States is also evident in Figures 7.2 and 7.3. We can see immediately that population growth in the Cascadia states and British Columbia is typically twice that of their parent countries, although volatility of population growth is also evident. The population growth statistics indicate that if the ups and downs of the Cascadian economy were dampened by the developments accompanying free trade—something we believe is likely to happen—the expansion of Cascadia would be overwhelmingly faster than on the remainder of the continent. Indeed, as Figure 7.4 indicates, Cascadian population growth as a whole is less volatile than that of its four components, so that with free movement of labor within Cascadia across its two international borders, the volatility in population growth would be noticeably less severe. Clearly, we are dealing with a region of enormous potential and ability to benefit from increased integration.

The growth of population in Cascadia is mirrored by the growth of the economy. Figure 7.5 shows the GDP and population percentages of the region relative to the United States plus Canada, where GDP is calculated by converting Canadian values at current exchange rates. The relative importance of the four components of Cascadia can be seen from Figure 7.6. This shows that Washington accounts for approximately half of the region's output, while Brit-

Figure 7.3
Population Changes: U.S. and U.S. Cascadia States

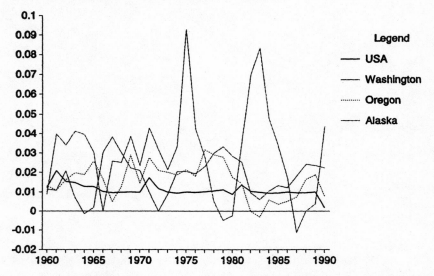

Source: U.S. Department of Commerce, Economics and Statistics Administration, Bureau of the
Census, *Statistical Abstract of the United States,* 1962–1991 issues.

ish Columbia and Oregon are each responsible for about one-fifth. Alaska grew
to well beyond 10 percent of Cascadia's economy with increasing oil prices,
but has slipped back.

THE ECONOMIC CHARACTERISTICS OF CASCADIA

Volatility

The population growth statistics in Figure 7.3 reflect the volatility of the
economies of the component units of Cascadia. This is because immigration
into and out of the Cascadia states and B.C. respond in large measure to job
opportunities. The income statistics supporting this claim are shown in Figures
7.7 and 7.8. For each component of Cascadia except Washington, the peaks
and troughs of the business cycle have a noticeably larger amplitude than the
underlying national economies.

An alternative way of evaluating the volatility of Cascadia's component units
versus the U.S. and Canadian economies is by computing the β's in regressions
between growth rates. This approach corresponds to the traditional risk analysis
measure in finance, where individual stock or portfolio returns are regressed
against the market index.

Figure 7.4
Population Growth: Cascadia Versus United States Plus Canada

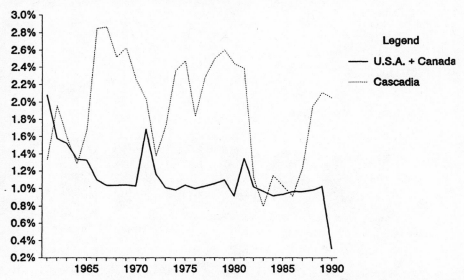

Sources: U.S. Department of Commerce, Economics and Statistics Administration, Bureau of the
Census, *Statistical Abstract of the United States*, 1991; Statistics Canada, *Postcensal
Annual Estimates of Population by Marital Status, Age, Sex and Components of Growth
for Canada, Provinces and Territories*, June 1991, pp. 34–35.

The results of the β analysis for Cascadia during the period 1963–1986 are
summarized in Table 7.1. The statistics shown are from

$$\%\Delta q_i = \alpha + \beta_i\%\Delta Q_i + \mu \tag{1}$$

where $\%\Delta q_i$ is the growth rate in real provincial or state product, and $\%\Delta Q_i$ is
the growth rate in real GNP or GDP of the United States or Canada.[4] The
constants in Table 7.1 are measures of the differences in average growth rates
of per capita personal income in each state/province versus the parent country.
In the cases of B.C., Washington, and Oregon these are not statistically different from zero. That is, despite the more rapid average population growth rates
in Cascadia, the *levels* of state/provincial incomes have kept pace with national
incomes, so *per capita* incomes have not moved further apart. This is as expected in an environment of mobile labor; people move if real income per
capita growth rates differ.[5]

The β's in Table 7.1 show that B.C., Oregon, and Alaska are indeed more
volatile than their parent countries. In the cases of B.C. and Alaska the β's are
significantly higher than 1.0. Of particular interest in the table is the substantially negative β for Alaska; what is good for Alaska is bad for the United States.
This is presumably the consequence of oil, because as a net importer of oil,

Figure 7.5
Cascadia as Part of Canada and the United States: GDP and Population

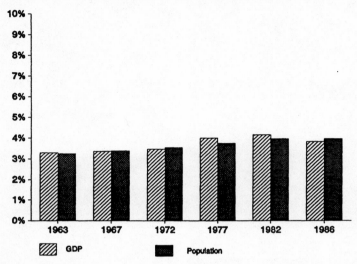

Sources: U.S. Department of Commerce, Bureau of Economic Analysis, *Survey of Current Busi-
    ness*, May 1988, pp. 44–45; Ministry of Finance and Corporate Relations, *B.C. Eco-
    nomic Accounts*, Victoria, British Columbia, 1964–1989; Statistics Canada, *Canadian
    Economic Observer—Historical Statistical Supplement Annual Date up to 1990*, Cat.
    No. 11-210, July 1991, p. 89, and *Postcensal Annual Estimates of Population by Marital
    Status, Age, Sex and Components of Growth for Canada, Provinces and Territories*, June
    1991, pp. 34–35; U.S. Department of Commerce, Economics and Statistics Administra-
    tion, Bureau of the Census, *Statistical Abstract of the United States*, 1964–1987 issues.

the United States is hurt by high prices, while Alaska as a major producer is
helped. Washington, being the largest and most diversified element of Cascadia, has a β of unity, as we might expect.

One of the benefits free trade could bring to the region is the diversification
that comes from bringing B.C. into closer economic association with Alaska
and the Lower Forty-Eight, and indirectly, from making Alaska less isolated.
To test this, we computed the β for Cascadia taken as a whole, against the
United States and Canada combined. The results are shown at the bottom of
Table 7.1. The statistically insignificant β means we cannot reject the null-
hypothesis that Cascadia has similar risk characteristics to North America. That
is, as a region, Cascadia is not significantly more volatile than the United
States plus Canada even though the component units are more volatile.

Economic Linkages

For obvious reasons, free trade within Cascadia should shift the axis of economic linkage from East-to-West to North-to-South. With so little experience

Figure 7.6
Shares of GDP in Cascadia

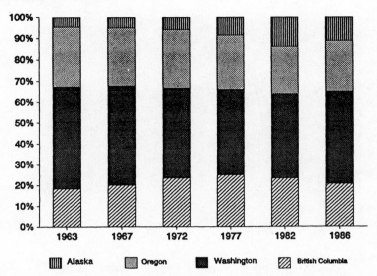

Sources: U.S. Department of Commerce, Bureau of Economic Analysis, *Survey of Current Business*, May 1988, pp. 44–45; Ministry of Finance and Corporate Relations, *B.C. Economic Accounts*, Victoria, British Columbia, 1964–1989.

of free trade, it is not possible to judge whether such a shift of axis has occurred. However, it is possible to see if there is room for such a shift by considering the before–free trade pattern of connectedness. While this cannot be done on trade flow data, which are not available in a usable form, we can judge connectedness from the extent to which individual sectors are linked. Specifically, by calculating correlations of sector growth rates for B.C. versus Canada, and B.C. versus U.S. Cascadia, we can see if B.C. is more closely tied to the Canadian economy than to U.S. Cascadia. Similarly, by comparing correlations of sector growth rates of U.S. Cascadia to B.C. with correlations between U.S. Cascadia to the entire United States we can see if U.S. Cascadia is part of a separate entity or part of the United States. The relevant correlations are shown in Table 7.2.

Comparing the first column of Table 7.2 to the next three columns shows that for the period studied, B.C. is distinctly tied into Canada; in just about every sector the correlation is lower for B.C. versus U.S. Cascadia than for B.C. versus Canada. One interesting feature of this comparison is the negative correlation between B.C. and U.S. Cascadia for the agriculture, forestry, and fishing sector. It would appear that what is good for B.C. is bad for U.S. Cascadia, and vice versa. While we would expect the fortunes on both sides of the border to have common roots if this sector is part of an open competitive international marketplace, this is not so if there is direct competition between

Figure 7.7
Changes in Real Personal Income Per Capita: Canada and British Columbia

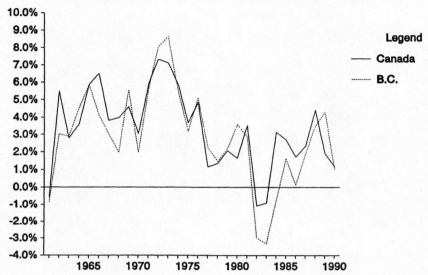

Source: Statistics Canada, *System of National Accounts—National Income and Expenditure Accounts—Annual Estimates 1926–1986*, June 1988, pp. 92–93.

B.C. and U.S. Cascadia, and where there are oligopolistic market situations.[6] This is a sign that before free trade this sector was not connected, but that potential benefits exist for Cascadia from integration under free trade.

Table 7.2 shows that Washington and Oregon are both closely tied into the U.S. economy. The table also shows that a large number of sectors in these two states are closely tied to each other. On the other hand, Alaska is almost entirely idiosyncratic, having little or no connection with the United States, B.C., or Washington and Oregon. This comes as little surprise; we recall that Alaska has a negative β with respect to the United States. The clear message from Table 7.2 is that before free trade, the borders between Alaska and B.C. and between B.C. and Washington were economically meaningful. Thus, there exist potential gains from free trade and increased cooperation.

Structural Distinctiveness

The more distinctive the elements of a trading arrangement, the greater the potential gains from free trade. Specifically, the gains from trade depend on the relative opportunity costs of different industries or sectors that are the basis of comparative advantage. The correlations in Table 7.2 relate like industries, and show that even here there are some differences. However, more important

Figure 7.8
Changes in Real Personal Income Per Capita: United States and U.S. Cascadia

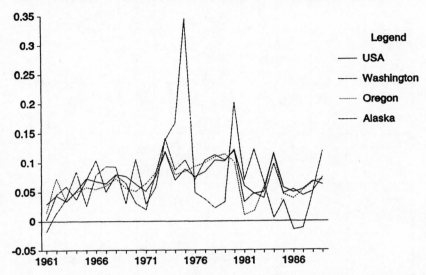

Source: U.S. Department of Commerce, Economics and Statistics Administration Bureau of the Census, *Statistical Abstract of the United States*, 1962–1992.

Table 7.1
"Risk Analysis" for Cascadia and Its Components, 1963–1986

	Constant (α)	Slope (β)	R^2	D-W
B.C.	-0.0086 (-0.0168)	1.4507* (0.2195)	0.68	1.24
Washington	0.0032 (0.0092)	0.9862 (0.2342)	0.46	1.23
Oregon	-0.0065 (0.0078)	1.2466 (0.1990)	0.65	1.00
Alaska	0.1578 (0.0344)	-2.5349** (-0.5354)	0.29	1.66
Cascadia	-0.0178 (0.0214)	1.2953 (0.2332)	0.60	1.08

Standard errors given beneath coefficients.
 * Significant at the 5% level, 2-tailed test
** Significant at the 1% level, 2-tailed test

Table 7.2
Growth Rate Correlations for Primary and Manufacturing Industries, 1962–1986

Sector	B.C. vs Canada	B.C. vs Wash.	B.C. vs Oregon	B.C. vs Alaska	Wash. vs USA	Wash. vs Ore.	Wash. vs Alaska	Ore. vs USA	Oregon vs Alaska	Alaska vs USA
Agr., frtry, fishing	0.03	-0.21	-0.15	0.62*	-0.01	0.58*	0.24	0.12	0.26	-0.07
Metals	0.06	-0.04	0.23	0.23	0.37	0.37	0.77*	0.50	0.15	0.32
Ind. materials	-0.07	0.04	0.21	-0.07	0.56*	0.52*	-0.01	0.61*	0.16	0.37
Pet. and gas	0.02	-0.03	0.07	-0.09	0.41	-0.03	0.25	0.19	0.29	0.62*
Coal	0.55*	0.57*	-0.40	0.22	-0.22	-0.30	0.20	0.14	0.17	-0.20
Food & Bev.	0.61*	0.40	0.42	0.08	0.90*	0.85*	0.50*	0.87*	0.36	0.40
Paper	0.84*	0.54*	0.53*	0.60*	0.76*	0.80*	0.52*	0.77*	0.63*	0.48
Pet. products	0.54*	-0.09	-0.52*	-0.03	0.31	0.34	0.15	0.29	0.16	0.39
Chemicals	0.18	0.04	0.26	0.21	0.40	0.12	0.06	0.92*	0.31	0.35
Other non-durables	0.46	0.23	0.37	-0.15	0.83*	0.78*	-0.09	0.84*	-0.09	-0.06
Wood	0.81*	0.37	0.51*	-0.24	0.89*	0.95*	0.13	0.94*	0.01	0.19
Furniture	0.55*	-0.03	0.21	0.35	0.89*	0.74*	0.43	0.89*	0.51*	0.37
Primary metals	0.59*	0.40	0.50	0.29	0.82*	0.89*	0.47	0.91*	0.47	0.46
Metal products	0.75*	0.24	0.47	-0.01	0.36	0.44	0.13	0.87*	-0.01	-0.11
Mach. and equip.	0.77*	0.61*	0.76*	0.39	0.75	0.77*	0.21	0.83*	0.21	0.13
Transport equip.	0.61*	0.21	0.26	-0.20	0.42	0.56*	0.13	0.68*	-0.05	-0.09
Electrical prods.	0.62*	-0.01	0.19	0.27	0.62*	0.58*	-0.24	0.72*	-0.21	-0.22
Misc. Manuf.	0.74*	0.14	0.01	-0.05	0.70*	0.42	0.07	0.04	0.15	-0.13
Construction	0.66*	0.12	-0.02	0.06	0.54*	0.62*	-0.12	0.79*	-0.26	-0.46
Utilities	0.59*	0.41	0.68*	0.09	0.53*	0.79*	0.01	0.70*	0.33	0.49*

* Significant at the 5% level, 2-tailed test

Sources: Ministry of Finance and Corporate Relations, B.C. *Economic Accounts 1990–1991*, February 1991, pp. 11–12, 18–21; Statistics Canada, Input-Output Division, *System of National Accounts—The Input-Output Structure of the Canadian Economy in Constant Prices 1961–1981*, December 1987, Cat. No. 15-511, pp. 78–89; U.S. Department of

Table 7.3
Structural Distinctiveness: Matched Sectoral Importance Correlations, 1986

	Washington	Oregon	Alaska	B.C.	U.S.A.	Canada
Washington	1.0000	0.9171**	0.1011	0.7794**	0.9376**	0.8031**
Oregon	0.9171**	1.0000	0.0713	0.8392**	0.9274**	0.7832**
Alaska	0.1011	0.0713	1.0000	0.0981	0.1950	0.2577
B.C.	0.7794**	0.8392**	0.0981	1.0000	0.8014**	0.9246**

*Significant at the 1% level

Sources: Ministry of Finance and Corporate Relations, *B.C. Economic Accounts 1990–1991*, February 1991, pp. 11–12, 18–21; Statistics Canada, Input-Output Division, *System of National Accounts—The Input-Output Structure of the Canadian Economy in Constant Prices 1961–1981*, December 1987, Cat. No. 15-511, pp. 78–89; U.S. Department of Commerce, Bureau of Economic Analysis, *Gross State Product 1963–1986* (Washington, D.C., 1988).

than idiosyncrasies within given, like industries, are differences in the industrial structures of the Cascadian states and B.C.

In order to see whether there are noticeable differences in industrial structures between B.C., Washington, Oregon, and Alaska that can contribute to the potential to gain from trade, values added by double-digit industrial categories were obtained for each state/province. These were put on a comparable basis, giving thirty-two common industrial sectors. That is, we obtained values added by thirty-two common industrial sectors for B.C. and the U.S. Cascadian states, where the thirty-two values added make up the provincial/state products. Next, we calculated the importance of each industry as a fraction of the provincial/state product. Finally, we calculated the correlation coefficients between the relative sizes of the industrial sectors. Correlations were calculated between all four units of Cascadia, as well as between each state/province and the U.S. and Canada. To reduce distortions from spuriously correlating a state/provincial industrial value added with itself included in the parent country's GDP, B.C. sectoral outputs were subtracted from Canadian sectoral outputs, and the combined U.S. Cascadian states sectoral outputs were subtracted from U.S. sectoral outputs. The correlation coefficients are shown in Table 7.3.

The top row of Table 7.3 shows that Washington's industrial structure is more similar to that of Oregon than to B.C., and is very different from Alaska. Washington is even more like the non-Cascadian United States than Oregon, and more like the United States than Canada. A similar picture emerges from the second row, which shows that Oregon is more like the United States than Washington, more like Washington than B.C., and unlike Alaska. Table 7.3, like Table 7.2, which was concerned with sectoral growth rate correlations, shows B.C. is more like Canada than the United States, more like Oregon than Washington, and unlike Alaska. Alaska is indeed unlike the other units of Cascadia, and reflecting its energy and resource output base, is more like

Canada than the United States. The overall picture that emerges from Table 7.3 is one of four units that have different structures, making Cascadia a place that offers potential comparative advantages.

CASCADIA'S POTENTIAL WITH FREE TRADE

Industrial Organization

The incorporation of market structure into international trade theory has shown that when there is imperfect competition, the conclusions of classical international trade theory may no longer apply. For example, it can pay to restrict trade when the market power of foreign producers would be used to exploit a country's consumers unless the country maintained local production.[7] The low correlations of growth rates between B.C. and the U.S. Cascadian states are indicative of imperfect market structures; in competitive markets producers typically rise and fall together, whereas in imperfectly competitive markets, one producer's gain may be at the expense of others. Furthermore, the imperfectly competitive environment may well have led to the barriers—hidden and explicit—that have been part of the trade picture between B.C. and the U.S. Cascadian states. This is suggestive of gains from trade, as market power is enhanced by Cascadian integration via removing international barriers.

Economies of Scale and Scope

The traditional theory of comparative advantage is cast in terms of constant returns to scale and ignores economies of scope. However, in reality both economies exist, especially in such industries as forestry and paper production. Cross-border integration means the chance to exploit these economies via, for example, bigger and more flexible paper mills, and via a wider product range. Increasing the product range would mean diversification benefits in a highly cyclical industry. With research and development being cross-border, and with larger-scale operations, Cascadia's producers would regain some of their losses in competitiveness vis-à-vis producers of similar products in the Southern United States and South America.

Scale and scope economies are not limited to forest products and other natural resources. For example, in software development the complementarities between products provide synergies from a wide range of producers. The more software development occurs in a region, the better the access of each firm to state-of-the-art products of other firms. These synergistic benefits are behind, for example, the close ties between Microsoft of Redmond, Washington and Consumers' Software of Vancouver, B.C., which led to Microsoft purchasing Consumers': Microsoft needed Consumers' network management systems. It is no accident that a large concentration of software firms already exists in Cascadia.

The magnificent physical surroundings of Cascadia appeal to talented professionals like software engineers who can pursue their careers from any location, but who need to be in face-to-face contact when integrating what they do. Similar advantages exist in the financial sector where, although communications technology allows institutions to select any location, personal contacts mean agglomeration economies from particular sites.

A sector with particular potential for Cascadia is international finance. The West Coast of the United States lacks an international financial center of global importance. Los Angeles during the 1980s supplanted San Francisco as the dominant West Coast financial center, but it is still largely a domestic center with little international finance vis-à-vis a true international financial center like London, Zurich/Geneva, Hong Kong, or Singapore.[8] Moreover, there is a need for a financial and managerial center in the Pacific time zone to fill a current gap (discussed in more detail below). Thus, there exists an opportunity for a true Zurich/Geneva-like international finance center (IFC) to evolve in the time zone, and Cascadia has a significant edge given its great-circle route location and the other attributes noted below relative to the Asia-Pacific region. Fortunately, Cascadia spans two nations and thus can avail itself of a host of international financial attributes present in Canada generally, and Vancouver specifically.[9] With reform of the U.S. financial system imminent and the free trade agreement providing national treatment for financial institutions involved across the forty-ninth parallel (and soon the Rio Grande as well if NAFTA proceeds according to plan), Vancouver, and possibly Seattle too, has the potential to fill this niche and exploit the Canada–U.S. FTA, NAFTA, and the attributes discussed below relative to Asia. Having Vancouver build on its considerably greater international financial expertise to take the lead for Cascadia might be the soundest strategy to follow, providing Seattle with a nearby successful niche-oriented IFC from which it might benefit, and with which it might cooperate to realize the economies of scale and scope focused upon here.

Tourism provides another means by which Cascadia could exploit global niches to attract a large enough client base to realize economies of scale and scope. Obvious synergies exist from tourists attracted from afar to any one part of Cascadia. With these synergies in mind, Cascadian governments could work together to coordinate advertising and promotion, training, and standards, so that the region could become an important international tourist destination. Joint marketing of ski packages, recreational and adventure tourism (e.g., white water rafting), and trade and convention activities could help create a sufficiently large tourist sector in Cascadia that real scale and scope economies could begin to be realized and built upon.[10]

Economies of scale and scope can derive from integration within Cascadia. However, Cascadia as a whole is still a relatively small market. To fully realize these economies Cascadia must take a more global view so that it can not only develop new products and niches, but also new and larger international markets along the lines suggested above. Fortunately, the most rapidly growing and potentially the largest regional economy lies at Cascadia's door, the Asia-Pacific region, and Cascadia has some unique attributes for dealing effectively with, and tapping into, this booming region compared with other regions of North America and Europe. We consider these next.

FRONT DOOR TO THE ASIA-PACIFIC

From being the back door to Europe, it is now widely recognized that Cascadia is a front door for the North American continent to the burgeoning economic region of the Asia-Pacific. This Asia-Pacific region is already important to Cascadia and likely to grow more so over time. Moreover, Cascadia will increasingly become, not just the North American gateway to the Asia-Pacific, but a vital link between Asia-Pacific and Europe, given its median location between the two continents. Indeed, Cascadia possesses numerous other natural advantages with respect to tapping the seemingly unbridled growth and potential of the Asia-Pacific region.

Links with Asia primarily, but with Europe secondarily, take numerous forms and combine to make Cascadia a cosmopolitan region. For example, there are investment links of all scales, from Japanese resort and hotel properties (West Coast Hotels in Vancouver and Westin International Hotels in Seattle), to Japanese paper, pulp, and lumber mills in British Columbia (Daishowa and Oji Paper), to numerous real estate and small manufacturing investments across the whole of Cascadia. There are also important immigration links. These have already been touched upon and provide powerful on-going commercial and cultural ties between Cascadia and Asia, especially through newer Asian immigrants.

A combination of extraordinary natural beauty, sophisticated and interesting cities, and a virtually unlimited diversity of recreational and adventure possibilities for tourists, has resulted in the region being one of the most successful tourist venues during the past half-decade, despite the global recession of 1991 and 1992. Whistler, B.C., for example, is now the number one international destination for Japanese skiers. International links are further reinforced by the gateway airports, modern bulk and container ports, and rail and road connectors in Vancouver and Seattle-Tacoma. The important transportation facilities provide vital and powerful physical infrastructural links between Cascadia, North America, and the Asia-Pacific. These physical ties enhance and interact with the other advantages noted here, once again to give Cascadia unique advantages vis-à-vis the Asia-Pacific.

The investment, cultural, tourist, and transportation links are key to the potential for growth of international trade for Cascadia. Indeed, Cascadia is already distinctive in its international trade orientation. Boeing is the largest supplier of airframes to the burgeoning Asia-Pacific airline industry. B.C., Washington, and Oregon are major providers of lumber, pulp, and wood products to Asia, particularly Northeast Asia and the People's Republic of China.

Figure 7.9
Foreign-Born Population (1961–1981): Canada and British Columbia

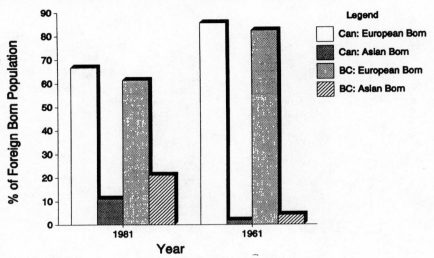

Source: *Canada Census of Population 1961–1981*, Ottawa, 1961, 1981.

Tourist trade is also growing, as is trade in high technology goods such as software and biotechnology. Physical proximity, transportation infrastructure, and the other attributes noted here all advantage Cascadia on the trade front with the booming Asia-Pacific region.

Complementing and helping to maintain the trade ties are the strong post-secondary institutions and related institutes of Asian research. International business is increasingly information and knowledge driven. Firms require the educated work force that post-secondary institutions provide, as well as the research capability of these institutions. Moreover, given the cultural differences that exist between North America and Asia, and even more so within the Asia-Pacific region itself, the ability to understand the cultures and their differences, an understanding greatly aided by Cascadia's universities, provides yet another edge for Cascadia to deal with the Asia-Pacific.

The final special link to the Asia-Pacific that Cascadia enjoys is provided directly by people through immigration. Figure 7.9 presents information for 1980 (the 1990 census data is not yet available) on the foreign-born population in the United States and each of the Cascadia states. Figure 7.10 presents analogous information for 1981 (again, 1991 Canadian census information is not published yet) for B.C. and Canada. It can be seen from these figures that both U.S. and Canadian Cascadia have a significantly higher proportion of Asian-born residents than do the U.S. and Canada on average nationally (including Cascadia). These proportions would be skewed even more in Cascadia's favor were we to consider data for 1990–91, since immigration patterns over

Figure 7.10
Distribution of Foreign Born (1980): U.S. and Cascadia States

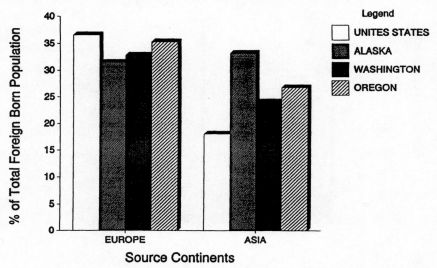

Source: Bureau of the U.S. Census, *1980 Census of Population*, Vol. 1, *Characteristics of the Population*, 1981.

the decade of the 1980s show that both U.S. and Canadian Cascadia received significantly higher proportions of immigrants from Asia than the United States and Canada as a whole.

This higher percentage of Asian-born residents gives Cascadia an additional boost in dealing with the Asia-Pacific region over and above those noted previously. Given that large, and growing, numbers of Cascadians either come from the Asia-Pacific or are North American–born children of Asia-Pacific immigrants, Cascadia boasts the ability to deal with the region through its own residents who are simultaneously linguistically and culturally Asian, and capable of tapping into extensive family and business networks in Pacific Asia. This cultural and linguistic edge, when combined with great-circle route proximity and the other advantages that Cascadia possesses vis-à-vis the Asia-Pacific region, provides Cascadia with a rather awesome capability to benefit from the continuing Asia-Pacific boom.

The foregoing advantages enjoyed by Cascadia in dealing with the Asia-Pacific region are considerable. However, perhaps the greatest potential advantage the region enjoys is that it is binational and thus able to benefit from the international strengths of both Canada and the United States.

Most of the economic regions of North America lie entirely in either the United States or Canada. Cascadia is different. As a result, Cascadia can take advantage of the different national strengths that Canada and the United States bring to international economic affairs. For example, the two countries have quite different world outlooks and are perceived differently by the international community. Specific Canadian strengths that are realizable for Cascadia through Vancouver include, on the international financial front, the fact that there is no history of exchange control or freezing/seizing foreign assets in Canada: Canada does not interfere in the international financial marketplace and has not imposed exchange controls nor frozen or seized foreign assets, making it relatively atypical. More broadly, Canada has no geopolitical aspirations. Canada is not involved in geopolitical maneuvers and is trusted widely as an honest international broker. Furthering these international financial opportunities is Canada's strong and stable national banking and financial system. Given the recent savings and loan and banking crisis in the United States, Vancouver's presence in Cascadia provides access to a very strong and well-regulated financial system that has continued to enjoy great international confidence.

Looking more generally at international trade, Canada is a trading nation and is open to international dealings as a result. Canada's open economy has also spawned an openness of attitude and a willingness (out of sheer necessity) to look outward and think more globally than the United States. This truly international orientation is particularly evident in Vancouver and can contribute greatly to inculcating a similar internationalism in Cascadia more broadly.

Greatly assisting Canada's and potentially Cascadia's trading abilities is the fact that, since World War II, Canada has been even more a nation of immigrants than the United States, creating business links all over the world. Broadly speaking, Canada has absorbed roughly three times as many international immigrants per capita as has the United States in the past half century, reinforcing its internationalism and providing a significant plus for Cascadia as a result.

Shifting our attention to the United States and some of its international strengths that are realizable for Cascadia through Alaska, Washington, and Oregon, we find the following heading the list. Because of its size and global political and economic bargaining power, the United States can bring international muscle to the aid of Cascadia. Whereas Canada is seen as the world's honest broker, the United States is often seen as the global enforcer. Both sets of responses are needed, and Cascadia can enjoy both.

From an international trade perspective, one of Cascadia's greatest strengths is the direct access it enjoys to the huge U.S. domestic market. Cascadia, especially with free trade, has unlimited access to the largest market in the world. Being part of North America and of the United States (for U.S. Cascadia) is obviously a great plus.

For continuing development and economic advancement, Cascadia's access to U.S. science and technology, and indeed its key role in computer and aerospace technology, is critical. U.S. science still outstrips the world by a considerable margin. Cascadia can access U.S. scientific and technological advances and bring them to bear on global markets very effectively, given its Pacific Rim location and increasingly international outlook.

Finally, and again of major importance, is Cascadia's access to U.S. finan-

Table 7.4
Water Area Per Capita, 1990

	Population (thousands)	Water area Sq. Km	Water per 1000 persons
British Columbia	3,213.2	1,8070	5.62
Washington	4,867	12,227	2.51
Oregon	2,842	6,127	2.16
Alaska	550	222,871	405.22
California	29,760	20,031	0.67

Sources: U.S. Department of Commerce, Economics and Statistics Administration, Bureau of the
Census, *Statistical Abstract of the United States* (Washington, D.C., 1991), p. 201;
Statistics Canada, *Canada Year Book 1992*, October 1991, p. 28, and *Postcensal Annual
Estimates of Population by Marital Status, Age, Sex and Components of Growth for
Canada, Provinces and Territories*, June 1991, p. 35; U.S. Department of Commerce,
Economics and Statistics Administration, Bureau of the Census, *Statistical Abstract of
the United States*, August 1991.

cial and human capital. Despite problems in the U.S. banking and finance
system, it is still a huge mobilizer of financial capital and still possesses the
most efficient and liquid capital markets in the world. The large pools of financial capital can combine with the perhaps even more impressive human capital
(and under free trade both can move quite readily anywhere they are needed
within Cascadia), to make a highly internationally competitive region ideally
located to benefit both from European integration and Pacific Asian boom
times.

CASCADIA, FREE TRADE, AND CALIFORNIA

One of the features of the 1989 Canada–U.S. Free Trade Agreement is
nondiscriminatory access to natural resources. While this has been widely viewed
in terms of U.S. access to Canadian energy, and perhaps fresh water, in the
context of Cascadia there is a second side to this, namely the free flow of
natural resources across the second U.S.–Canadian border, that between B.C.
and Alaska. The freedom of movement of gas, fresh water, and other resources
over the border from Alaska to B.C. has implications that are relevant to the
entire continent, but are especially important to California.

Despite lengthy discussions and substantial planning, the Alaska–B.C. natural gas pipeline has not been built. Economic integration in Cascadia should
clear some of the hurdles that led to the shelving of this huge project, with the
flow of gas ultimately benefiting the U.S. Southwest and California. Similar
consequences of integration apply to water. As Table 7.4 shows so clearly,
California has relatively little water compared to the Pacific Northwest, and
especially compared to Alaska. Washington and Oregon are reluctant to sell

water to California when they periodically face shortages themselves. Similarly, Canada has resisted bulk sales of fresh water to the United States, understandably fearing that any precedent would open the taps, allowing the diversion of rivers.[11] With an opening of both U.S.–Canadian borders to free trade, Alaskan water might conceivably be moved to the Lower Forty-Eight via B.C. river systems, or water might be "traded down the coast," from Alaska to B.C., from B.C. to Washington, and so on. With the drop in aquifers in California and water shortages that have blocked development, benefits from the freer flow of water resulting from Cascadian integration could be substantial well beyond the region of Cascadia.

Eliminating Cascadia's two international borders could provide for the freer flow of international cargoes as well as water. The land-bridge concept, whereby goods can be shipped from Asia to central and eastern North American locations, has been touted for several decades. An integrated Cascadia would allow it to blossom, since goods could enter North America at Prince Rupert or Vancouver, B.C. or Seattle-Tacoma, Washington and proceed unimpeded across the continent with savings of many days shipping time, which is extremely important in light of just-in-time inventory systems. B.C. and Puget Sound ports have a huge edge over other regions of North America because of their proximity to Asia along the great-circle air and shipping lanes, as noted above. Overcoming border barriers and such regulatory barriers as the Jones Act would cement Cascadia's role as the gateway to and from Asia.

CONCLUSION

This chapter has developed a number of arguments in favor of viewing the Pacific Northwest region as an integrated economic unit, which we and others call Cascadia. Evidence presented above suggests that Cascadia already exhibits close ties among its four components: Alaska, British Columbia, Washington, and Oregon. Furthermore, significant gains can be realized in the future from eliminating barriers resulting from the two international borders dividing Cascadia.

We are not urging here political integration. Instead, we are stressing that economic cooperation and integration in Cascadia as a result of free trade and Cascadia's natural advantages for bridging Asia, Europe, and North America can bring major benefits to the region. A number of such cooperative efforts are already well under way.[12] Our evidence and discussion argues that present and expanded cooperation within the region are likely to bear significant economic fruits, the first of which are already discernible.

NOTES

The authors are indebted to Hadar Ben-Moshe and Yuming Fu for research assistance, and to the Centre of International Business Studies at the University of British Columbia for financial support.

1. Some of the fascinating historical accidents that shaped the political division of Cascadia are described in David J. Mitchell, "Continental Stalemate: How the Alaska Purchase Treaty Led to Canadian Confederation," *The New Pacific*, no. 4 (Fall 1990), 25–40, and J. S. Galbraith, *The Hudson's Bay Company as an Imperial Factor, 1821–1869* (Los Angeles: University of California Press, 1957).

2. For a discussion of the domain of Cascadia based on common values and contemporary culture see Ian Gill, "A Green Island in a Sea of Envy: Welcome to Cascadia, the West Coast Ecotopian's Dream State," *The Georgia Straight*, June 5–12, 1992.

3. Paul Krugman's contributions to trade theory, including the importance of economies of scale and scope and of endogenous trade policy, span a vast range of articles and books. For examples of his ideas, see Elhanan Helpman and Paul R. Krugman, *Market Structure and Foreign Trade: Increasing Returns, Imperfect Competition and the International Economy* (Cambridge, Mass.: MIT Press, 1985); Paul Krugman, ed., *Strategic Trade Policy and the New International Economics* (Cambridge, Mass.: MIT Press, 1986); *Rethinking International Trade* (Cambridge, Mass.: MIT Press, 1990); and *Geography and Trade* (Cambridge, Mass: MIT Press, 1991).

4. In the case of the United States, GNP statistics are used, while for Canada GDP is employed. We can note that because the component state/province is also included in the country, the β's are biased toward zero. This strengthens our test. If a β in (1) differs from zero, this is a true *a fortiori* of the true β.

5. While this is generally true, it is also possible to envision circumstances where above-average per capita incomes could persist over time in a region if there were skill requirements (either legislated or associated with the principle sectors in the regional economy) such that free movement of people into the region would not eliminate per capita income differences because these jobs carried with them higher wages and salaries and were disproportionately represented in the region. The Silicon Valley (south of San Francisco) and Route 128 (around Boston) regions would be examples of high skill requirements leading to persistently high wages and salaries.

6. This is not really an unexpected result. Given the presence of marketing boards for dairy and poultry products in British Columbia and the importance of these products in Washington and Oregon, there should be a strong negative correlation. Also, British Columbia competes directly with Washington and Oregon in tree fruits. Similar head-to-head competition exists between the British Columbia and Washington and Alaska fishing industries, where catches are strictly regulated and one country's gain comes at the other's expense. Forestry similarly provides this sort of zero-sum game for B.C. versus Washington and Oregon, for example with respect to countervailing duties, which advantage Washington and Oregon lumber producers, and spotted owl cutting restrictions, which advantage B.C. producers.

7. For an example involving European airframe manufacturing as a counterbalance to U.S. market power see James A. Brander and Barbara Spencer, "Export Subsidies and International Market Share Rivalry," *Journal of International Economics* 18 (February 1985): 83–100.

8. For documentation of the limited role of San Francisco and Los Angeles in international finance see Michael A. Goldberg, "The Evolution of International Financial Centers on the Pacific Rim," in Dilip Das, ed., *North-South Economic Relations* (New York: Praeger, forthcoming 1993).

9. Vancouver's desire to become an international financial center, and its considerable progress toward this goal, have been documented in Michael A. Goldberg, "In-

ternational Finance on the Pacific Rim and the Emerging Network of Pacific International Financial Centers," Paper presented at the Metropolis '90 Conference, Melbourne, Australia, October, 1990.

10. Tourism is already the second biggest industry in British Columbia and one that is rapidly growing and outperforming its counterparts in other states and provinces over the past five years (B.C. Economic Accounts, Ministry of Finance and Corporate Relations, 1991). B.C.'s experience could readily be shared with and built upon for Cascadia as a whole.

11. For decades, engineers have studied diverting the Thompson River in B.C. into the Columbia River, allowing the Columbia to be linked to the Colorado, and sending vast amounts of water to California. At one point the Thompson and Columbia rivers are only a few miles apart.

12. Several joint initiatives have been undertaken by the governments of British Columbia and Washington, for example. A formal economic cooperation agreement has been in effect since the late 1980s. The state and the province jointly share a booth at the annual Las Vegas Computer Show promoting the exceptional software capabilities of the "Evergreen triangle" (Seattle-Vancouver-Victoria). The premiers of Alberta and British Columbia meet with the governors of Idaho, Washington, Oregon, and Alaska, with the B.C.–Washington cooperative agreement being talked about as a model for broader provincial and state agreements. See for example, T. Brainerd Chadwick, "Hands Across the Border: The Pacific Northwest Economic Partnership," *The New Pacific*, no. 1 (Fall 1989): 1–20; and Vancouver Stock Exchange, "The Pacific Northwest: A New Trading Alliance," *VSE Business Report* 2, no. 1 (May 1992): 4.

PART III

Keys to a Free Trade Zone in the Western Hemisphere: History, Opportunity, Motivation, and Timing

8

The Rocky Road Toward Hemispheric Economic Integration: A Regional Background with Attention to the Future

Joseph Grunwald

The Western Hemisphere has arrived at an ironic juncture. The United States, for many years the champion of multilateralism and promoter of global free trade, is now pushing regionalism. Latin American countries, for many years limited by import-substituting industrialization and failed regional economic integration efforts, have finally moved toward opening their economies to the world, but now they are tempted by a U.S. initiative to join a regional bloc. An additional irony is that Latin American countries' past attempts to band together in various kinds of economic unions were in large part aimed to make the region less dependent on the United States. Now most Latin American countries seem eager to join the United States in free trade arrangements. What is the background of this state of affairs?

THE HISTORICAL SETTING

Until very recently, the image of Latin America was one of stagnating economies laboring inefficiently behind high trade walls erected to promote domestic industrialization. Within the broad historical context, that picture had some validity for only a brief time period, although even then it did not truly reflect reality given the fact that between the 1950s and 1970s many Latin American countries' growth rates were among the highest in the world.

For most of Latin America's history, free trade dominated protectionism. Ever since colonization, Latin American countries have been viewed as export economies dedicated to the sale of their natural resources overseas. True, during the colonial period Spain and Portugal dominated trade through trade monopolies, but these obviously were not intended to benefit Latin America.

After independence the British arrived, but their domination did not require conquest, colonization, or annexation. They penetrated the region through treaties of free trade and friendship. Some historians referred to this hegemony as "the imperialism of free trade."[1] At its peak, at the turn of the century, British economic interests owned about a quarter of the region's total commercial assets.

Even before the end of the last century the United States started to replace Europe as the principal source of capital. The free exchange of Latin American primary commodities for U.S. manufactured goods became the basis of U.S. economic power in the region. Unlike Britain, which seldom needed to intervene in Latin America during its period of "informal" imperialism, the United States frequently intervened militarily in the Caribbean basin on behalf of U.S. economic interests. The "exercise of an international police power" contained in the 1904 Roosevelt Corollary[2] to the Monroe Doctrine dominated U.S. hemispheric relations until the 1930s, when the United States renounced military coercion in its Good Neighbor Policy.[3]

During the hegemony of Europe and, more recently, of the United States, local Latin American economic interests benefited and cooperated with the outside powers to preserve the conditions that supported international commerce. Since its citizens first became significantly involved in economic relations with the region in the second half of the last century until the early postwar period, "the United States continued to see the Latin American republics as simple agrarian countries and producers of raw materials for export [and importers of manufactures] even while Latin America turned toward industrialization."[4] This served well the need of not only the United States but also of the local elites to expand economically. Already before World War I the United States had become Latin America's most important trading partner,[5] and soon after that war U.S. investment surpassed that of Britain or any other power. "By 1930 the United States dominated virtually everywhere in the hemisphere."[6]

When in the post–World War II period major Latin American countries seriously embarked on import-substituting industrialization, inter-American relations changed. The intense wartime economic cooperation, under which the region supplied strategic raw materials (at set prices) to the United States and the United States provided production assistance (primarily through the Export-Import Bank) to regional economies, gave way to a period of disappointment for Latin America. The United States focused on Europe and the world economy and U.S. private business interests. U.S. officials expressed their strong distaste for Latin American import-substitution policies of trade restriction and state intervention, and aid to the region dried up. The United States lectured Latin America on the benefits of free private enterprise, while U.S. manufacturers discovered that they could prosper by setting up subsidiaries in the region behind high trade barriers.

THE WESTERN HEMISPHERE IDEA

Geography and history, reinforced by economic and political considerations, have from time to time stimulated a special relationship between the United States and Latin America. The "Western Hemisphere idea" emerged in the 1880s as a counterweight against the strong and growing European influence in Latin America.[7]

An early highlight of Pan-Americanism was the First International Conference of American States, held in Washington in the winter of 1889–90. The prime mover of the conference was U.S. Secretary of State James G. Blaine, an advocate of expansionism at the turn of the century, who sought to create a hemispheric customs union. He as well as other U.S. policy makers were deeply concerned with eliminating European political and economic influence in Latin America and expanding U.S. foreign trade. Blaine and others were convinced that the United States could easily compete with Europe in supplying the region with manufactures. The conference's agenda included not only the creation of an American customs union, but also the establishment of regular communications between American ports, building of a Pan-American railway, setting up of customs regulations, standards of weights and measures, laws to protect copyrights and trademarks, and institution of a common silver coin.[8]

Regarding the key issue of a continental customs union, the conference failed. Because of its close economic ties to Europe, Argentina led the opposition. There was little enthusiasm for the scheme elsewhere in Latin America, possibly anticipating some countries' desire to advance their own industrialization. The growing protectionist sentiment in the United States, culminating in the 1890 McKinley Tariff Act, did not help.

Ever since then, the Western Hemisphere idea has waxed and waned in irregular cycles. Thus, at the Second International Conference of American States held in Mexico City in 1901–02, the idea of a continental customs union was not presented. With a few exceptions, notably U.S. Secretary of State Cordell Hull's tariff-cutting proposal for increasing hemispheric trade at the Seventh International Conference of American States in 1933, economic integration did not play a positive role in inter-American policy until the 1961 Alliance for Progress.

The Alliance for Progress

The Alliance was referred to as "the renascence of the Western Hemisphere idea . . . ; for a few brief years, that program represented the apparent triumph of Pan-Americanism."⁹ There are various reasons for the flagging of the Alliance soon after it was established. One of the basic factors was that Latin American countries did not take seriously the Alliance's call for reforms, such as land reform, tax reform, education reform, and administration reform. Latin American policy makers knew that the fundamental motivation for that U.S. initiative was the emerging threat of Castro in Cuba and fear of Soviet penetration into the hemisphere. Most countries, therefore, surmised (correctly) that they could get U.S. assistance anyway, reforms or not. (They did meet another condition for aid, the preparation of economic and social development plans, which was easily done because they were nonbinding, often containing fancy models supplied by contracted foreign econometricians.) Furthermore, by the end of the 1960s the Castro threat had largely evaporated.

Probably the grandest hemispheric conference was the 1967 Punta del Este summit meeting of heads of state in the Americas. Ostensively still within the era of the Alliance, it was promoted with great fanfare by U.S. President Lyndon B. Johnson to push Latin American economic integration. He offered financial support for a Latin American common market. President Johnson's request for a $1.5 billion five year aid commitment for Latin America was not supported by the U.S. Congress. (Interestingly, the 1967 $1.5 billion in 1990 dollars is about four times as much as the 1990 $1.5 billion fund under the Enterprise for the Americas Initiative.) Although the summit was hemisphere-wide, the United States, as the world's main defender of multilateralism, did not propose to be included in the common market.¹⁰

It did not take long for the summit elation to fizzle. First, fear of balance of payments losses was not overcome by any concrete U.S. aid. Perhaps more importantly, the specter of domination by external private investors emerged as a strong hindrance to Latin American integration progress. Suddenly it appeared that a Latin American common market might be highly vulnerable to economic penetration by the United States. The early experience of the European Economic Community showed that subsidiaries of giant U.S. international corporations in Europe had grown faster than European firms.¹¹

Latin American apprehensions were kindled by unilateral U.S. economic moves such as the withholding of aid to Peru during that country's dispute with a U.S. oil company in the early 1960s and the 1962 Hickenlooper amendment to the U.S. foreign assistance and sugar acts. The amendment, arising from expropriation disputes in Brazil, provided for the cutoff of assistance to any government that expropriates the property of U.S. citizens or corporations without "equitable and speedy" compensation. Thus it could limit diplomatic flexibility by the possibility of triggering major policy action almost automatically. This and other similar congressional restrictions "were inevitably seen in Latin America as forms of economic coercion: they seem to give foreign investors decisive status in determining the legitimacy of policies followed by sovereign states."¹²

Table 8.1
U.S. Trade with Latin America* as Percentage of Total U.S. Trade, Various Years,
1950–1991

Years	US Exports to Latin America as Percent of Total US Exports	US Imports from Latin America as Percent of Total US Imports
1950	28	35
1958–59	23	28
1963–65	16	21
1974–76	14	12
1979–81	17	14
1984–86	14	13
1989–91	14	13

*The International Monetary Fund changed the definition of Latin America, starting with the 1985 Yearbook of Direction of International Trade Statistics, affecting post-1977 data. After 1977, Latin America conforms to the IMF definition of Western Hemisphere, all of the Western Hemisphere less the United States, Canada, and Cuba. The percentages calculated on the basis of the new series, the last three rows in the table, are about two points higher compared to the previous definitions. Thus the 1979–81 average Latin American share is 15 percent of U.S. exports and 12 percent of U.S. imports calculated on the basis of the old series.

Sources: For 1950: A. Fishlow, "The Mature Neighbor Policy," in J. Grunwald, ed., Latin America and World Economy (Beverly Hills, Calif.: Sage Publications, 1978), Table 2.1, p. 38. For 1958–1976: Direction of Trade Annual 1958–62, Annual 1963–67, and Annual 1970–76 (Washington, D.C.: Joint Publications of the International Monetary Fund and the International Bank for Reconstruction and Development, 1963 and 1967). For 1979–1991: Direction of Trade Statistics, Yearbooks 1985, 1991, and 1992 (Washington, D.C.: International Monetary Fund, 1985, 1991, and 1992).

Globalism

By the 1970s the United States again had abandoned a special relationship with Latin America and reemphasized global interdependence. It was recognized that, except for the two world wars, Latin America played a relatively small role in U.S. foreign trade (Table 8.1), compared to Europe and East Asia, not to mention Canada. U.S. investment also turned elsewhere. Although it has been clear since early in this century that the United States is much more important to Latin American economies than the other way around, the ratio of trade with the United States to total trade has declined for many, if not most, Latin American countries (Table 8.2).

Table 8.2
Latin America and Selected Countries: Trade with the United States as Percentage of Total Trade, Various Years, 1950–1991

	Exports to U.S.as % of Total Exports			Imports from U.S. as % of Total Imports		
	1950	1961–1965	1989–1991	1950	1961–1965	1989–1991
Latin America*	52	36	38	49	42	38
Argentina	19	8	12	20	25	25
Brazil	54	36	23	35	32	22
Chile	52	35	18	48	38	20
Colombia	82	54	43	70	50	36
Mexico	86	59	72	84	68	69
Peru	26	34	23	53	40	29
Venezuela	56	35	51	69	53	47

*Latin America includes all Latin American countries except Cuba in 1950; for all other years, Latin America includes all of the Western Hemisphere less the United States, Canada, and Cuba (corresponds to the *Western Hemisphere* definition of the IMF for 1989–1991, and approximately to the *Latin America* definition of the Inter-American Development Bank used for 1961–1965).

Sources: For 1950, J. Grunwald, M. S. Wionczek, and M. Carnoy, *Latin American Economic Integration and U.S. Policy* (Washington, D.C.: The Brookings Institution, 1972), Table A-4, pp. 168–71. For 1961–1965, *Annual Report* (Washington, D.C.: Inter-American Development Bank, 1967). For 1989–1991: *Direction of Trade Statistics, Yearbook 1992* (Washington, D.C.: International Monetary Fund, 1992).

So Latin America was put on the back burner in U.S. foreign policy. It lost its extraordinary relationship with the United States. "No special privilege can be conceded to Latin America because equally important interests elsewhere in the world would be adversely affected."[13] That policy did not change noticeably until President Bush's declaration of regional interdependence in the 1990 Enterprise for the Americas Initiative.

LATIN AMERICAN ECONOMIC INTEGRATION

Ever since Simón Bolívar, Latin Americans have dreamt about a Pan-Latin America. Despite fervent exhortations by influential Latin American intellectuals and policy makers, the idea of regional economic integration remained rhetorical until the middle of this century, when the Central Latin American Common Market (CACM) and the Latin American Free Trade Association (LAFTA) were negotiated. Both treaties were signed in 1960. While CACM made significant progress in its first decade, it became clear within less than a decade that LAFTA was not going anywhere.[14]

The Latin American Free Trade Association and Its Successor

Eventually, LAFTA included the ten South American countries (Argentina, Bolivia, Brazil, Chile, Colombia, Ecuador, Paraguay, Peru, Uruguay, and Venezuela) and Mexico, and provided for the gradual elimination of all intraregional trade barriers within twelve years. During the first few years, hundreds of tariffs were reduced in item by item negotiations, primarily on products in which there was little or no trade among the member countries. Progress quickly evaporated when it came to cutting trade barriers on products in which partners competed. At the 1967 summit meeting the target date for a common market was extended from 1973 to 1985. The euphoria surrounding the birth of LAFTA at the beginning of the 1960s gave way to bitter disappointment soon after the summit.

Finally, in 1980, the partner countries signed a new treaty, superseding LAFTA, and established the Latin American Integration Association (LAIA). Fixed targets, such as yearly tariff reduction commitments, schedules for the freeing of trade by certain percentages, and the common market date were abandoned. LAIA allows a multiplicity of different forms of economic cooperation instead of LAFTA's rigid economic commitments. As an informal, open-ended arrangement LAIA has emphasized integration by projects and has not put pressure on the member countries to liberalize their external trade.

The Andean Group

When LAFTA difficulties became apparent in the mid-1960s, the six Andean countries—Bolivia, Chile, Colombia, Ecuador, Peru, and Venezuela—banded together (under LAFTA) to form the Andean Subregional Integration Agreement. The idea was that it would be easier for a smaller group of neighboring countries to integrate than for LAFTA as a whole, where Argentina and Brazil seemed to dominate. Mexico, the other big Latin American power, was not considered a threat because of its historically minimal economic interaction with other South American countries (less than 2 percent of its imports came from South America, Central America, and the Caribbean combined during 1961–1965, and about 3 percent in 1991;[15] see also Memo Items in Table 8.3).

The original Andean Pact of 1969 was much more ambitious than LAFTA. It provided for automatic and irrevocable reduction of tariff and nontariff barriers to intra-Andean trade, a common external tariff within ten years, establishment of sectoral industrial development programs, harmonization and coordination of economic policies and development plans, and a controversial common regime for the treatment of foreign investment and technology.

So far, the Andean Group has not gotten any closer to economic integration than LAFTA did. One of its major achievements has been the establishment of the Andean Development Corporation (CAF, by its Spanish acronym) to

Table 8.3
Latin America: Share of Intraregional Exports, Various Years, 1938–1990

Year	Intra-LAIA Expt as % of Total	Intra-AND Expt as % of Total	Intra-CAC Expt as % of Total	Intra-CAR Expt as % of Total	Intra-LAT Expt as % of Total
1938	6	na	na	na	6
1950	8	na	3	na	8
1960	8	1	7	5	8
1970	10	3	27	8	13
1980	14	3	22	9	15
1990	10*	4	15	13*	16

Notes: LAIA includes AND, MERCOSUR, Chile, and Mexico. AND = Andean Group; CAC = CACM; CAR = CARIFTA; LAT = All of Latin America and Caribbean. na = not available. * 1989.
Memo Items: in 1991, intra-MERCOSUR exports were 9 percent of total MERCOSUR exports, Chile's Latin American exports were 14 percent of its total exports, and Mexican Latin American exports were 4 percent of its total (see last source below).

Sources: For 1938, D. W. Baerresen, M. Carnoy, and J. Grunwald, *Latin American Trade Patterns* (Washington, D.C.: The Brookings Institution, 1965), Table II-b, p. 76. For Andean Group and CARICOM in 1960, U. Lächler, "Regional Integration and Economic Development," The World Bank Industry and Energy Department, PPR, Working Paper No. 14, November 1989, Table 7, p. 18. For all other in 1950 and 1960, J. Grunwald, M. Wionczek, and M. Carnoy, *Latin American Economic Integration and U.S. Policy* (Washington, D.C.: The Brookings Institution, 1972), Table 3, p. 46. For Latin America in 1970 and 1980, *Statistical Yearbook for Latin America and the Caribbean, 1988 Edition* (Santiago, Chile: United Nations Economic Commission for Latin America and the Caribbean, 1989), Tables 287 and 289, pp. 558–59 and 564–65. For all others in 1970, 1980, and 1989, A. Inotai, "Regional Integration Among Developing Countries, Revisited," World Bank, The Policy, Research, and External Affairs Complex, WPS 643, April 1991, Table 2, p. 50. For 1990, J. Nogués and R. Quintanilla, "Latin America's Integration and the Multilateral Trading System," World Bank and CEPR Conference on New Dimensions in Regional Integration, April 2–3, 1992, Table 8, p. 20; and International Monetary Fund, *Direction of Trade Statistics, 1992* (Washington, D.C.: IMF, 1992).

function as a subregional development bank. CAF has contributed to regional investments but has not been able to increase the importance of trade within the zone, which has the lowest proportion of intraregional trade of any integration scheme in Latin America (Table 8.3). Balance of payments concerns have been obstacles to progress, and the facts that the member countries have similar factor endowments (in all of them mineral products play a major role) and the connecting infrastructure among the countries is poor have been detrimental.

Intra-Andean transportation costs have often been higher than the costs of shipping goods to outside the region.[16]

After opening its economy during the military regime, Chile formally withdrew from the Andean Group in 1976. Subsequently, the group relaxed its targets, taking into consideration the movement of partner countries toward more open economic systems. More recently, the Andean Group has introduced what it hopes will be more realistic goals toward a common market. Despite several invitations, Chile has refused to rejoin the group even after the restoration of its democracy. Chile considers its own economic liberalization too far ahead of the other countries for it to benefit from subregional integration.[17]

The Central American Common Market

The small Central American countries constituted one republic for a short period after their independence early last century. That union "disintegrated after fifteen years into five small units [Costa Rica, El Salvador, Guatemala, Honduras, and Nicaragua] ravaged by external invasions, regional wars, and domestic strife."[18] For more than a century the memories of past bloody struggles and local prejudices against neighboring countries have made some three dozen attempts at uniting Central America end in dismal failure.

It is not surprising, therefore, that the postwar Central American integration movement started from a much lower base of intraregional commerce than LAFTA. In 1950, intra-CACM exports were 3 percent of total CACM exports, compared to 8 percent of intraregional exports in LAFTA (Table 8.3). Beginning in 1951, careful preparation for regional economic cooperation under the leadership of the United Nations Economic Commission for Latin America overcame past hostilities, and by the time the common market treaty was signed in 1960 intraregional trade had reached 7 percent.

Because of the closeness of the Central American countries, the lower economic disparity between them, compared to LAFTA, and fairly stable macroeconomic conditions, intraregional commerce thrived. Despite the El Salvador-Honduras war of 1969, intra-CACM exports reached 27 percent of total CACM exports in 1970. During that period, El Salvador, followed by Guatemala, seems to have benefited the most from the integration agreement. The other three CACM members, Costa Rica, Honduras, and Nicaragua, experienced significant intraregional trade deficits.[19]

In the 1970s, CACM started to weaken because of the unhappiness of the three lagging partners—Honduras suspended its membership—and also because of macroeconomic instability, including rising fiscal and balance of payments deficits, foreign exchange controls, and declining foreign demand for the region's products. In the 1980s, the armed conflicts in Nicaragua and El Salvador overwhelmed the region and wrecked economic relations. By 1987 intraregional exports had fallen to less than 12 percent of total exports. With the end of hostilities, the decline in the debt crises, and substantial economic reforms, Central America is poised to resume its march toward economic integration.[20]

Other Integration Schemes

MERCOSUR. By far the largest, and also newest, subregional arrangement is the South American common market, MERCOSUR by its Spanish acronym, comprising Argentina, Brazil, Paraguay, and Uruguay. Emerging from bilateral trade agreements between Argentina and Brazil in the mid-1980s, the common market treaty was signed in 1991, providing for the elimination of all trade barriers between the four countries, common external tariffs, and harmonization of economic policies by mid-decade. Chile, more than half of whose Latin American trade is with Brazil and Argentina, was invited but refused to join because of economic instability and high trade barriers in MERCOSUR countries, particularly Brazil. Since 1990, when intra-MERCOSUR exports were only 9 percent of total MERCOSUR exports (Table 8.3, Memo Items), Argentina-Brazil trade has surged upward.

CARICOM. The smallest integration program in the Western Hemisphere is the Caribbean Community, or CARICOM, established in 1972 and succeeding the Caribbean Free Trade Area, which was a loose association, formed in the mid-1960s, of former and present British Commonwealth countries and territories. Of CARICOM's thirteen member countries, Jamaica is, with its 2.5 million inhabitants, by far the most populous, although Trinidad and Tobago, with half of Jamaica's population, has a per capita gross domestic product more than twice as high and its economy is probably more important for the United States because of its petroleum resources. CARICOM also looks toward a common market before the end of this century.[21] Its intragroup trade is still small, although it rose from 5 percent in 1965 to almost 13 percent at the end of the 1980s (Table 8.3).

SELA. The Latin American Economic System (SELA, by its Spanish acronym) is a promoter of Latin American economic cooperation rather than an integration agreement. Sparked by Mexican and Venezuelan initiatives during the height of the Third World push toward a "new international economic order," it was established in 1975 to "arrange common positions [in international forums] and galvanize cooperation for economic and social progress in the 25 Latin American member countries."[22] Fostering economic integration has been a principal objective of SELA.

LATIN AMERICAN ECONOMIC INTEGRATION AND THE EAI

An important motivation for the Latin American integration movement of the 1950s was to establish a counterweight against the overwhelming economic power of the United States in the region. Economic dependency was keenly felt. Guided by the European integration process, Latin American countries hoped that opening up markets to one another would strengthen their economies and get them better conditions in the world economy, particularly vis-à-vis the United States. Economic strength would derive from the expanded benefits of regional, rather than national, import-substituting industrialization.

At that time the United States was cool, if not actually opposed, to Latin American economic integration. U.S. discomfort with that idea was not due to any fear of Latin American economic power, but rather to a strong U.S. belief in multilateralism. Regional blocs, particularly among underdeveloped countries, would go against the optimum allocation of resources. For special reasons, European integration was considered an exception.

U.S. policy changed with the Alliance for Progress. In the East-West struggle, the United States needed a secure hemisphere and became interested in the region's economic development. It was recognized that integration might not be so inefficient after all, and might contribute to regional economic growth. The United States became supportive of Latin American economic integration, leading to the 1967 summit meeting discussed earlier.

After the subsequent disenchantment with Latin American cooperation efforts and occasional Latin American rebuffs of U.S. overtures, the United States disengaged from regional integration enterprises. It continued to provide some funding to such regional institutions as the Central American Bank for Economic Integration and CAF, and there was major U.S. support for the Inter-American Development Bank, which has financed integration projects.

Despite the depressing failures of regional integration, Latin Americans have never given up the idea of economic union. Integration agreements, although languishing during most of the last three decades, have survived. Stimulated by the debt crisis and its aftermath, the movement revived at the end of the 1980s. Bold new initiatives were undertaken, including the strengthening of common market commitments by all subregional groups and the emergence of MERCOSUR.

Although accompanied by mighty skepticism nourished by past disappointments, the most recent efforts seem to be more than intensified rhetoric. While from the vantage point of late 1992 the time frame of the common market targets appear unrealistic, the dramatically changed Latin American economic environment is more conducive to intraregional cooperation. Since the mid-1980s, most countries' regional trade has grown faster than their total trade. Part of this is due to the debt crisis and the subsequent economic downturn, which may have induced strapped Latin American countries to shift imports from extraregional hard currency suppliers to regional sources. Nevertheless, the newly modified Latin American trade agreements are more efficient because Latin American countries have opened their economies, unilaterally reducing trade barriers and bureaucratic obstacles to international commerce.

The possibility that the EAI may provide a more effective impulse to Latin

American integration than Latin Americans had been able to muster in the past is ironic, since integration was originally conceived in part as a means to increase the region's bargaining power with the United States. Latin American countries that may have sought refuge from being overwhelmed by the U.S. economy by banding together are no longer afraid of the United States. This is not because the U.S. economy is weaker, but because many Latin American countries have undergone severe reforms, reaching higher levels of productivity, and, therefore, greater self-confidence. They have seen that attempts to unite economies with similar levels of economic development may not be enough. Several of them suspect that a real integration stimulus may now come from linking up with the U.S. economy, even though the importance of trade relations with the United States has declined since the early postwar period (Table 8.2). The EAI takes into account the possibility of free trade agreements between subregional integration pacts and the United States. Just as France and Germany have taken the leadership in the economic union process in the European Community, so the United States may be the catalyst not only in Western Hemisphere but also in subregional Latin American integration.

WESTERN HEMISPHERE INTEGRATION: PROBLEMS AND PROSPECTS

Because Latin American trade barriers are still much higher than those of the United States, an FTA with the United States will require the continuation of unilateral trade liberalization by Latin American partners. Obviously, the more Latin American countries and subregional groups can liberalize their trade regimes before entering into an FTA with the United States, the less difficult the adjustment problems will be afterwards.

Integration Fears and Objectives

During the earlier period of intra–Latin American integration, the principal obstacle was the fear of deindustrialization and of balance of payments losses. Almost every member of an integration agreement perceived a danger in lowering trade barriers: its own industries might not be competitive and the country might be flooded with imports, bankrupting many firms and causing a deterioration of the balance of payments, aggravated by a loss of exports. Furthermore, imports might be diverted from lower-cost extraregional suppliers to higher-cost intraregional producers.[23]

While these perceptions still persist, the grounds for them have weakened. Unilateral trade liberalization combined with other economic reforms in most Latin American countries have eliminated grossly inefficient firms and international competitiveness has increased. Armed with these improvements, Latin American countries still prefer to trade with developed industrial countries rather than with themselves. In addition to the desire for linkages with advanced economies in order to obtain higher technology, Latin American firms can derive significant practical advantages by dealing with exporters and importers in developed countries, such as being able to obtain supplier credits that most often are not available in their trade with other Latin American countries.[24]

Most of the trade of Latin America, excluding the largest oil producers, Mexico and Venezuela, is still with countries outside the Western Hemisphere (compare Tables 8.2 and 8.3). This has led to a fear of high trade diversion costs for Latin American countries joining an FTA with the United States. Yet, trade diversion is not considered terribly relevant in Latin America. Not that such costs would be insignificant, but they are viewed as short-term in nature and a proper price to pay for attaining long-term objectives.

The near-term goal of joining an FTA with the United States is not trade expansion. It is to build confidence abroad and domestically in the Latin American economy that has become a partner with the U.S. economy. With the increased confidence it is hoped that domestic and foreign resources will become available for badly needed infrastructure. When transportation and communications improve and the labor force is being upgraded through effective education and training, private investment, domestic and foreign, can thrive. After new investments bear fruit, exports will be able to expand vigorously. It is possible that this kind of reasoning has led Mexico to be willing to pay the costs of the significant trade diversion that may occur because of severe rules of origin insisted on by the United States in the NAFTA negotiations.

While trade diversion may not greatly worry Latin American countries contemplating an FTA with the United States, investment diversion is a serious concern. For example, NAFTA may attract investments to Mexico at the expense of Caribbean basin countries, or of Brazil. Apprehension of losing investments to countries in a U.S. FTA are more real than balance of payments considerations, which seem to have receded into the background.[25]

FTA Expansion

Not only countries outside an FTA with the United States might suffer investment diversion, but also latecomers to an FTA can be assumed to be at a disadvantage compared to early joiners. Moreover, the benefits of the early joiners could be diluted. It will depend on how hemispheric integration proceeds.

If Latin American countries accede to NAFTA will it weaken or strengthen Mexico's position? If only trade were involved, then the accession of another country to NAFTA would benefit both Mexico and the new member, provided that NAFTA's trade with the outside world does not diminish.[26] But, as indicated earlier, more than trade is involved, and Mexico's immediate FTA goal is confidence building. It is not clear whether a NAFTA expansion will enhance or weaken Mexico's potential for attracting resources.

Separate FTAs between individual countries or regional blocs and the United

States—a hub-and-spoke system—could create competition between the FTAs for investment and other resources, which might lower Latin American benefits in all FTAs. It must be assumed that a hub-and-spoke system is less efficient than a large FTA covering the same countries, because in the former, trade barriers between the FTAs persist.[27]

Asymmetry

Until NAFTA, all formal economic integration arrangements, whether in Europe, Africa, Asia, or Latin America, had been negotiated between countries at similar levels of development. While there was a significant difference in per capita income between, say, Italy and France in the 1950s when the European Economic Community was formed, or between Paraguay and Argentina in 1960 when the original LAFTA agreement was signed, the huge gap between Mexican and U.S. income levels is many times greater.[28]

Gaps in Labor and Environmental Standards. The lack of experience in joining into open trade arrangements such disparate economies as the United States on one side and countries in Latin America on the other, has brought to the surface problems that were not encountered as severely in previous integration efforts in Europe and elsewhere. Above all, the enormous disparity in wage levels raises the specter of unilateral moves of industries from the high-wage to the low-wage country. This image is compounded by other factors that characterize differences between economically advanced and less developed countries. Prominent among them are labor standards and environmental protection. Why should it be surprising that First World and Third World countries are not equal in such standards or in their enforcement? No matter how intensive the negotiations, differences in the way in which labor and environmental matters are dealt with cannot be bargained away. Such differences are among others that define the gap between the First and Third Worlds. They may be covered by cosmetics in order to make an FTA acceptable, but they can disappear only in the long term, possibly with the help of such instruments as a free trade agreement.

The Infrastructure Problem. Obviously, deficiencies in physical and human infrastructure are another manifestation of underdevelopment. Unlike the gaps in wage levels, labor codes, and environmental standards and in their enforcement, all of which may act as incentives for firms in high-wage/high-standards economies to shift production to low-wage/low-standards partners, an inferior infrastructure acts as a deterrent to such moves. Thus, the quantity and quality of private investment will be limited by the inadequacy of roads and other transportation facilities, communications, supply of water and electricity, worker housing, labor skills, worker training facilities, and other infrastructure.

Therefore, if a Latin American country would measure the success of its entering into an FTA with the United States by the speed with which private investment will increase, its first priority should be to upgrade its infrastructure.

Until this can be achieved, the United States will remain the main attraction for investment. Not only is U.S. infrastructure superior, but the United States is also by far the largest market in any FTA. And, by definition, firms in the United States would also have access to other markets in an FTA.

On the other hand, a highly deficient infrastructure can protect high-cost domestic industry in a developing country, even if tariffs fall to zero. Transportation and other import costs may make U.S. exports uncompetitive with domestic production in the less developed country market. Obviously such a situation is incongruous with the idea of an FTA.

Undoubtedly, firms that need to escape high wages and/or strict enforcement of labor and environmental codes in order to remain competitive might move or shift production to the less developed FTA partner. Such transfers will be limited for several reasons. As indicated, available infrastructure, if not upgraded, will become exhausted. Very low wages may temporarily help maintain an internationally competitive edge as long as a large share of production is for exports and demand for unskilled labor-intensive production endures. Extremely low wages, however, cannot generate the purchasing power to support dynamic domestic production for local markets, and therefore will hinder economic development. Nor can low wages alone assure the maintenance of international competitiveness, as the East Asian countries have demonstrated. These newly industrializing countries have given highest priority to education and training so that the upgraded labor force will absorb higher technology for more efficient production. Rising wage levels that inevitably follow improvement in skills have not deterred the East Asians from becoming formidable international competitors.

The weak partner country in an FTA must rely on the confidence-building process to enable it to obtain necessary resources. Because of probable difficulties in getting private funds for infrastructure improvement, official agencies such as the World Bank, Inter-American Development Bank, and national governments need to be tapped. That would set the stage for private investment growth sustained by a sound physical and human environment and not based only on very low wages or on poor enforcement of labor and environmental codes.

CONCLUSION

In the Latin American context, unilateral trade liberalization and the progress toward freer markets seem to have made regional integration more viable. This moves one to ask—returning to the questions implicit in the very beginning of this chapter—Why go to regionalism when there already is a movement in Latin America toward global free trade? Are regional blocs detrimental to the multilateral trading system? Or are they building blocks for open world trade? Those who might be inclined to answer the second question in the affirmative may concede that regional integration could be a second-best solution. "If regionalism is the form that new openness in trade takes, then regionalism is more desirable than the alternative of a blocked or eroding multilateralism and is good."[29]

So a convergence could emerge between the globalists and those who view regional blocs as training grounds and stepping-stones on the way to global free trade. In that function, Latin American countries must do more than reduce trade barriers among themselves, otherwise their economic growth would be limited by regional import substitution. Their integration must be accompanied by continued multilateral trade liberalization if they want to remain on the path toward international competitiveness. So far, multilateralism seems to have been more successful than economic integration in Latin America. With the advent of the EAI, the introduction of extreme asymmetry in FTAs with the United States may do more for Latin American integration than the more symmetrical existing subregional free trade arrangements have achieved in the past.

The United States and Latin American countries reach for hemispheric integration with similar motives. First, the emergence of regional blocs in the world economy has induced the United States to increase its attention to its own hemisphere and has encouraged Latin American countries to seek a safe haven through an economic association with the United States. Second, recent U.S. experience has shown that exports can be an important engine for economic growth not only in other countries but also in the United States. Markets in this hemisphere offer a great potential. On the Latin American side, economic links with the United States provide legitimacy in the world economy, enhancing a country's image as having a promising economic future and therefore being worthy of investment risks. Third, the United States and Latin American countries perceive hemispheric integration as strengthening their bargaining power with the rest of the world.[30]

Because of its asymmetry, NAFTA is a singular experiment. To include South American countries would be even more unique. The United States and Mexico share one of the world's longest borders, and the size of their trade ranks among the top three or four trading volumes between any two countries around the globe. No other Latin American country's trade with the United States comes near it. For Mexico, therefore, the potential benefits of a free trade agreement with the United States would be much more concrete than for any other Latin American country. If symbolism plays a significant role for Mexico in entering NAFTA, it is immensely more important for other Latin American countries in signing up with the United States.

The hemispheric experiment, absent any previous experience elsewhere, will have to rely on its own devices. It appears that little can be learned from the most successful integration experiment so far—the European Community— that will be useful for the EAI. Perhaps the one important lesson is that it takes a lot of money to smooth the way toward a common market. The resources available currently and foreseen for the EAI and its hemispheric integration objective are only a tiny fraction of what the Europeans have been spending yearly.

NOTES

The author wishes to thank his colleagues at the University of California at San Diego, Lawrence Krause and John McMillan, for commenting on an earlier draft of this chapter.

1. John Gallagher and Ronald Robinson, "The Imperialism of Free Trade," *Economic History Review* 6 (August 1953), pp. 1–15.

2. Quoted in Albert Fishlow, "The Mature Neighbor Policy: A Proposal for a United States Economic Policy for Latin America," in Joseph Grunwald, ed., *Latin America and World Economy* (Sage, 1978), 30.

3. See Bryce Wood, *The Making of the Good Neighbor Policy* (Columbia University Press, 1961). In the postwar period, the United States has resumed military and non-military intervention in the region. These have been based not on economic interests, as in the past, but on cold war and other political considerations.

4. Joseph Grunwald, Miguel S. Wionczek, and Martin Carnoy, *Latin American Economic Integration and U.S. Policy* (The Brookings Institution, 1972), 65.

5. In 1913, just before World War I, 31 percent of Latin America's exports went to the United States, compared to a 21 percent export share to the United Kingdom. Donald W. Baerresen, Martin Carnoy, and Joseph Grunwald, *Latin American Trade Patterns* (The Brookings Institution, 1965), Table A, p. 20.

6. Fishlow, "The Mature Neighbor Policy," 31.

7. See Arthur P. Whitaker, *The Western Hemisphere Idea: Its Rise and Decline* (Cornell University Press, 1954).

8. Grunwald et al., *Latin American Economic Integration*, 67.

9. Fishlow, "The Mature Neighbor Policy," 37.

10. For the Declaration of the Presidents of America and the resulting Action Program, see Grunwald et al., *Latin American Economic Integration*, Appendix D.

11. See Jean-Jacques Servan-Schreiber, *Le Défi Américain* (Paris: Editions Denoël, 1967). That book, expressing French concern about the rapid emergence of U.S. enterprise in the European community, allegedly sold more copies in Brazil than in France.

12. Fishlow, "The Mature Neighbor Policy," 46.

13. Ibid., 40.

14. Special analyses and information on Latin American and Caribbean economic integration can be found in the issues of INTAL, *integración latinoamericana*, published in Buenos Aires monthly by the Instituto para la Integración de América Latina (INTAL), an entity of the Inter-American Development Bank.

15. Joseph Grunwald, "Hemispheric Economic Integration? Some Reflections," in Sidney Weintraub, ed., "Free Trade in the Western Hemisphere," THE ANNALS 526, (March 1993), The American Academy of Political and Social Science, Table 1 and sources cited therein.

16. In addition to the illegal drug trade, there is significant smuggling of legitimate goods across borders, particularly between Colombia and Venezuela, and Ecuador and Colombia.

17. In the words of Chile's minister of finance, "Chile is not considering rejoining the Andean Pact, but is looking instead to reach free-trade agreements with various countries without subscribing to a specific subregional entity" (Alejandro Foxley quoted in CORFO, *Chile Economic Report*, New York, no. 253, September 1992, p. 7). Although Chile, the principal promoter of the original Andean Pact, may not return to the group, it has accepted a 1992 invitation to rejoin CAF.

18. Grunwald et al., *Latin American Economic Integration*, 42.

19. Guillermo Noriega Morales, "Breve historia del Mercado Común Centroamericano y su situación y funcionamiento durante la crisis de la década de 1980," in INTAL, *integración latinoamericano*, Buenos Aires, 17, no. 179, June 1992, Tables 2 and 3, p. 21.

20. Current agreements provide for the establishment of a complete common market by the year 2000 with a common external tariff instituted before mid-decade. Honduras is about to reenter CACM. Recent discussions strive to incorporate Belize and Panama into the common market.

21. In mid-1992 CARICOM members agreed to establish a monetary union with a common regional currency by the year 2000. OAS-CECON, *TRADE NEWS* 17, no. 8, Washington, D.C., August 1992, p. 4.

22. Free translation by the author of Iris Mabel Laredo, "Definición y redefinición de los objectivos del proceso de integración latinoamericanas en las tres últimas décadas (1960–1990)," INTAL, *integración latinoamericana* 16, no. 171–172, September–October 1991, p. 10.

23. For a discussion of integration fears, see Grunwald, "Hemispheric Economic Integration?"

24. See, for example, Luis Escobar Cerda, "Aspectos financieros de la integración de América Latina," INTAL, *integración latinoamericana* 17, no. 178, May 1992, p. 55.

25. Investment diversion worries are, of course, not confined to Latin America; thus, East Asian countries have expressed concern that they might lose investments to Mexico because of NAFTA. For a discussion of issues of investment location in a Latin American common market, see Joseph Grunwald, "Some Reflections on Latin American Industrial Integration," in José Núñez del Arco, Eduardo Margain, and Rachel Cherol, eds., *The Economic Integration Process of Latin America in the 1980s* (Inter-American Development Bank, 1984).

26. For a theoretical discussion of the FTA expansion problem, see John McMillan, "Does Regional Integration Foster Open Trade? Economic Theory and GATT's Article XXIV," in K. Anderson and R. Blackhurst, eds., *Regional Integration and the Global Trading System* (Harvester Wheatsheaf, 1993).

27. Chile signed an FTA with Mexico in September 1991. It does not give the country access to NAFTA. As of 1992, Chile is seeking either to join NAFTA or to enter into an FTA directly with the United States. By the end of 1991, the United States had signed sixteen framework agreements (possible precursors of FTAs) covering all of Latin America and the Caribbean, with the exception of Cuba, Haiti, and Surinam. Two of the agreements were signed with regional integration pacts, MERCOSUR and CARICOM.

28. Using current rates-of-exchange conversion factors, the per capita income gap between Mexico and the United States is more than 10:1. When adjustments are made, smoothing out fluctuations in order to approach a more realistic conversion factor (the

"Atlas" method), the gap diminishes to somewhat less than 9:1. In using estimates of the respective purchasing power of the peso and the dollar (the method employed by the United Nations International Comparison Program (ICP), the difference declines to less than 4:1. No matter how calculated, the Mexico–U.S. gap in NAFTA is still a large multiple of any other gaps that have existed in other integration agreements. (For the latest Atlas and ICP per capita GDP figures, see The World Bank, *World Development Report 1992* (Oxford University Press, 1992), World Development Indicators, Tables 1 and 30 respectively and the corresponding technical notes).

29. John Whalley, "Regional Trade Arrangements in North America: CUSTA and NAFTA," World Bank and CEPR Conference on New Dimensions in Regional Integration, Session 3, Paper no. 6, April 2–3, 1992, Washington, D.C., p. 23. The McMillan article cited above ("Does Regional Integration Foster Open Trade?") comes to a similar conclusion, albeit under well-defined conditions.

30. In a nationally televised debate on free trade, Henry Kissinger stressed that the important U.S. rationale for NAFTA is the enhancement of U.S. global bargaining power (Public Broadcasting System, "Firing Line," University of Mississippi, September 11, 1992).

9

The Enterprise for the Americas Initiative: Empty Gesture, Shrewd Strategic Gambit, or Remarkable Shift in Hemispheric Relations?

_____ *Joseph S. Tulchin*

On June 27, 1990, telephone calls were made all over Washington summoning ambassadors and top level bureaucrats to the White House at noon to hear a major address by President George Bush. The extent and urgency of the summons was rare in Washington, and several Latin American ambassadors who attended the session reported that they had the impression of participating in a momentous occasion, of watching history being made. Gathered in the East Room of the White House, the ambassadors, the cabinet, and government's top advisers heard the president deliver a formal address in which he announced the Enterprise for the Americas Initiative.

The president began by referring to the dramatic events in the world in the previous year, linking the changes to the "rising tide of democracy never before witnessed in the history of this beloved hemisphere." He stated that the "political transformation sweeping . . . Latin America and the Caribbean has its parallel in the economic sphere." As a result of the meeting in Cartagena, Colombia in February 1990 with the heads of the Andean nations, the president had begun a comprehensive review of economic policy toward "this vital region. . . . That review is now complete," he said, "and the need for new economic initiatives is clear and compelling." He went on,

All signs point to the fact that we must shift the focus of our economic interaction toward a new economic partnership because prosperity in our hemisphere depends on trade, not aid. I've asked you here today to share with you some of the ideas, some of the ways we can build a broad-based partnership for the 1990s—to announce the new Enterprise for the Americas Initiative that creates incentives to reinforce Latin America's growing recognition that free market reform is the key to sustained growth and political stability.

The new policy would have three pillars—trade, investment, and debt—and would include action to strengthen environmental policies in this hemisphere. After a reference to the upcoming quincentenary, he declared, with a rhetorical flourish,

Today, the bonds of our common heritage are strengthened by the love of freedom and a common commitment to democracy. Our challenge, the challenge in this new era of the Americas is to secure this shared dream and all its fruits for all the people of the Americas—North, Central, and South.

The comprehensive plan that I've just outlined is proof positive the United States is serious about forging a new partnership with our Latin American and Caribbean neighbors. We're ready to play a constructive role at this critical time to make ours the first fully free hemisphere in all of history.

The reaction in Latin America to the president's speech was immediate and enthusiastic. More than a few officials in the United States and in Latin America professed to see the Enterprise for the Americas Initiative as the herald of a new era in hemispheric relations. Representatives in Washington of several nations announced their intention to sign up to negotiate free trade agreements at the earliest possible moment. Several research centers began comprehensive projects to study the EAI and its consequences for the region. Students from Argentina to Mexico began to write term papers comparing the EAI to the Alliance for Progress and the Good Neighbor Policy.

The administration emphasized that the president's new policy was part of a worldwide phenomenon—part of the broad swing toward market economies and democratic polities. The policy itself, according to Roger B. Porter, one of the president's advisers on economic matters, was part of a "vision for Latin America that is built on a foundation of partnership: partnership between Latin America and the Caribbean on the one hand and the United States on the other; partnership among the governments in the Hemisphere and their private sector; and partnership among the private sectors of the countries in the region."[1] This official explanation of the EAI recognized that there were scant government resources involved. That was the point: the EAI was about markets, eliminating barriers to trade and to entrepreneurship, and reducing statism. "The challenge to Latin governments under the Bush initiative," Porter said in a speech to the Americas Society in the fall of 1990, "is to remove obstacles to efficiently functioning markets, and to create a climate for entrepreneurship." States should not be involved in production, but should "implement regulations which safeguard foreign investments and facilitate the entry and exit of capital."[2]

Nearly two years later, in his testimony before the U.S. International Trade

Commission, David R. Malpass, deputy assistant secretary for inter-American affairs of the State Department, restated the themes first adumbrated by President Bush:

First, that the changes now underway are revolutionizing the economic and political structures of Latin America. I am convinced that by the time this decade closes, we will be living in a hemisphere very different and a lot better than what we saw in the 1980s.

Second, that the changes in Latin America offer unprecedented opportunities for us here in the United States to improve our lives. A growing and democratic Latin America is vital to U.S. welfare and security.

Malpass pointed out that exports create jobs and that the $60 billion in U.S. exports to Latin America represent approximately one million jobs. If U.S. trade to Latin America increased to $100 billion by the end of the decade, it would mean the creation of nearly another million jobs. Increased trade would be the key to improved relations between the United States and Latin America; it would lead to cooperation in other areas such as drugs and terrorism; and, he concluded, it would lead to "joint efforts to preserve and enhance the environment, [and] political cooperation to preserve the peace throughout the hemisphere and the world. The transformation of Latin America into a democratic and market-oriented community of nations means that we share common goals and common values. Nothing enchances U.S. security more than to be part of a community of nations with shared commitments to peace, democracy, and economic freedom."

As President Bush's term has now drawn to a close, it is appropriate to ask what has been accomplished—what all the fuss was about—and whether the EAI has fulfilled its promise from the U.S. perspective and from the Latin American perspective. It is the purpose of this chapter to evaluate the Enterprise for the Americas Initiative from the vantage point of the United States: how it fits into U.S. policy toward the region and globally; how it fit into the policy apparatus of the Bush administration; and, how, if at all, it will affect U.S. relations with Latin America during the coming years.

To begin, we must understand the strategic and political context out of which the Initiative emerged. For nearly a decade, the United States had been the subject of study after study concerned with the nation's decline relative to the emerging economic communities in Europe and Japan. Even the most optimistic of the studies was convinced that the days of U.S. dominance of the international economy were over and that the best that might be anticipated in the years ahead would be some sort of tri-polar world in which economic influence might be divided evenly, with the West confronting the East, led by the Soviet Union.[3] Then, stunningly, the Soviet Union collapsed. While the process of reform in the Soviet Union had accelerated to the point where it became increasingly obvious that what had been called the East Bloc and the

Evil Empire scarcely were what they had been, still it came as a shock when the Berlin wall was torn down by a crowd of joyous celebrants on November 9, 1989 and the nations of Eastern Europe, one after the other, declared their independence of the Soviet Union and their determination to form democratic states linked to the rest of Europe. Almost overnight, the Soviet Union had been transformed—imploded was the word most popular among journalists— into a loose, quarreling confederation of states perilously close to impotence. Now, instead of worrying about mutual destruction and the threat of military attack from a powerful enemy, the Western allies were concerned to coordinate their efforts to provide the economic aid deemed necessary to keep the former Soviet Union from sliding into chaos.

Leaders in the West were unclear as to how to react to the events in the East. Some wanted to declare victory in the cold war and one analyst wrote of the "end of history."[4] In the United States, members of Congress called for a "peace dividend" that would be used to stem the decline of the U.S. economy and restore its competitiveness, while dealing in a more generous fashion with the homeless, the poor, and the other dilemmas ripping at the nation's social fabric. President Bush, by nature an optimist, saw a global trend toward market economics and democratic politics. He was particularly encouraged by the movement toward freer international trade. He believed profoundly in the efficacy of untrammeled international exchange.

This was the government's recognition of what had come to be called the Washington Consensus concerning the transformation of the international market. Reflecting a view long advocated by the international lending agencies and the International Monetary Fund, it stressed the virtues of the free market and the need to restructure the command economies of the former socialist bloc and the protectionist economies of the Third World along lines congenial to the policies of the industrialized nations of the developed West.[5] According to this view, with the end of the cold war, there was a growing trend toward openness in the international economy, based on increasingly free trade and growing ease of movement of capital, labor, and information across national boundaries, for the benefit of the world community. Such restructuring or reform by the developing nations would permit their reinsertion into the increasingly competitive world economy, where efficiency and comparative advantage appeared to be the keys to success.

The end of the cold war freed the nations of Eastern Europe to join in a movement already well advanced in the Western Hemisphere, where, with the exception of Cuba, all of the nations were ruled by civilian, elected governments, an alignment unique in the region's history. Moreover, prodded and pushed by the international banks and the demands of the U.S. Treasury Department, many of the governments had set out on economic reforms of profound significance, turning away from import-substitution models of development that had dominated policy making virtually since the Great Depression and had been an article of faith since the 1950s, to open their economies to the international market. The Washington Consensus seemed global in its reach.

Nevertheless, while these trends were enormously encouraging to President Bush, he had been upset by the lament of the presidents of the Andean nations with whom he had met early in 1990 to discuss the vexing issue of drug traffic. The end of the cold war had prompted a shift in U.S. interest in Latin America from security issues to hemispheric free trade, democracy, drugs, migration, and the environment, and President Bush had gone to the meeting in Cartagena expecting enthusiastic cooperation from his Latin American colleagues. Instead, the leaders of Bolivia, Peru, and Colombia had reported to him that their nations—and the other nations of the region—were caught in an economic tailspin. They reported that the 1980s had been a lost decade for Latin America. The region had gone backward in economic terms, pinned down by the heavy burden of the enormous unpaid international debt that had brought the flow of private capital to a standstill and dragged most of the hemisphere into a recession that was undermining the new and fragile democracies. In the face of severe recession, the civilian governments were unable to raise the revenue to satisfy the legitimate needs of their population.

To compound the problem, the restructuring programs that were imposed on them by the international banks as a condition for renewed loans, and by the U.S. Treasury in some cases as a condition for credits by the Export-Import Bank or other federal agencies, were sapping the strength of the state precisely at a time when a strong state was needed to consolidate the new democracies and to respond to legitimate social needs such as staggering unemployment and to threats such as drug traffic, environmental degradation, and terrorism, which were at the top of the U.S. agenda for the hemisphere.

But President Bush was not attracted to a program of official aid. It went against his own philosophy and he knew that even if he were to adopt such a program, he would have a tough time selling it to the Congress and to the American people who were leary of the lingering recession and of the costs of the savings and loan scandal hanging over their heads. Historically, with the exception of the Alliance for Progress, the United States had responded to Latin American requests for economic help by urging them to open their markets and allow U.S. capital to solve their problems. "Trade not aid," was the response of U.S. officials after the Second World War to Latin American colleagues who asked for a hemispheric equivalent of the Marshall Plan. Bush was not the first U.S. president to believe in the magical healing powers of the international market.

These general concerns were focused for the president and his immediate advisers on the specific case of Mexico, where the young Harvard-educated president, Carlos Salinas de Gortari, had embarked on a bold reform program designed to open the Mexican economy, jumpstarting it with massive infusions of foreign capital and privatizations. Mexico had been a special case in Latin

America for the United States for many years. Aside from the obvious ties created by intertwined histories, a 2,000 mile shared border, and a high level of economic interdependence, the two nations were forced to confront together the most significant migration—legal and illegal—in the hemisphere. As Texans, President Bush and Secretary of State James Baker had a greater awareness of Mexico than most Americans, and an acute sense that they should do something about and for Mexico. As Texans, too, they tended to confuse the rest of Latin America with Mexico. What was good for Mexico undoubtedly would be good for the rest of Latin America.

Gathered on the president's ranch in southern Texas, they took into account their recent decision to begin talks with Mexico for a free trade zone, which when added to Canada, would constitute a North American Free Trade Area. They took into account also the president's forthcoming trip to South America in September.[6] What emerged—the result of policy planning within the Treasury Department by a small group called together by Secretary Nicholas Brady— seemed the perfect package. It was designed to deal with the major preoccupations of the nations in the region—debt, trade, and economic well-being. It was aimed at Mexico but would include the rest of the hemisphere. It was consistent with the policy of the administration in the Uruguay Round of the GATT negotiations and would strengthen the commitment of the Latin American nations to the multilateral trade reform central to those discussions. Finally, by insisting on partnership and hemispheric togetherness, it was designed to still the deep-seated anxieties of Latin Americans about the residual urges of the United States toward hegemonic behavior in the hemisphere.

The end of the cold war had left many leaders in Latin America more than a little nervous. They were concerned that the United States would pay even less attention to the region now that its strategic importance was called into question. On the other hand, the invasion of Panama had made some people in Latin America nervous that, with the end of the cold war, the United States would use its power unilaterally, without paying adequate attention to Latin American interests. It was hoped the EAI would calm those fears and create a wellspring of good will toward the United States, while supporting the U.S. efforts toward worldwide free trade and reenforcing efforts to strengthen the ties with Mexico.

The problem in getting the EAI off the ground was that it had very little specific content and no guidelines for putting the general policy into effect. The simple truth of the matter is that the announcement in June caught the U.S. bureaucracy off guard. The talks with Mexico had been in the works for months, but this was different. As the policy had been cooked in the Treasury Department, the Commerce and State departments were virtually out of the loop. It took a week for the Commerce Department to set up an office to deal with the EAI and the director of that office admitted not long after setting up shop that he hadn't the foggiest idea of what he was supposed to do and that he had no staff to do anything anyway. It was six months before the Commerce

Department would be in a position to deal effectively with the new policy. By that time, the Office of the U.S. Trade Representative (USTR) had staked a claim to leadership in the policy, since it was based on trade, although there, as at Commerce, the first note struck was one of bureaucratic unpreparedness. One of the senior officials responsible for Latin America told a public audience in Washington at the end of 1990 that the USTR simply did not have the staff to negotiate all the free trade treaties contemplated in the EAI and that it could only deal with subregional groupings, even though such groupings were contrary to Treasury Department policy on negotiating the debt.[7]

The State Department was the slowest to respond, perhaps because there were several divisions that felt they had the right to participate. By the beginning of the new year, activity concerning the EAI was centered in the office of the assistant secretary for Latin American affairs, acting as a liaison with the Agency for International Development. And, as so little of the EAI had to do with debt, Treasury had begun to cede the turf it had staked out during the policy-formulating process. Still, for nearly a year after the president's address, the EAI was a policy without a home and without any coherent leadership. During that time, there was virtually no attention paid to it in the press and the Congress displayed little interest in anything except the fast-track authorization for negotiations with Mexico. No one on Capitol Hill could get excited about the EAI until the Mexican case had been decided, and people throughout the country had difficulty distinguishing the EAI from NAFTA. When, for example, at the anniversary of the original announcement of the EAI, the president called the cabinet and the diplomatic corps into the Rose Garden of the White House to extol the successes of the EAI in the previous year, in the press conference that followed, not a single question was asked about the EAI; everything asked had to do with domestic politics.

Giving the EAI its specific content has not been easy, with much of the initiative coming from Latin America. The trade "pillar," as it is called, rests on a complex set of broad, general commitments to freer trade, known as framework agreements, which have been signed with virtually every nation in the hemisphere, and a bold commitment to create a free trade area "from Alaska to Tierra del Fuego." By the end of 1992 only Cuba, Surinam, and Haiti had not signed framework agreements with the United States. To facilitate the negotiation of trade agreements with the nations of the region, the administration asked for and won fast-track authorization under which Congress commits itself to vote only up or down on the entirety of a trade agreement presented to it, disallowing approval of some provisions and not others. Furthermore, it must vote on implementing legislation within a fixed period of time. On May 24, 1991 Congress approved a two year extension of fast-track authorization to June 1, 1993. While the fast track might benefit EAI, it was intended to make the Mexican treaty easier to deal with, and the political tensions associated with the Mexican treaty during a presidential election threatened to spoil fast-track handling for the rest of Latin America.[8]

The debt pillar is the weakest of the three pillars of the EAI—trade, investment, and debt. It deals exclusively with official bilateral debt, which amounts to only $12.5 billion for the entire region out of a total foreign debt in excess of $400 billion. Of course, there are some countries, all in the Caribbean basin, for whom the amount represents a considerable portion of their total foreign debt, but it is trivial and insignificant for the major debtors in the region—Argentina, Brazil, and Mexico—whose official debt amounts to $524 million, $2.5 billion, and $1.6 billion, respectively. Debt forgiveness must be approved by Congress, and the executive began the process by requesting modest authorizations from Congress in each of the fiscal years 1992 and 1993. Such requests were entirely unsuccessful until the Foreign Aid Bill for fiscal 1993 was passed in October 1992, with trivial amounts for debt.

The investment pillar was the least defined in the original document and remains unclear to this day. After a period of floundering and indecision, the Bush Administration gave over the investment portion of the EAI to the Inter-American Development Bank in the form of a Multilateral Investment Fund, which was to reach $1.5 billion with major contributions from Japan, Germany, and other creditor nations. In addition, a small amount was set aside, again through the IDB, to support investment sector reforms.

Trade, on the other hand, seems to have been an idea whose time had come. Almost without being asked, Latin American nations began to lower their tariff barriers or to accelerate processes of trade reform begun before June 1990. As the representative of the Brazilian government, Minister Sergio Amaral, stated at hearings conducted by the U.S. International Trade Commission in January 1992:

If I had been invited by the ITC to appear before the Commission three years ago, I would have felt uncomfortable explaining and justifying:

- the existence of a list of 1,300 products the import of which was suspended;
- very high tariff levels, which when combined with additional taxes may have reached 300 percent;
- the invocation of Article XVIIIB of the GATT, for almost two decades, to cover for an array of import restrictions, despite the fact that BOP imbalances were real.

Today, however, I am pleased with this opportunity to provide you with an update on the far-reaching liberalization program which has been implemented in Brazil in the last two years and to inform you that, to the best of my knowledge, there are no remaining barriers to the access of U.S. products to the Brazilian market, except for a few restrictions in the area of informatics, which will be eliminated by October 1992. A sea change has taken place in Brazil's trade policies, which had an immediate impact on U.S.–Brazil trade relations.

Later in his testimony, Minister Amaral complained that the United States was lagging behind Brazil and other Latin American nations in the liberalization of its trade policies and he urged the United States to take a more aggressive stance in collaboration with the nations of the hemisphere in confronting the protectionist tendencies of some European nations within the GATT. Frustration with the GATT was expressed also by the Argentine representative in Geneva, Ambassador Archibaldo Lanus, who complained that only Latin America was following the suggestion of the developed nations to remove the barriers to trade and that they might find themselves exposed in the near future in a world market in which only the primary product exporters had lowered or eliminated trade barriers while the developed countries, their logical markets, had left their trade walls as high as they had been.[9]

The link between GATT, the EAI, and NAFTA is crucial to understanding the U.S. approach to the EAI and its political fate in Washington. The congressional leadership saw the fast-track authorization for Mexico as part of the nation's effort to get something out of the Uruguay Round of the GATT talks and not as part of the EAI. The leadership of both houses made this clear in a letter to the president from Senator Lloyd Bensten and Congressman Dan Rostenkowski on March 7, 1991, in which they indicated their concern for the unresolved issues of the environment and the vast differential in labor standards between the two countries. The president's response on May 1, emphasized his commitment to the free trade negotiations and stressed President Salinas's commitment to high environmental standards. At the same time, he reiterated his willingness to work closely with the Congress in the coming months. Deputy U.S. Trade Representative Ambassador Julius Katz told the Senate Committee on Finance that it was the administration's intention to consult Congress at every step of the negotiations with Mexico, so that fast-track did not mean eliminating Congress from the treaty process, and that it was in the administration's interest not to get caught up in an adversarial relationship with the Congress during the negotiations.[10]

Fruit of the executive's cooperative posture came during the summer months as Congress included in the annual appropriations legislation approval for the modest debt-reduction promises extended in the EAI. The government moved quickly to sign bilateral agreements with Chile, Bolivia, and Jamaica to reduce those nations' debt under P.L. 480, the Food for Peace Program. These successes were offset by the embarrassment suffered at the beginning of the new fiscal year, from September until December, when Congress could not pass a budget and left the government to be financed by continuing resolutions that held expenditures to the levels of the 1991 budget, which meant that EAI was held at zero. Once the budget was approved, the debt forgiveness program could begin.

The multilateral investment fund suffered an even more frustrating fate. Congress postponed acting on the commitment of the United States to contribute $100 million, while the Europeans stated publicly that they would not put in their share unless the United States were to increase its commitments to the reconstruction of the former Soviet Union and Eastern Europe. Japan, after some hesitation, agreed to match the U.S. contribution when that contribution actually was made. Nothing came out of the Congress until the Foreign Aid Bill in October. The IDB was organizing to disburse the funds but did not receive anything to disburse for more than a year.

Even if the MIF were completed at the desired levels, the total appears insignificant—25 cents per capita—compared to the efforts by the Germans to incorporate their brethren from the former Democratic Republic—$3,000 per capita—or the monumental efforts mounted to rescue the economies of Eastern Europe and the former Soviet Union. But the paltry sums in question are justified by the Bush Administration on the grounds that they are symbolic—commitments to start the ball rolling and get the private sector involved, to stimulate entrepreneurship.

The private sector in the United States slowly made its voice heard, at hearings conducted around the country by the U.S. Trade Representative. Firms large and small indicated their support for the NAFTA and for the president's vision of a free trade zone throughout the hemisphere. The consensus was that there was a lot of money to be made in the hemisphere for U.S. businesses and that jobs would be created, hundreds of thousands of jobs, as a result of the treaty. The only warning came from manufacturers of light machinery and textiles who insisted that unless the treaties with the low-wage countries in the hemisphere included strict provision for the addition of local inputs, the Asian exporters would simply use them as reexport platforms and flood the U.S. market with cheap goods.[11]

The only public objection to the EAI at these early hearings came from organized labor and those who professed to speak for labor. In a formal presentation to the USTR in Boston, four economists, led by Samuel Bowles of the University of Massachusetts, asserted that the NAFTA would lead to dramatic increases in U.S. direct private investment in Mexico, which, in turn, would lead to the loss of more than half a million jobs in the United States by the year 2000.[12] This testimony was meant to contradict a report submitted to Congress in June 1991 by the Department of State, which estimated that 15 percent of any rise in Mexican income would be spent on U.S. goods. Each extra $1 billion in U.S. exports would mean that approximately 22,000 new jobs would be created domestically.

In October, Lloyd Bentsen, chairman of the Senate Finance Committee, asked the U.S. International Trade Commission to produce a report on the trade policies of the countries in Latin America and their implications for future U.S. trade. Because the president had indicated his intention to negotiate with Chile after concluding the treaty with Mexico, Bentsen asked the USITC to pay particular attention to that country. The hearings were held in January, but consistent with the entire history of the EAI, stirred more interest in Latin America than in the United States.

As the year wore on and public fears of the recession increased, the argument of lost jobs took on greater salience. Opposition to President Bush's re-election emerged within the Republican party in the person of Patrick Buchanan, who hit hard at the president's failure to pay attention to U.S. problems at home. The same argument was raised by Harrison Wofford in his successful campaign for senator in Pennsylvania against Richard Thornburgh, who had the complete backing of the president. After the campaign, Wofford thought it necessary to distance himself from Buchanan by publishing an article in the *Washington Post* affirming that he was no isolationist.[13]

The press generally took up the question of protectionism, as a reflection of Buchanan's impact on the campaign.[14] The fear that lost jobs might become the key issue in the negotiations with Mexico led the president to tell President Salinas at their meeting in Camp David on December 14 that it might be necessary for Mexico to make further concessions in the negotiations. At the same time, the administration assumed a lower public profile on the talks and stopped all mention of the possibility of beginning negotiations with Chile in the near future. The president mentioned free trade in general terms in his State of the Union address in January and relaunched the EAI with some ceremony in February.

Once the Buchanan threat was overcome by March, the president became more aggressive and expressed his annoyance that he could not get the treaty with Mexico before the elections. In April, he told the Council of the Americas that he would not let the campaign interfere with his plans to sign a free trade treaty with Mexico.[15] At the same time, however, administration officials in the State and Commerce departments said privately that there was no way the treaty draft could be ready before the end of the year. When pressed publicly to estimate when the talks would be concluded, Trade Representative Carla Hills indicated that dates were not important. What was important, she said, was a good agreement that would be supported enthusiastically by a broad segment of the American people.[16] Members of Congress doubted that it would be presented before March 1993. In fact, most congressional staff of both parties were convinced that the jobs issue was so delicate that the administration would get the treaty through the Congress only by a strong presidential effort that would stress long-term geopolitical interests of the treaty and deemphasize all short-term economic benefits.

As it turned out, the pessimists were wrong. The NAFTA was signed—twice. The first time was symbolic, in time for the Republican party convention in August. The final signing came a month later. But Bush was playing a high stakes game and he gambled with the fate of the EAI by pushing the NAFTA into the presidential campaign. Backed into a corner by Clinton's attack on his handling of the economy, Bush urged Carla Hills to conclude the agreement with Mexico in time for the convention so that he could use it to accuse his Democratic opponent of being a protectionist. Clinton's response was that he favored free trade agreements, he just didn't like this free trade agreement, although he promised to accept it if it could be adjusted slightly and accompanied by compensatory domestic job programs. Salinas meanwhile was forced to defend himself against domestic nationalists by insisting that Mexico would not negotiate with candidate Clinton: Mexico would deal only as one sovereign state with another.[17] Looking beyond NAFTA to EAI, there is a real danger that the U.S. bureaucracy will not move fast enough. The fast-track authorization expires in June 1993, and without it, negotiating multiple free trade treaties is inconceivable.

The Mexicans were more than a little disturbed at suffering the consequences of U.S. domestic politics. Following the meeting at Camp David, in December, the Mexicans leaked word of their concern to the press.[18] In March, President Salinas delivered a major address in which he indicated how Mexico might react to the failure to establish a NAFTA and how his government would turn to "Social Democracy" instead of the free market policies it had been following for the previous three years.[19]

The question of the environment is one that causes considerable tension in the talks between Latin America and the United States. A speech by Brazilian Ambassador Rubens Ricupero suggested that this would be a major bone of contention in negotiations between the United States and the nations of the future free trade zone.[20] The Latin Americans were concerned that the United States might use the environment as a weapon in their trade negotiations. Indeed there was evidence that environmental groups were prepared to do just that. Again, however, it is important to point out that these groups already had raised the specter of unfair disparities in environmental regulations in the public discussions of the GATT negotiations and would deny strenuously that they were discriminating against Latin Americans by inserting these concerns into the debate over NAFTA and EAI. The fact of the matter is that the Europeans are quite close to the United States in their environmental policies and even are ahead of the United States on some issues. That certainly is not the case with Latin America, and the environment would be a blunt weapon used against the Latin Americans in any talks in which environmental regulations were a condition of free trade benefits.

Through all of the political bickering over NAFTA, the EAI became lost from view. If NAFTA had become "Bush's Treaty," then the EAI had become "Bush's Initiative." Clinton said nothing about the EAI during the campaign and his advisers suggested that a new Democratic administration would do something different with regard to Latin America.[21] At the very end of the congressional session, Congress passed the Foreign Aid Bill with most of the EAI provisions. The MIF was funded at $90 million and debt reduction was authorized, although at anemic levels—only $50 million for bilateral debt. The bill passed because the congressional leadership, convinced Clinton would win, wanted what they thought the American people would consider a "give away" to be passed under a Republican president, so that a new Democratic administration would not have to worry about it in January 1993. All major international aid programs—the development banks, IMF, Russian aid, and Israeli housing subsidies—were included in the omnibus bill.[22]

Thus far, the results of the EAI have been minimal. In and of itself, the

EAI has accomplished virtually nothing. There has been little direct or short-term gain. A more serious problem is, as Peter Hakim has pointed out, quoting a World Bank study, that the EAI has been oversold in Latin America.[23] Even if all barriers to trade with the United States were eliminated, even nontariff barriers, Latin American exports to the United States would increase only 8 percent. That will not be enough to solve Latin America's economic woes nor fuel the engines of growth for very long. The success of the export models may prove ephemeral.

However, the indirect gains have been significant. At the very least, in a worst case scenario, the possibility of a free trade area in the hemisphere would protect the Latin American nations against a resurgence of U.S. protectionism, although nontariff barriers have become so complex and the asymmetry between the U.S. economy and the economies of the Latin American nations so vast that true free trade would be decades away under the best of circumstances and hopelessly delayed under more difficult circumstances. Still, there have been important indirect benefits of the EAI, even if we take a harsh or cynical view of its accomplishments in the short term. There has been a palpable increase in investor confidence in Latin America, as shown by the impressive demand for securities on a growing number of exchanges in the region, and there has been significant inflow of private capital, at least into a few of the countries, mainly Chile and Mexico. If the EAI provides a buttress for free trade policies that are historically anamolous, politically vulnerable, and subject to domestic attack, then it may prove to be a self-fulfilling prophesy of the most positive sort by making the economies of the Latin American nations more competitive in the international marketplace.

Furthermore, the EAI has provided a powerful stimulus to intraregional integration efforts, pushing them further toward realization than at any previous time. Indeed, even if the Bush Administration failed to realize its part of the EAI partnership, if such projects as MERCOSUR and the Andean Pact are brought to fruition they will strengthen the economies of Latin America at a critical time and prove to be a powerful support for the self-esteem of the peoples of the hemisphere. Ironically, by pushing the Latin American nations to restructure their economies, then leading them to expect great things from an EAI given a splashy inauguration, and then frustrating them by bureaucratic inadequacy and partisan wrangling, the United States may end up strengthening Latin American regionalism.[24] Historically, the United States has preferred to deal with Latin American nations one on one and has gone to great lengths to discourage joint or multilateral efforts. Today, in the aftermath of the cold war, the United States needs Latin America to join in the settlement of hemispheric disputes, just as it needs European and other allies to deal effectively with crises in Yugoslavia, Cambodia, Iraq, and elsewhere, whether it be through the United Nations or through other forms of collective effort. In the Western Hemisphere, the United States needs allies to deal with crises in Haiti or Peru. It needs allies to deal effectively with drug traffic, with terrorism, or with threats to the environment. That need for allies, for partners as George Bush put it, may produce some changes in U.S. policy that were not entirely anticipated and that run counter to the U.S. historic need for a free hand in hemispheric action. The Bush Administration gave every indication that it preferred to act alone. Historically, the Democrats have been more inclined toward multilateral cooperation with Latin America.

What can we expect of the EAI in the United States in the new administration? It is virtually certain that a Bush administration would have continued to support the EAI because it fit so well with its global policies. The EAI was utterly consistent with the Bush Administration's policy toward GATT and its bias toward free trade. The EAI has the virtue of supporting U.S. efforts for a global community and yet also holds open the possibility of strengthening the U.S. as the leader of a hemispheric bloc, should such a strategic coalition become necessary in the years ahead. Such a strategy is put forward by those who anticipate that the Uruguay Round will fail and that the world economy will drift toward increasing competition among three blocs: the European Community, Japan and its Asian subsidiaries, and the United States and Latin America.[25] In the language of game theory, the EAI is a win-win situation. Moreover, in such a situation, Latin America has nowhere to go, since its European and Asian trading partners would become increasingly preoccupied with intrabloc trade and less concerned with the well-being of their Latin American trading partners. Finally, under any future scenario of world trade, the EAI is a plus because it will stimulate the economies of Latin America, which will enhance the political stability of the countries in the region, always a concern in Washington, and, by expanding their economies, make it easier for their governments to satisfy the demands of their populations while they become more attractive markets for the United States.

On the domestic front in the United States, the EAI is inextricably linked to the NAFTA negotiations with Mexico. Nothing of moment will happen until the treaty is approved. The fate of the treaty in Congress will be determined by the evolution of the recession in which the United States is mired and the conclusion of the Uruguay Round. Should the GATT talks stall, the new administration will redouble its efforts to conclude the NAFTA treaty. If the recession ends, getting the treaty through Congress will be easier. Even if the recession lingers, the president probably has the votes to push the treaty through Congress; but, he must commit himself publicly and with energy to gain his objective.

When all the speeches are finished, it will be the private sector that will determine whether or not the EAI fulfills its promise. Only with a strong expansion of hemispheric trade and significant direct investment of foreign capital can we expect growth to resume in Latin America. And without growth, the EAI will end as a failure. But some in Latin America feel it already has succeeded.[26] It has linked democracy and economic integration, and it has helped to legitimize the necessary, inevitable, and politically difficult policies designed to make the nations of the region into global traders. If this view is correct, the EAI will have taken on a life of its own in Latin America, pulling the United States along with the rest of the hemisphere.

NOTES

1. Roger B. Porter, "The Enterprise for the Americas Initiative: A New Approach to Economic Growth," *Journal of Interamerican Studies and World Affairs* 32, no. 4 (Winter 1990): 2.

2. Ibid, 6.

3. The classic statement of what has come to be called "imperial overreach" is in Paul Kennedy, *The Rise and Fall of the Great Powers* (New York: Random House, 1987). Other examples of similar arguments are: David P. Calleo, *Beyond American Hegemony* (New York: Basic Books, 1987); Josef Joffe, *The Limited Partnership* (Cambridge, Mass: Ballinger, 1987); and Joel Krieger, *Reagan, Thatcher and the Politics of Decline* (New York: Oxford University Press, 1987). For a very different opinion, see Henry R. Nau, *The Myth of America's Decline* (New York: Oxford University Press, 1990).

4. See Francis Fukuyama, "The End of History?" *The National Interest*, 16 (Summer 1989).

5. John Williamson, "What Washington Means by Policy Reform," in John Williamson, ed., *Latin American Adjustment: How Much Has Happened?* (Washington, D.C.: Institute for International Economics, 1990).

6. The trip subsequently was postponed until December 1990.

7. Don Abelsen made the remarks during the colloquium of Sidney Weintraub at the Woodrow Wilson International Center for Scholars, December 1990, subsequently published as part of Working Paper No. 195. Professor Weintraub incorporated Abelson's remarks into his own argument for the growing regionalism in U.S. trade policy in his paper, "The New U.S. Economic Initiative Toward Latin America," *Journal of Interamerican Studies and World Affairs* 33, no. 1 (Spring 1991), 1–18. The lack of staff was a constant preoccupation of the USTR; for example, see the interview with Carla Hills, *New York Times*, May 2, 1992, D11. At the end of 1992 it still was USTR policy to do one treaty at a time, and to consider Mexico not finished until Congress had ratified the treaty.

8. *New York Times*, May 2, 1992, A35.

9. Presentation to FLACSO seminar, Buenos Aires, March 6, 1992.

10. Ambassador Julius Katz, testimony before the Senate Finance Committee, April 24, 1991. The same attitude was expressed by Myles Frecchette, assistant U.S. trade representative for Latin America, the Caribbean and Africa, in a speech at American University, June 12, 1991.

11. Testimony before the Trade Policy Staff Committee, Atlanta, Ga., August 29, 1991.

12. Samuel Bowles et al., "Estimates of the Impact of the Free Trade Agreement on Direct U.S. Investment in Mexico," Study submitted to the Trade Policy Staff Committee Public Hearings, Boston, September 11, 1991. Progressive economists continued to oppose NAFTA. See Ricardo Grinspun and Maxwell A. Cameron, eds., *The Political Economy of North American Free Trade* (New York: St. Martin's Press, 1993).

13. Harris Wofford, "I'm No Isolationist," *Washington Post*, December 26, 1991, A23.

14. See, for example, "Free Trade Politics," *Christain Science Monitor*, December 23, 1991, 18.

15. *New York Times*, April 24, 1992, D1.

16. Press briefing by U.S. Trade Representative Carla Hills, The White House, December 13, 1991.

17. *Excelsior*, September 23, 1992, II,1.

18. "Mexico Worries U.S. May Stall Trade Pact," *Los Angeles Times*, December 12, 1991, A4.

19. Speech by President Salinas, March 23, 1991.

20. Speech before Trans Atlantic Futures, Washington, D.C., February 23, 1992.

21. Comments made by Samuel Berger at a meeting of the D.C. Liaison Committee on Latin America, September 14, 1992.

22. Interview by author with lobbyist Barry Hager, October 13, 1992.

23. Peter Hakim, "The Enterprise for the Americas Initiative," *Washington Quarterly* 15, no. 2 (Spring 1992). Also, see his "The Enterprise for the Americas Initiative, What Washington Wants," *The Brookings Review* (Fall 1992).

24. Weintraub, "The New U.S. Economic Initiative."

25. Lester Thurow, *Head to Head: The Coming Economic Battle Among Japan, Europe, and America* (New York: William Morrow, 1992).

26. Felix Peña, "Competitividad, Democracia e Integracion en las Americas," presentation to the seminar on Hemispheric Integration at the Fundaçao Getulio Vargas, Rio de Janeiro, August 21, 1992.

PART IV

The North American Free Trade Negotiating Track: Agenda Setting for the Enterprise for the Americas Initiative

10

Argentina, the Southern Common Market, and the Prospects for Success of the EAI

_____ *Roberto Bouzas*

The Enterprise for the Americas Initiative is the most comprehensive U.S. policy proposal toward Latin America since President Kennedy's Alliance for Progress. Notwithstanding the modesty of the resources involved, the announcement of the EAI raised expectations of a constructive U.S. approach to some of the most daunting problems faced by the countries of the region. As a result, it laid the groundwork for improved political relations in the Western Hemisphere. The EAI addressed three key issues of the international economic agenda of the Latin American countries: international trade, direct investment, and external debt. It also contributed to the ongoing debate about the strategic options for Latin American countries in a world of rapid and far-reaching economic change.

This chapter briefly reviews the implications of the EAI for Argentina and, given the critical role of its trade component, its potential effects upon the ongoing process of subregional economic integration. The first section underlines the remarkable political impact of the EAI as opposed to its limited economic significance in the short run. The second section addresses U.S.–Argentine trade relations and the implications of the trade component of the EAI. The third section discusses its potential effects upon the Southern Common Market, MERCOSUR, from the standpoint of its two largest partners. A final section presents some concluding remarks.

THE EAI AND ARGENTINA: POLITICS AND ECONOMICS

The main and most immediate effect of the Enterprise for the Americas Initiative upon Argentina was political. Its announcement in June 1990 coincided with a period of sea-changes in the domestic political economy. Following almost a decade of frustrated attempts at economic stabilization and reform, since mid-1989 the Menem Administration intensified policies aimed at trade liberalization, fiscal consolidation, and public sector divestiture. The new government also abandoned the traditional nonaligned posture of Argentine foreign policy and adopted a pragmatic approach based upon a clear-cut identification with U.S. objectives and interests. In this new political environment, the announcement of the EAI created expectations of improved bilateral relations and served as a boost to the process of domestic economic reform.

Prior to taking office, Argentine and foreign economic elites regarded Carlos Menem as a poorly suited candidate to implement the tough stabilization and structural reform policies required to stop the slide toward fiscal collapse and hyperinflation. Menem was generally regarded as a mainstream Peronist/populist leader who advocated state intervention and income redistribution, rather than the "pro-market and conservative fiscal and monetary policies" recommended by the so-called Washington Consensus.[1] As a result, Menem's victory in the May 1989 polls was viewed as a preamble to irresponsible policies that could end up in economic chaos and, eventually, lead to the collapse of Argentina's newborn democracy.

To the surprise of most observers and of its own electorate, immediately after taking office the new president appointed as finance minister a high-ranking official of a large Argentine conglomerate and empowered him with the explicit task of implementing a tough stabilization and structural reform program. After several failed policy packages and a second hyperinflationary bout in 1990, in April 1991 Congress passed the Convertibility Law, which established a fixed exchange rate and full convertibility of the domestic currency.[2] The Convertibility Plan formally took monetary policy away from government's hand and placed strict limits on the public sector's ability to finance fiscal deficits. These policies opened the door to negotiations with international financial institutions and private creditors and, eventually, to the conclusion of a "Brady-type" debt reduction package.

In the foreign policy realm the new administration implemented an unprecedented change of direction, certainly for an elected government and particularly for a Peronist one. The new approach included an open identification of Argentine interests and policy objectives with those of the United States. The incoming Administration criticized Alfonsin's foreign policy as idealistic (or "principist") and replaced it by an overt effort to align its policies and attitudes with U.S. regional and global priorities. The notion that the challenge to U.S. policies was based on a misguided search for self-satisfaction rather than the promotion of self-interest became the foundation stone for the new policy.[3] This argument was reinforced by the changing international environment of the post–cold war era: advocates of the new approach argued that Argentina faced a historic opportunity to actively participate in the building of a new world order and strategically improve its relations with the hemispheric hegemonic power.

In this policy environment, the EAI effectively served one of the purposes presumably envisioned by its proponents, namely, to provide a breath of support to Latin American governments implementing tough stabilization and reform policies at practically no economic cost. The EAI emphasis on policy reform and conditionality reinforced the Menem Administration's belief that it was on the correct policy course and gave hopes that Argentina would be among the first beneficiaries of the fallouts of a renewed U.S. interest in the Western Hemisphere.

In contrast to its political significance, the immediate economic impact of the EAI upon Argentina was largely irrelevant. Although Argentina is the third largest Latin American debtor ($58.2 billion by year-end 1991), the vast majority of its liabilities are due to private banks and multilateral organizations. Argentine bilateral debts owed to U.S. official agencies amount to just over $500 million (predominantly nonconcessional debts to the Export-Import Bank). If the nonconcessional debt reduction component of the EAI is eventually passed by the U.S. Congress, a share of these liabilities (10 to 15 percent) may be sold to facilitate debt-for-nature, debt-for-development, or debt-for-equity swaps, and hence retire part of Argentina's obligations to the U.S. government. However, the effect upon Argentina's total external liabilities clearly will be negligible.

The investment component of the EAI, seeking to promote and support liberalization of investment regimes in Latin America through a new Inter-American Development Bank (IADB), Investment Sector Loan Program (ISLP), and an IADB-administered Multilateral Investment Fund, is also of relatively minor importance to Argentina. On the one hand, the proposed MIF will be extremely modest, with total projected resources of $1.5 billion for a period of five years. On the other, the IADB investment sector loan program has not been the result of increased financial resources made available to the IADB, but of a reshuffling of existing funds. This line of sectoral credits, however, is largely compatible with prevailing Argentine policies in the fields of privatization, deregulation of labor and goods markets, and investment reform. According to official sources, by late 1992 Argentina is likely to conclude negotiations to obtain a $300 million IADB loan to increase private sector participation by removing policy and institutional obstacles from those financial and non-financial areas that play a major role in private sector development.

ARGENTINA AND THE TRADE COMPONENT OF THE EAI

The trade pillar, particularly the proposal to negotiate free trade agreements with countries or groups of countries in Latin America, is by far the potentially most influential component of the EAI. The United States is an important trade partner for Argentina and its share in total Argentine exports and imports expanded in the 1980s. However, since Argentine trade flows are regionally well diversified, the U.S. share of Argentine foreign trade is relatively low when compared to that of other Latin American countries: in 1990 the United States absorbed less than one-sixth of Argentine total exports and supplied about one-fifth of Argentine total purchases abroad (Table 10.1). The importance of the U.S. market is enhanced when manufactured exports are considered: in contrast to the commodity composition of overall Argentine sales abroad, exports to the United States are tilted toward manufactured products, particularly intermediate goods and processed food products.[4]

In 1990 about 40 percent of Argentine exports to the United States entered duty-free, under either the most favored nation clause or the benefits of the Generalized System of Preferences (Table 10.2). The remaining 60 percent generally payed low tariffs. In 1986, a year for which more disaggregated data is available, the weighted average tariff rate paid by Argentine exports to the United States was just 2.9 percent. Some individual products, however, paid relatively high duties (among others fruit juices, scrap tobacco, ceramic floor and wall tiles, and woven wool fabrics). According to one estimate, in 1986 about a quarter of Argentine exports with trade of $50,000 or more paid duties of 5 percent or higher.[5] However, most observers agree that nontariff barriers (NTBs) are more relevant obstacles to Argentine exports to the United States than import duties. According to the United Nations Conference on Trade and Development (UNCTAD), in 1986 more than a quarter of Argentine exports to the United States were subject to some kind of NTB, especially specific taxes (19.6 percent of total exports), countervailing duties (4.1 percent), quotas (3.9 percent) and variable import fees (1.9 percent).

Foreign (and U.S.) access to Argentine domestic markets has greatly improved in the last few years as a result of rapid liberalization of the trade regime. Since the mid-1980s, but especially after 1987, Argentina implemented a series of trade liberalization packages that greatly diminished tariff and nontariff protection. The most recent set of trade policy initiatives (April 1991) removed the few remaining NTBs and established three tariff levels (5, 13, and 22 percent) and a temporary 35 percent rate for electronic products. Quantitative restrictions were temporarily maintained for the automobile sector in the context of a sectoral restructuring program.

For the last two decades, Argentina has been under U.S. pressure to remove certain practices considered unfair by U.S. legislators and trade practitioners. Since the late 1970s Argentina has been subject to five Section 301 investigations, although none of them led to the application of sanctions.[6] More recently, following the enactment of the 1988 Omnibus Trade and Competitiveness Act, Argentina was included on a special Section 301 "watch list" on the grounds of allegedly inadequate protection of intellectual property rights, particularly pharmaceutical patents. Although rapid trade liberalization and policy reform in Argentina has greatly diminished trade frictions, it has not eliminated all U.S. trade complaints.[7]

However, trade liberalization in Argentina has been inconsequential to a major area of bilateral trade disputes, namely, U.S. agricultural subsidies. As an efficient nonsubsidizing agricultural producer and exporter, Argentina has suffered extensively from the subsidies war among the United States and the

Table 10.1
NAFTA/MERCOSUR Trade Flows, 1990 (Percentage of Total Trade)

Exports from/to	Canada	Mexico	U.S.A.	NAFTA	Argentina	Brazil	Paraguay	Uruguay	MERCOSUR	Total (millions of US$)
Canada	-	0.4	72.7	73.0	0.0	0.3	0.0	0.0	0.4	131,278
Mexico	2.4	-	73.1	75.5	0.4	0.7	0.0	0.2	1.2	29,982
United States	21.1	7.2	-	28.3	0.3	1.3	0.1	0.0	1.7	393,106
NAFTA	15.1	5.2	21.2	41.5	0.2	1.0	0.1	0.0	1.4	554,366
Argentina	0.7	2.6	13.8	17.0	-	11.5	1.2	2.1	14.8	12,352
Brazil	2.3	1.3	23.4	27.0	2.0	-	0.9	1.0	3.9	32,266
Paraguay	0.0	0.0	4.1	4.1	5.8	32.6	-	1.2	39.6	959
Uruguay	0.8	1.9	9.8	12.4	4.8	29.6	0.9	-	35.4	1,694
MERCOSUR	1.8	1.6	20.0	23.4	1.7	4.7	0.9	1.2	8.6	47,270

Imports of/from	Canada	Mexico	U.S.A.	NAFTA	Argentina	Brazil	Paraguay	Uruguay	MERCOSUR	Total (millions of US$)
Canada	-	0.4	62.9	63.3	0.1	0.6	0.0	0.0	0.7	119,681
Mexico	1.3	-	70.8	72.1	0.7	1.0	0.0	0.1	1.9	32,687
United States	18.1	5.5	-	23.6	0.3	1.7	0.0	0.1	2.1	517,020
NAFTA	14.1	4.3	14.7	33.1	0.3	1.4	0.0	0.1	1.8	669,388
Argentina	0.6	2.8	21.5	24.9	-	17.6	1.0	2.8	21.5	4,079
Brazil	2.0	0.9	21.1	24.1	6.7	-	1.5	2.7	10.9	22,440
Paraguay	0.0	0.0	12.3	12.3	12.7	17.5	-	0.7	30.9	1,193
Uruguay	1.0	2.9	10.5	14.4	16.8	23.0	1.1	-	40.9	1,317
MERCOSUR	1.7	1.2	20.3	23.3	6.5	4.2	1.3	2.5	14.6	29,029

Source: International Monetary Fund, *Direction of Trade Statistics* (Washington, D.C.: IMF, 1991).

Table 10.2
Structure of U.S. Imports from MERCOSUR and Conditions of Access to the U.S. Market, 1990 (Percent)

	Arg.	Bra.	Par.	Uru.(1)	MERCOSUR	World	Share of imports from MERCOSUR in total imports
Structure of US imports							
Foods and feeds	31.3	23.6	23.0	16.8	24.7	5.8	8.7
Agricultural materials	1.0	3.2	2.5	4.1	2.8	1.9	3.0
Coal & petroleum	23.4	6.7	0.0	0.0	9.2	13.3	1.4
Ores & metals	1.5	5.9	0.0	5.8	5.1	3.0	3.4
Manufactures	41.7	59.7	71.0	64.3	57.0	72.7	1.6
Non classified	1.1	0.9	3.4	7.0	1.1	3.3	0.7
Total	100.0	100.0	100.0	100.0	100.0	100.0	2.0
Conditions of access to US market							
MFN duty-free imports	17.0	27.0	17.0	20.0	25.2	n.a.	
GSP duty-free imports	22.0	18.2	59.4	32.6	16.8	n.a.	
Tariff-paying imports	61.0	57.8	23.6	65.4	58.0	n.a.	
Total	100.0	100.0	100.0	100.0	100.0	n.a.	

Weighted Tariff Rates (2)						
Foods and feeds	4.1	11.1	3.3	0.8	n.a.	3.0
Agricultural materials	1.2	0.0	0.0	2.8	n.a.	0.7
Coal & petroleum	0.4	0.6	0.0	0.0	n.a.	0.6
Ores & metals	0.0	0.3	0.0	0.0	n.a.	0.6
Manufactures	3.3	4.7	4.5	11.3	n.a.	4.5
Non classified	2.9	5.8	3.3	2.5	n.a.	3.6
Imports with trade of at least $50,000 paying tariffs equal to or higher than 5%	22.5	27.9	27.2	43.1	n.a.	n.a.
Non-tariff Barriers Coverage Ratio	28.6	26.1	14.0	6.8	n.a.	n.a.

Notes: n.a.: Not available

1. Because exports of nonmonetary gold contracted markedly between 1986 and 1989, comparison of trade (1989) and tariff data (1986) for Uruguay is misleading.

2. 1986 trade weights

Source: Based on United Nations, *Commodity Trade Statistics 1989* (New York: United Nations, 1991); Refik Erzan and Alexander Yeats, "U.S.-Latin American Free Trade Areas: Some Empirical Evidence," in Sylvia Saborio et al., *The Premise and the Promise: Free Trade in the Americas* (New Brunswick: Transaction Books, 1992); and *Boletin Comercial* (Washington, D.C.: OAS-CECON, several numbers).

European Economic Community. In particular, Argentine exporters have been adversely affected by unfair competition from U.S.–subsidized sales in world markets. So far, U.S. negotiators have insisted that agricultural subsidies can only be effectively dealt with in a multilateral context.[8]

A prior article by the present author provided a preliminary assessment of Argentine (and MERCOSUR) overall incentives and obstacles to enter into an FTA with the United States.[9] In short, most direct economic benefits (which could not be reaped from unilateral trade liberalization) would arise as a result of obtaining preferential and more secure access to a large market, which in turn could enable the exploitation of scale economies (when possible due to the technical characteristics of activities in which comparative advantages exist), enhance private sector expectations, and foster capital inflows from abroad. Furthermore, an FTA with the United States could provide more certainty as regards the future course of economic policy, locking in recent and (still perceived as) fragile reforms. Preferential trade liberalization vis-à-vis the United States may also prevent the partner from being discriminated against in the U.S. market (as a result of agreements concluded by the United States and third parties) and provide an insurance in case of a deepening process of regionalization in the world trading system.[10]

On the other hand, there are costs that need to be taken into consideration. Given the diversified productive structure of the United States, for Argentina an FTA with the United States would be tantamount to free trade. However, preferential trade liberalization would be burdened by trade diversion. In this restricted sense, discriminatory liberalization would be clearly inferior to a unilateral elimination of trade barriers.[11] In the case of Argentina, the welfare costs associated to trade diversion may not be negligible due to the large share of non–U.S. suppliers in Argentine imports, the relatively high protection still conferred on certain domestic producers, and the fact that the United States is not necessarily the most efficient supplier by international standards.[12] A regionally well-diversified import structure may also enhance the potential for trade retaliation from third parties, which will see their trade shares negatively affected by the preferences granted to the United States.

The issue of adjustment costs—inherent in any transition to free trade policies—deserves some attention as well. Although these are theoretically transient and the counterpart of higher productive efficiency (in the medium term), their very existence could make an agreement politically unfeasible unless dynamic benefits begin to compensate rapidly for lost jobs and investments. The prevailing disparity in size between the United States and Argentina also underlines the issue of the distribution of costs and benefits and, particularly, the need to smooth the burden of adjustment over time.

If it were a likely candidate to enter into FTA negotiations with the United States, the Argentine government should also take into consideration that the latter would involve far more than the gradual elimination of tariffs and NTBs to trade in goods. In fact, free trade agreements have become a means by which

U.S. trade negotiators have advanced U.S. objectives in a wide variety of areas, including the so-called new issues of intellectual property protection, foreign investment rules, and trade in services. As the U.S.–Canada Free Trade Agreement demonstrates and the draft of the North American Free Trade Agreement suggests, commitments made by Canada, Mexico, and the United States in those areas go well beyond those that might reasonably be expected as a result of multilateral negotiations. However, recent policy initiatives put forward by the Menem Administration, such as the protection of intellectual property rights and the bilateral investment treaty with the United States, suggests that Argentina may be prepared to acquiesce in a variety of issues pushed forward by U.S. negotiators with no immediate *quid pro quo*.

An FTA with the United States may also reduce Argentina's relative autonomy in economic policy making and eventually constrain the ability to pursue sectoral and/or industrial public policies that may be considered inappropriate by U.S. legislators or policymakers. Certainly, the weight of this factor would be largely dependent upon the extent to which independent policies would be effectively constrained by an FTA as well as upon the prevailing perception regarding the ability of individual countries to pursue autonomous policies.[13]

ARGENTINA, MERCOSUR, AND THE EAI

The announcement of the EAI coincided with the deepening of the process of economic integration in the Southern Cone, its origins going back to the bilateral integration and cooperation program launched by Argentina and Brazil in the mid-1980s.[14] In 1988, the original initiative was complemented by a bilateral treaty which bound the two countries to create a common market by the end of the century. Two years later, the then newly elected governments halved the term planned to constitute the common market, and in March 1991 Paraguay and Uruguay joined in by signing the Asunción Treaty. The treaty committed the four countries to establish the Southern Common Market (MERCOSUR) by January 1, 1995, therefore binding them to common policies in trade and other areas. For the transition period, it established an automatic and across the board mechanism to progressively bring tariffs to intraregional trade down to zero and to eliminate all NTBs. It also established that any member of the Latin American Integration Association (ALADI) could be admitted into MERCOSUR if it was not already part of a subregional or extraregional integration scheme.[15]

The process of economic integration between Argentina and Brazil and, later on, among the four MERCOSUR countries, has taken place in a context radically different from the past. In contrast to the high protection, emphasis on domestic markets, and import-substitution characteristic of Latin American integration schemes in the 1960s and 1970s, recent efforts at economic integration have been accompanied by widespread trade liberalization and an overhaul of prevailing development regimes. However, the rhythm and intensity of the reform process have varied from country to country, with Brazil generally lagging behind its other partners in MERCOSUR. This divergence extends to the balance of real or perceived costs and benefits of an FTA with the United States. To a large extent, they have been at the basis of the initially divergent reactions to the EAI by the two largest MERCOSUR partners (Argentina and Brazil).

Available estimates suggest that Brazil ranks among the Latin American countries whose exports would expand most as the result of an FTA with the United States.[16] In effect, such an agreement may provide more secure access to the U.S. market and remove some of the obstacles (particularly NTBs) faced by Brazilian exporters. This would enable Brazil to reap dynamic gains arising out of scale economies, improve business expectations, and attract larger investment flows. It is uncertain, however, how strong these effects would be if the prospective FTA is signed once NAFTA has been in place for several years. However, in the case of Brazil, defensive reasons may play an important role in encouraging FTA negotiations. This incentive, which is already present in the case of NAFTA (there is a wide overlapping in the effective and potential supply of Mexican and Brazilian exports to the United States), would be enhanced if FTA agreements flourish throughout the Western Hemisphere.

The counterpart of these potential benefits are several real or perceived costs. In the first place, notwithstanding the process of trade liberalization launched in the late 1980s, Brazil still is a relatively highly protected and diversified economy, which would bear large adjustment costs as a result of preferential trade liberalization vis-à-vis the United States. Second, since the overall reform process has lagged behind, an FTA with the United States could not be regarded as a vehicle to lock in reforms, a role that has been emphasized in the case of Mexico. Third, Brazilian policymakers are persuaded that, as a global trader and a weak partner in the world economy, the fundamental economic interests of Brazil lie with multilateralism. Furthermore, they do not seem to perceive an unavoidable trend toward regionalism and, as a result, show skepticism toward any move that may be regarded as consolidating the shift toward economic blocs. Fourth, U.S. negotiating priorities are not necessarily regarded as compatible with those of Brazil. Perceptions regarding Brazilian policy autonomy and the role of sectoral and industrial policies also suggest a relatively low degree of convergence between likely U.S. demands and Brazilian readiness to comply.

The balance of costs and benefits and the relatively more gradual reform process (in the context of an unstable domestic economic situation) probably explain the cautious Brazilian reaction to the EAI from both the government and public opinion.[17] In fact, since the EAI was launched in June 1990, a wedge between Argentine and Brazilian reactions to the U.S. policy initiative has become somewhat evident. Negotiations to sign a framework agreement between the United States Trade Representative and the four MERCOSUR countries have been an indicator of these divergencies.[18]

Different perceptions on the part of Argentine and Brazilian private and public sectors as to the implications of the EAI (particularly of its trade component) have not been a source of serious difficulties to the process of subregional economic integration yet, mainly because negotiations with the United States have remained within the modest boundaries set by the immediate action agenda of the minilateral framework agreement (concluded by a small number of countries).[19] However, should the option of an FTA negotiation arise in the near future, the cohesion of MERCOSUR may be placed under stress.

CONCLUSION

So far, the impact of the EAI has been mainly political. In the economic field, where its trade component is potentially the most significant, progress has been slow. A cursory overview suggests that a clear-cut economic reason does not seem to exist for MERCOSUR countries to enter into an FTA with the United States, particularly if the multilateral trade scaffolding does not deteriorate markedly. Successful completion of the Uruguay Round of multilateral trade negotiations would greatly contribute to this benevolent scenario. Should the international environment further deteriorate or FTAs with U.S. participation proliferate in the hemisphere, incentives to enter into an agreement on defensive grounds would mount.

It seems that different preferences regarding pace and depth of trade liberalization and the extent and content of economic reform initiatives prevail among MERCOSUR partners, particularly the two larger ones. In the same vein, prevailing perceptions and ideologies regarding policy options and alternative international scenarios also seem to differ. If an FTA negotiation with the United States were feasible in the short term, these differences may place MERCOSUR under considerable pressure. However, this looks like an implausible scenario: in effect, it is likely that before entering into any new agreement, the United States would have to make a detailed examination of NAFTA's impact in order to build the domestic political coalitions necessary to get new agreements approved.

This scenario supports a "wait and see" attitude as regards an FTA negotiation with the United States. In the meantime, Argentina and its MERCOSUR partners should pursue the process of subregional economic integration forcefully, progressively ironing out the above-mentioned divergencies and dealing effectively with the problems that a lack of macroeconomic coordination will increasingly pose as trade liberalization proceeds. Eventually, if an FTA with the United States is not forthcoming and MERCOSUR progresses smoothly, Chile may find it attractive to join the subregional process.

As far as relations with the United States are concerned, the framework agreement can provide an adequate instrument to deal with the most compelling bilateral trade issues, including the impact that the implementation of

NAFTA may have upon trade flows between MERCOSUR and the United States.

Two final caveats are in order. First, much of the favorable Latin American reaction to the proposal to negotiate FTAs in the Western Hemisphere with the participation of the United States has been fostered by domestic political considerations and/or short-term economic (balance of payments) reasons. Private and public actors in Latin America should be careful in assessing available alternatives so as not to confuse long-run strategic options and short-term immediate constraints.

Second, U.S. policy actions will remain very influential (probably more than at any time in the recent past) as regards the future of the process of economic integration in Latin America. This influence should be factored in by U.S. policymakers in the context of a long-run and strategic approach to the region. An undue concentration on immediate considerations may result in lost opportunities, the costs of which will only be adequately realized in the future.

NOTES

1. On the Washington Consensus policy recommendations see John Williamson, "What Washington Means by Policy Reform," in J. Williamson, ed., *Latin American Adjustment: How Much Has Happened?* (Washington, D.C.: Institute for International Economics, 1990), 5–20.

2. For an overview of Argentine stabilization and reform policies since the mid-1980s see Roberto Bouzas, "Beyond Stabilization and Reform: The Argentine Economy in the 1990s," in R. Bottome et al., *In the Shadow of the Debt: Emerging Issues in Latin America* (New York: The Twentieth Century Fund, 1992), 83–109.

3. For an exposition of this approach see Carlos Escude, "La Politica Exterior de Menem y su sustento teorico implicito," *AMERICA LATINA/Internacional* 8, no. 27 (February/March 1991).

4. For an analysis of U.S.–Argentine trade relations see Roberto Bouzas, "U.S.–Mercosur Free Trade," in Sylvia Saborio et al., *The Premise and the Promise: Free Trade in the Americas* (New Brunswick: Transaction Books, 1992), 259–60.

5. See Refik Erzan and Alexander Yeats, "U.S.–Latin American Free Trade Areas: Some Empirical Evidence," in Saborio, *The Premise and the Promise*, 136.

6. Two investigations referred to subsidies (differential export taxes on oil-seeds and vegetable oils and a ban on exports of untanned hides), two to services trade restrictions (marine insurance and couriers) and one to protection of pharmaceutical products.

7. In 1991 the Menem Administration submitted to the Argentine Congress a bill to grant protection of intellectual property rights, which closely follows U.S. demands. Also in 1991 Argentina and the United States signed a bilateral agreement on subsidies (Argentina is not a signatory of the GATT Subsidies Code) and a bilateral investment treaty.

8. The conflict on the agricultural subsidies issue peaked when Brazilian importers announced that they intended to purchase U.S. subsidized wheat in 1991 and, again, in 1992.

9. See Roberto Bouzas, "U.S.–Mercosur Free Trade," 261–67.

10. In a scenario of fragmentation of the world trading system, even economies with a highly diversified regional pattern of trade are likely to do better as members of an "unnatural" trade bloc than as independent participants in a conflictive trade environment. In the same vein, the larger the number of countries entering into FTAs with the United States, the higher the incentives for Argentina (and MERCOSUR) to follow suit on defensive grounds.

11. See Winston Fritsch, "The New Minilateralism and Developing Countries," in J. Schott, ed., *Free Trade Areas and U.S. Trade Policy* (Washington, D.C.: Institute for International Economics, 1989), 337–52.

12. These factors weight even more heavily in the case of Brazil.

13. One author argues that an indequate assessment of costs and benefits and an exaggerated fear of international isolation may lead to mistaken decisions, involuntarily strengthen the trend toward regionalism, and eventually compel far-reaching concessions in exchange for admittance to a regional agreement. See John Whalley, "Regional Trade Arrangements in North America: CUSFTA and NAFTA," mimeo, 1992.

14. For an overview of the evolution of the Argentine-Brazilian Cooperation and Integration Program and MERCOSUR record and prospects see Monica Hirst, "Avances y desafios en la Formación del MERCOSUR," *Documentos e Informes de Investigación*, no. 130 (Buenos Aires: FLACSO, 1992), 1–40.

15. In practice, this implied leaving the door open for an early accession of Chile, an ALADI member that quit the Andean Pact in the mid-1970s.

16. Mexico and Brazil would account for 90 percent of the expansion of exports that may result from a preferential removal of U.S. trade barriers to Latin American exports. See Erzan and Yeats, "U.S.–Latin American Free Trade Areas," 139–40.

17. For a discussion see Luiz Carlos Bresser Pereira, "From Mercosur to the American Integration," Paper presented to the Eighteenth International Congress of the Latin American Studies Association, Los Angeles, September 24–27, 1992, pp. 25–30.

18. Two issues (external debt and technology transfer) became the centerpieces of differences between U.S. and MERCOSUR negotiators. Eventually, as a result of the increasingly isolated position of Brazil, the framework agreement excluded any reference to the external debt issue and made only a superficial reference to technology transfer.

19. The first two meetings of the Trade and Investment Council (held in Washington and Buenos Aires in November 1991 and April 1992) did not produce major breakthroughs but provided a mechanism to air mutual trade complaints and policy conflicts. Some of the issues raised have been: (1) U.S. agricultural subsidies, (2) intellectual property rights protection, and (3) submission of the Asunción Treaty under Article XXIV of the General Agreement of Tariffs and Trade.

11

The Chilean Perception of the Americas Initiative

————————————————————— Mladen Yopo H.

INTRODUCTION

The Enterprise for the Americas Initiative to create a free trade zone from Anchorage to Tierra del Fuego was a surprise to all. Nobody, except the president's closest advisors, knew the magnitude of what President Bush was to announce in Washington on June 27, 1990 at a White House ceremony with the Latin American ambassadors and their attachés.[1]

After the initial impact wore off, the Initiative received a warm, post–cold war welcome from the Latin American countries as the beginning of a new and better era in hemispheric relations after a long period of "nonpolicy" from the United States toward Latin America.[2] However, along with academic researchers and policymakers, Latin American governments have begun to change their initial optimistic view and hasty support toward a more realistic attitude.

The reasons for this change can be found in the international context surrounding the announcement and in the Initiative itself. In this sense, there are four possible complementary hypotheses to explain President Bush's interest in launching the EAI.[3]

In the first place, the Initiative reflects the interest of policymakers—especially in the Republican administration—in realigning the U.S. presence in the new world scheme. The new distribution of world power following the collapse of the Soviet Union, and even after the Gulf War, clearly did not lead to U.S. hegemony—Pax Americana II. The new issues on the international agenda—the drug trade, migration, global warming, markets, technology—which are not dealt with most effectively by military means, have brought about a diffusion of power through transnational interdependence and impact, in which no great power—not even the United States—will alone be able to provide solutions.

This new reality has not only altered factors related to security and power, it has also shaped new alliances among the world's players that, in some cases, aim to be more than regional economic blocs. The conclusion was clear to the U.S. government: the dispute over hegemony would be between regional blocs rather than states, thus the creation of NAFTA and the Enterprise for the Americas Initiative.[4]

A second explanation can be found in the demands made by the Mexican government of Carlos Salinas de Gotari before the signing of its treaty with Washington. NAFTA represents the happy ending of Mexico's new diplomacy goal of securing and legalizing a preferential relationship with the United States, following a tendency toward a growing and silent integration of the two economies. However, for domestic purposes, Mexican authorities had to link this objective to the traditional task of diplomacy established since the Revolution of 1910: not to lose its cultural roots and close relations with the rest of Latin America. To appease charges of dependence and subordination, coming especially from supporters of the left-wing Democratic Revolutionary Party, Salinas de Gotari demanded from Washington an equivalent measure for the rest of Latin America.[5]

A third hypothesis stems from pressure exerted by some European countries—France and Italy—during the 1990 G-7 summit meeting for more cooperation from the United States and more attention to the great economic problems facing Latin America's fragile democracies. Given that U.S. response to this European request was generally evasive and that the 1990 G-7 meeting was going to be held in Houston, President Bush pressed his advisors to improve on this point.

And fourth, the Americas Initiative is closely tied to the Uruguay Round of GATT on free trade that began in 1986 and is still unfinished. The U.S. government tried to make GATT the principal mechanism for building a new world trade framework, based primarily on multilateral free trade agreements. However, problems with the European Community and Japan—especially in the area of agricultural products—have created obstacles to this,[6] so the Bush Administration had to secure its own space and negotiating power in GATT.

No matter which of these hypotheses is the correct one—or if all of them are[7]—the truth is that, in the beginning, the Americas Initiative was more a general concept than a consistent policy that could be put into practice. This is illustrated by the Bush administration's response to Chilean Finance Minister Alejandro Foxley, who was in Washington when the president announced the Initiative. Foxley quickly supported the plan and demonstrated his willingness to begin immediate negotiations in order to reach a quick agreement. U.S. authorities replied that negotiation was impossible at that time, because the president's announcement only marked the beginning of plans to put the Initiative into effect.

This is highlighted by the U.S. government's decision to take a preliminary approach through the signing of a framework agreement on investment and trade, and to secure other goals such as copyright agreements before signing a major agreement.[8] The framework agreement that was signed with all interested Latin American countries in mid-1990[9] would not, according to Commerce Department officials, necessarily lead to the final signing of a Free Trade Agreement.

It is now partially clear that this Initiative will not be applied in homogeneous terms for all Latin American countries, considering that it is open to those with free market economies that are willing to satisfy other U.S. requirements. It is likewise clear that those countries not at the top of the U.S. agenda for this issue will be excluded, at least temporarily.

Because of the complex domestic and foreign situation facing the United States, the Republican government could not afford to make generous concessions with other countries. This explains why the Initiative had to be selective and not costly to the United States. This is also why the focus of the Initiative is on trade, investment support, and debt reduction, excluding fresh money or grants.

COSTS AND BENEFITS

At any rate, the idea of becoming partners with the United States, even when the costs and benefits are still not very clear, has made the Initiative very stimulating for Latin American countries. In Chile's case, few issues in the country's current history have generated such consensus without previous discussion than the idea of signing the Americas Initiative.

When the democratic government of the Concertación (a coalition of centrist parties led by the Christian Democrats) came to power in Chile in December 1990, several conflictive issues remained on the U.S.–Chile bilateral agenda as holdovers from the Pinochet dictatorship. During the eighteen months after the Initiative was announced, most of these were resolved,[10] which explains President Aylwin's statement that "relations with the United States have entered a stage of open cooperation."[11]

Chile is a small and distant market that cannot be compared in commercial and geographical importance to Canada and Mexico—in 1991, Chile ranked thirty-eighth among countries importing from the United States and thirty-second among those exporting to the U.S.—nor in strategic weight to Israel. Nonetheless, all U.S. authorities, including President Bush, have said that, after Mexico, Chile is next in line for a trade agreement with the United States. There are three possible explanations for this: first, the cost of an agreement with Chile would be low for the United States; second, Chile has a stable democracy and one of the best economic records in the region, with stable macroeconomic management and a broad range of trade liberalization (see Table 11.1); and, third, an agreement with Chile would play a symbolic role for the rest of the countries, using Chile as a model to show what can be done. Chile, in fact, was the only country not part of a subregional bloc that was named as a candidate for the Americas Initiative in a request by President Bush to the Senate to extend the fast track.[12]

With this in mind, just a week after President Bush announced the Initiative, Chile quickly got to work on reaching an agreement with the United States. A framework agreement was signed in September 1990, and in June 1991 another step was taken with the establishment of a bilateral working group that would process the necessary information to facilitate future negotiations before the fast-track procedure ends in June 1993. In February 1992, Finance Minister Alejandro Foxley and U.S. Ambassador Curtis Kamman signed an environmental agreement that contemplates a fund and a board of directors. In any case, U.S. officials were very clear in saying that no informal negotiations had begun with Chile, and the U.S. Trade Representative added that any other bilateral negotiations will have to wait until a final agreement is signed with Mexico, and perhaps until some progress has been made in the Uruguay Round of GATT.

Chile has significantly diversified trade[13] since its trade liberalization policy went into effect in 1974, with Japan being its number one individual trading partner in 1991 and the European countries topping the list as a bloc, and it has already signed or is discussing trade agreements with other Latin American countries.[14] Still, Chile's principal economic and political relations are with the United States. It is also true that neither Japan nor Europe has offered Chile a similar agreement, and that the Latin American markets potentially open to Chile through bilateral agreements do not compensate for the 17 percent represented by the U.S. market—18.5 percent if we include Canada and Mexico after NAFTA.

On the other hand, the importance of the U.S. market for Chile is being cut down by the slowed growth of the U.S. economy and the Chilean resolution to reduce copper exports after the failed dumping charges against Chilean producers. The balance of trade with the United States is advantageous for Chile, with $14.364 million in Chile's favor in 1991 ($1,596,255,000 in exports and $1,581,891,000 in imports). Nevertheless, Chile's surplus is shrinking (see Table 11.2). Products exported to the United States have also diversified: copper and other metals make up about 40 percent (it used to be much more), while fruit, vegetables, and fish reach almost the same percentage.[15]

If Chile and the United States sign the Initiative, preliminary estimates predict a growth in trade of $260 million, which is important for Chile. U.S. average trade tariffs currently reach 3.3 percent (1990), being higher for those goods with more added value. The tariff on canned fruit and jam, for example, is between 20 and 35 percent. Since Chilean exports are mainly raw materials,

Table 11.1
Statistical Synopsis of Chile

	1982	1987	1991
Real Gross National Product (GNP)			
GNP total	-13.6	5.8	6.0
Agriculture, forestry, fishing	-0.6	3.4	1.8
Mining and quarrying	6.4	0.0	4.8
Manufacturing	-20.9	5.6	5.5
Construction	-23.4	10.1	5.0
General government (% GNP)			
Current income	36.7	31.4	27.7
Current expenses	34.0	23.5	21.0
Current savings	2.7	7.8	6.6
Fixed investment	2.2	2.8	2.6
Deficit or surplus	-2.6	2.4	1.6
Domestic financing	3.1	-2.5	-0.9
Money and credit (% GNP)			
Domestic credit	68.6	92.5	56.5
Public sector	-0.4	38.2	17.7
Private sector	69.0	54.3	38.8
Monetary supply (Mi)	6.2	4.3	4.6
Prices and wages			
Consumer prices	8.7	20.2	21.8
Real wages	-0.1	-0.2	4.9
Exchange rate (Pesos/dollars)			
Market rate (1980=100)	50.9	219.5	394.4
Real cash (1980=100)	91.0	180.0	187.6
Terms of exchange (million dollars)	76.3	81.5	83.0
Balance of payments (million dollars)			
Balance on account	-2,304.0	808.0	92.7
Balance of trade	63.0	1,280.0	1,575.9
Export goods (f.o.b.)	3,706.0	5,224.0	8,929.4
Import goods (f.o.b.)	3,643.0	3,994.0	7,353.5
Balance of services	-2,476.0	-2,164.0	-1,814.7
One-way transfers	109.0	126.0	331.5
Capital balance	1,034.0	1,021.0	867.6
Non-monetary sector	639.0	1,517.0	1,149.5
Official	150.0	714.0	-55.3
Private	489.0	803.0	1,204.8
Monetary sector	395.0	-496.0	-281.9
Reserve variation (- increase)	1,339.0	252.0	-1,245.5
Errors and omissions	-69.0	-78.0	285.2
Total foreign debt (million dollars)			
Debt paid	17,314.7	21,471.5	19,312.5
Debt service			
Effectively paid	3,676.1	2,366.7	2,972.7
Accrued interest paid/exports of non-factoral goods and services (%)	49.5	26.4	14.6

Source: Inter American Development Bank, *Economic and Social Progress in Latin America*, Report 1992.

Table 11.2
Trade Between Chile and the United States, in Thousands of U.S. Dollars

Period	Exports	Imports	Trade Balance	Total Exchange
1978	327,730	684,201	-356,471	1,011,931
1979	413,920	954,325	-540,405	1,368,245
1980	586,048	1,582,552	-996,504	2,168,600
1981	614,406	1,496,237	-881,831	2,110,643
1982	800,709	916,083	-115,374	1,716,792
1983	1,083,302	703,497	379,805	1,786,799
1984	951,245	747,837	203,408	1,699,082
1985	870,741	654,559	216,182	1,525,300
1986	915,226	641,497	273,729	1,556,723
1987	1,140,539	773,127	367,412	1,913,666
1988	1,393,222	1,002,048	391,174	2,395,270
1989	1,455,960	1,347,932	108,028	2,803,892
1990	1,469,150	1,373,399	95,751	2,842,549
1991	1,596,255	1,581,891	14,364	3,178,146

Source: Central Bank of Chile, *Monthly Bulletin*, January 1992.

tariffs were lower (2.5%), but with Chile's reincorporation into the Generalized System of Preferences (GSP), the tariff average should be no more than 2 percent, with 0 percent for about half the products.

Trade negotiations between Chile and the United States will have to deal not only with tariffs but also with technical barriers such as marketing orders, quotas, drawbacks, environmental and sanitary regulations, and others. With good results, Chile could then enter the U.S. market with new products like cheese, that are subject to a quota, and those products with added values such as canned fruit and vegetables, shoes, textiles, and processed metals. At worst, the U.S. market could remain open in a scheme of growing protectionism involving the so-called trade war.

This optimistic view of the trade issue is not shared by everyone today. Some businessmen not only doubt that they could increase their participation in the U.S. market with the Initiative, they also foresee that the agreement would raise some potential problems like environmental issues or other barriers. A cautious view was expressed by the president of the powerful Production and Commerce Confederation, José Antonio Gúzman, who said that, "Although the Initiative is seen as positive, it would not benefit all economic sectors in the same way, and in more than one case it could have a negative impact. The Initiative would not greatly improve our access to the U.S. market because the barriers are already relatively low." [16] (See Table 11.3.)

It is now partially clear that optimism about short-term trade is not shared by either the Chilean government nor private business. Nor are the prospects

Table 11.3
Tariffs on Chilean Exports to the United States

Product	Tariff		Total Export %
	MFN	GSP	
COPPER			
Non and refined	1.00	1.00	15.63
Alloy, wire, ingot and others	1.20	0.00	1.57
Copper commodity	3.60	0.00	0.02
FRUIT AND VEGETABLES			
Fresh fruit, legumes			
and vegetables	1.20	1.00	31.30
Prepared fruit and vegetables	10.80	10.62	4.06
FISH			
Fresh	0.20	0.03	9.47
Other	5.10	0.08	0.72
Fish flour	0.00	0.00	0.44
WOOD			
Wood	1.10	0.00	2.31
Raw wood	0.00	0.00	1.56
Others	1.48	0.00	0.48
Wood articles	6.80	0.00	0.27
Cellulose	0.00	0.00	0.58
Paper	4.80	0.00	0.04
Furniture	3.20	0.00	0.68

Source: A. Butelman and A. Frohmann, "Towards a Free Trade Agreement Between Chile and the United States," *Relaciones Economicas Internacionales*, FLASCO-CIEPLAN, No. 3, February 1992.

for debt reduction in its different modalities very exciting, since it could at best reach $200 million. (Chile has already been favored with a reduction of $16 million.) Until 1990, the official Latin American debt with the United States was nearly $12 billion (corresponding to 3 percent of the region's total foreign debt), and of this amount, only $7 billion were not commercial loans that could enter the debt-reduction process.

However, the third aspect of the Americas Initiative, investment support, is seen as the most realistic and important outcome for Chile. Even when the amounts are not very significant, they could, according to SELA, be a "seed investment" that could grow in the near future.[17] Chile was thus the first country to receive an Inter-American Development Bank loan for $150 million in the context of the Initiative. Chile is also willing to accede to a $30 million no-return loan from the Multilateral Investment Fund.

Even when the real benefits or costs are not clear, an agreement between the United States and Chile in the context of the Americas Initiative represents

Table 11.4
Materialized Foreign Investment, 1974–1989, in Millions of U.S. Dollars

United States	2,454
Australia	289
Cayman Islands	275
England	260
Spain	251
Japan	222
Bermuda	194
Norway	168
Panama	165
Canada	76
Others	653
Total	5,007

Source: A compendium made by the author, Committee of Foreign Investment, Central Bank of Chile, Indicators of Exterior Commerce, 1978 to 1990.

a symbolic certification of Chile's good image as a country in a full process of development and modernization—a kind of certificate of quality—that would not only attract more investment and trade but would also reinforce this process. The United States still remains the principal investor in Chile. (See Tables 11.4 and 11.5.)

Table 11.5
Authorized Foreign Investment, 1990, in Thousands of U.S. Dollars

Canada	491,688
United States	228,971
Cayman Islands	226,633
England	105,505
Holland	76,922
Bahamas	75,000
France	45,859
Japan	45,454
Australia	31,083
Panama	29,302
Others	86,047
Total	1,436,464

Source: Committee of Foreign Investment, Central Bank of Chile, Indicators of Exterior Commerce, 1990.

CONCLUSION

Will Chile be next? This is a key question, and the answer was uncertain until the middle of November 1992. Although both the Aylwin and the Bush administrations intended to sign the agreement before the fast track ends, there are several obstacles in the way. In the first place, the Initiative must overcome disagreements inside the U.S. Congress and between Congress and the Administration. This dispute was heightened by the presidential election and by the U.S. budget deficit. This is reflected in a statement made by Paula Stern, Bill Clinton's trade advisor, a few weeks before the election, in which she declared that President Bush's promise to Chile "is just an issue that will remain in the public opinion memory." Bill Clinton himself said that NAFTA had to change toward an improvement in the position of the United States.[18] It also seems that North American workers are not very happy with this type of agreement.

On the Chilean side, neither the workers nor the businessmen are so sure now about the benefits of the Americas Initiative. Chile's foreign trade is diversified today (32 percent with Europe, 18 percent with the United States, 18 percent with Japan and 14 percent with Latin America), and an agreement with articles of exclusion could shrink other opportunities. The discussion is also still open on whether Chile should first reinforce its agreements with other Latin American markets like MERCOSUR or should negotiate the Initiative on regional terms.

A national debate is just getting started, and even if the Aylwin Administration has a strong desire to sign the Americas Initiative, the government adopted an observer's stance while waiting for a sign from the United States, which seems to have come in the words of President Clinton in favor of ratifying the next agreement with Chile.

NOTES

1. The only significant official clues to the Initiative can be found in U.S. Commerce Department representative Carla Hills' remarks to the OAS General Assembly in Paraguay during the first week of June 1990. At that time, Carla Hills stated that the new world economic scene required a closer understanding between the United States and Latin America.

2. In general, the Americas Initiative was seen as the first complete outline of a hemispheric policy made by the United States since the Alliance for Progress. See Francisco Rojas Aravena, "Toward a New Doctrine in U.S.–Latin American Relations? The Americas Initiative." *Cono Sur* (FLACSO, Chile) 10, no. 4 (July-August 1991).

3. See Luis Maira, "An Examination of The Americas Initiative in the Context of the United States Political Process," preliminary draft. Institute of Latin American Transnational Studies (Chile), 1992.

4. A good examination of this was done by Ray Cline in his book *World Power Trends and U.S. Foreign Policy for the 1980's* (Boulder, Colo.: Westview Press, 1980).

5. President Salinas recently declared that "NAFTA is totally compatible with our

liberalization toward other markets. . . . That is why we have to strengthen our relations with Latin America." *El Diario* (Chile), October 19, 1992, 9.

6. See Sidney Weintraub, "The New U.S. Economic Initiative Towards Latin America," *Journal of Interamerican Studies and World Affairs* 33, no. 1 (Spring 1991): 4.

7. Undersecretary of the Treasury David C. Mulford described the Americas Initiative as the personal view of President Bush on a long-term hemispheric relationship based on partnership and prosperity. After his trip to Cartagena, Colombia, President Bush ordered a deep examination of U.S.–Latin American relations. David C. Mulford, "The Americas Initiative: The United States View," *Capitulos* (SELA, Venezuela) 28 (January–March 1991): 20.

8. Former Chilean Economy Minister Carlos Ominami discarded the suggestion of negotiating other economic topics before the start of free trade negotiations. In terms of copyrights, Chile already has a law that was passed with difficulty. *El Diario*, June 17, 1992.

9. Argentina, Brazil, Colombia, Bolivia, Ecuador, Chile, Paraguay, Uruguay, Venezuela, the Central American and Caribbean countries, with the exception of Cuba, Haiti, and Surinam.

10. Relations have normalized in all areas. In the political sphere, for example, the Kennedy Amendment was removed, Chile returned to the GSP and to the UNITAS operations, the *Letelier* case is in the hands of the Chilean judicial system, and the families received an indemnity through a commitment based on the Bryan-Suárez Treaty of 1916. The poison grape case is being solved through diplomacy or possibly through judicial action.

11. Patricio Aylwin, Presidential Address, May 21, 1991.

12. See Andrea Butelman and Alicia Prohmann, "Towards a Free Trade Agreement Between Chile and the United States," *Relaciones Económicas Internacionales* (FLACSO-CIEPLAN) 3 (February 1992): 25.

13. In 1991, Chile traded with 167 countries, with a total balance of $16 billion and a surplus of $1.595 billion. *El Mercurio* (Chile), February 15, 1992.

14. An agreement with Mexico is already set; the first step is a 10 percent tariff reduction in 1992, perhaps reaching 0 percent in 1996. Chile has also signed a halfway agreement with Venezuela that contemplates a differential tariff reduction reaching 0 percent in 1994. An agreement signed with Argentina would facilitate trade, investment, and physical integration. With Bolivia, Colombia, and the MERCOSUR subregional bloc there have been some talks toward establishing future free trade negotiations.

15. See Butelman and Frohman, "Towards a Free Trade Agreement," 16.

16. *El Diario*, October 21, 1992.

17. When Undersecretary Bernard Aronson visited Chile to participate in an investment meeting, he began his speech by saying, "I cannot think of a better place to invest than Chile." *El Mercurio*, May 5, 1992.

18. See *El Mercurio*, October 16, 1992, and *El Diario*, October 23, 1992.

12

An Analysis of Colombian Reactions to the EAI: Prospects for Success

_____ *Mauricio Reina and Gladys Cristina Barrera*

INTRODUCTION

Two years after being launched, the Enterprise for the Americas Initiative still appears to be in a state of beatitude. Everyone is talking about it and is anxious to put their faith in it; all that is lacking is a verification of miracles that would elevate it to the status of sainthood.

In the case of Colombia, this syndrome has been particularly notable. Amid a dense fog of misinformation, everyone is scrambling to jump on the bandwagon. Colombian government officials triumphantly announce the signing of an Agreement in Principle with the United States, as if that alone were not only necessary but sufficient. Newspapers announce with delight that Colombia is protected by the Bush Initiative, upon discovering that Colombia has current concessional loans with the United States. Businessmen, meanwhile, sway between uncertainty and hopefulness.

In fact, the concrete steps taken by Colombia regarding the Enterprise for the Americas Initiative can be divided into two categories. On the one hand, specific actions have been taken as explicit responses to EAI. On the other hand, economic reforms that make up part of the government's overall macroeconomic strategy, although not inspired by the new U.S. policy, nevertheless are convergent with those elements contained in the EAI considered fundamental for eventually obtaining its benefits. As might be expected in an incipient process like the Initiative, the elements pertaining to the second category are much more numerous than those in the first.

The first part of this chapter reviews some of the background of the development strategies and foreign trade policies adopted by Colombia in the last twenty-five years. Emphasis has been placed on the role of the EAI within Colombian foreign policy for the 1990s. The second, third, and fourth parts present an evaluation of the progress that has been made within the trade, investment, and foreign debt proposals contemplated by the EAI. Finally, some general considerations are made about the prospects for EAI in Colombia.

COLOMBIAN FOREIGN TRADE POLICY

During the 1980s, referred to by some as the lost decade in Latin America, Colombia had the highest level of economic growth (GNP per capita) in the region.[1] This was due—among other factors—to having a more diversified economy and to several decades of stable macroeconomic management.

Most Latin American countries have only recently applied neoliberal policies to diversify their export products and markets and liberalize their foreign economic policy. However, since the late 1960s, Colombia has tried to apply a variety of schemes for promoting new exports and reorienting its development strategy toward establishing stronger ties with the international economic system. Even though these objectives have been pursued, the results were very poor up to the 1990s. Perhaps the most important factor in the orientation of development strategies and in the formulation of Colombia's foreign trade policy has been the presence of a traditionally bipartisan political system.

The continuous domination of two traditional political parties (liberal and conservative) since the so-called National Front period (1958–1974) has generated three important phenomena. First was the consolidation of a "restricted democracy," which led to the formation of a homogeneous political class with broad consensus on matters of economic development strategies for the country. Second was the strengthening of presidential power, which allowed the executive to exercise strong control over the decision-making process in economic affairs, while promoting rationalization of the process itself. Such a technocratic orientation came about through the creation of decentralized institutes, practically independent and somewhat isolated from political pressures and debates. Third was the important role played by business groups, which have not only legitimized the political system—by acting as social intermediaries and supporting the government—but have directly influenced the formulation and application of the nation's economic policies. They not only provide the government with valuable economic information and analysis, but have, on occasion, taken responsibility for carrying out economic policies—as in the case of the National Coffee Growers Federation and its role in the coffee producing policy.[2]

In summary, a series of factors have converged in Colombia to allow development of a stable macroeconomic policy along with a great effort to diversify, and to a lesser extent, to liberalize the economy since the late 1960s. Nonetheless, the results were very limited. Consideration of the foregoing provides an understanding of the changes that have occurred in Colombian economic policy since 1966. From the beginning of the National Front until that year, Colombia followed a development model based on import-substitution industrialization. However, in the late 1960s, a process for obtaining a greater level of economic diversification was begun. Without tearing down the previous model, promotion of nontraditional exports—other than coffee—became central to the new foreign market–oriented development strategy. But to be fair, however, the impacts of economic diversification and liberalization did not meet expectations. The transition from the import-substitution model to the export promotion model culminated at the beginning of the 1990s.

It was during the late 1980s, and especially during César Gaviria's government (1990–1994), that Colombia's process of modernization and economic internationalization really started. This process has been called *economic opening* by the Gaviria Administration. Economic opening not only relaxed finance, foreign investment, foreign exchange, taxation, and labor regimes, but also introduced important reforms in foreign trade. The opening has emphasized regional economic integration as an indispensable mechanism for trade and political negotiations with integration schemes elsewhere in the world. As a result, economic opening falls within the terms of Colombia's foreign trade for the 1990s, and is characterized by the pragmatic nature of international relations and the development of a multilateral policy. This is a way of seeking greater autonomy on the international level, diversifying international relations not dominated by ideological criteria, and maximizing the country's negotiating power—emphasizing the pursuit of economic objectives. In addition to significant economic reforms, the present government put forward an important political reform in 1991, which was necessary not only to legitimize the political regime by promoting a more participatory democracy, but also to provide a new institutional framework for managing international economic relations.

In this context, trade negotiations with the United States, the European Economic Community, and the countries of the subregion are of transcendental importance for Colombia. Colombian expectations for the EAI should be understood both in terms of its overall foreign policy at this moment, and in reference to the importance of its bilateral relations to the United States. This should be understood in two different senses. First, the U.S. has been Colombia's principal trading partner and source of external financing. Second, relations with the U.S. have determined almost all aspects of Colombian foreign policy since the beginning of the century.

Subjects of mutual interest, such as the Uruguay Round of the GATT and the Andean Trade Preferences Act (ATPA) are included, respectively, in the 1990 Bilateral Agreement in Principle between the United States and Colombia, and in the Immediate Action Agenda—the starting point of discussion of the agreement in principle. The GATT negotiations represent an attempt to highlight the harmonization of positions and efforts by both countries favoring a successful outcome of the Uruguay Round. The United States has taken leadership in confronting the European Economic Community's protectionist policies through liberalization of world agricultural trade. Through its participation in the Cairns Group (made up of Argentina, Australia, Brazil, Canada, Chile, Colombia, Hungary, Indonesia, Fiji, Philippines, Malaysia, New Zealand, Thailand, and Uruguay), Colombia has supported the U.S. position, since both countries agree that the success of these negotiations is strategic for the development of free trade in the world, in general, and could benefit Colombian agricultural exports, in particular.[3] On the other hand, the ATPA or Andean Initiative was signed in July 1992 by President Bush. It provides special tariff reductions to various exports coming from Bolivia, Colombia, Ecuador, and Peru, as the *quid pro quo* for their efforts in the fight against drug trafficking. Even though ATPA does not benefit many Colombian exports to the United States, it is a good opportunity to establish a market for new products. But to do that will require a joint effort between the Colombian government—through the Ministry of Foreign Trade—and the private sector, especially the potentially benefited exporters.

The European Economic Community is Colombia's most important trading partner after the United States. Although Colombia's relationship with the EC, like that of the rest of the Latin American countries, is asymmetrical, it shows a more favorable tendency than for the region as a whole. During the 1980s overall trade with the EC grew by 42.8 percent, political ties were strengthened, and an aid agreement was signed with the Andean Pact.[4] Although the Common Agricultural Policy is still a thorn in Latin America's trade relations with the EC, a new trade opportunity was also created: the Special Cooperation Plan for those countries committed to fighting drug trafficking (Bolivia, Colombia, Ecuador, and Peru) was signed and set in motion in January 1991. At that time, a package of commercial preferences was approved, giving products from these Andean countries access to the EC for four years, including them in the group of "less advanced" countries in the Generalized System of Preferences. Colombia is aware of the advantage of this opportunity to consolidate its position in the new unified European market.

In the context of its multilateral policy, it is especially important for Colombia to consider strengthening its relations with the other countries of the subregion, through multilateral or bilateral integration agreements that allow creation of free trade zones. Examples of these are the Andean Group (Bolivia, Colombia, Ecuador, Peru, and Venezuela), the Group of Three (Colombia, Mexico, and Venezuela), and a bilateral accord with Venezuela. Colombia believes that regional integration is a necessary mechanism for increasing its political and economic negotiating power. Until now, however, the formation of subregional free trade zones has presented various obstacles, even though recent progress has been made especially within the Group of Three and in bilateral relations with Venezuela.

In the case of the Andean Pact, after more than twenty years of frustrated attempts at integration, it was reactivated in 1990 through the La Paz Agreement. There, the five countries agreed on the creation of a subregional free trade zone—based on the establishment of a Common External Tariff (CET)—by January 1992. This was to be the first step toward the creation of a Common Andean Market in 1995. These goals, however, have proven to be difficult. By October 1992, internal tariff barriers had been completely eliminated between Bolivia, Colombia, Ecuador, and Venezuela, but did not include Peru. Peru, in fact, has requested to be temporarily excluded from all subsequent free trade measures up to December 1993. Additionally, it has not yet been possible to establish the CET, a key instrument in achieving the Common Andean Market. Within the Group of Three, there are two main achievements oriented toward the creation of a free trade zone among the member countries: first, the definition of a timetable for tariff reductions to be concluded in July 1994; and second, the establishment of a commonly agreed bilateral mechanism to define the list of products exempt from this free trade agreement. The final important development for Colombia in subregional integration has been the bilateral negotiations with Venezuela. During February and March 1992, these countries adopted a CET and agreed to abolish the existing exempt products list. Finally, they began discussions on the possibility of common macroeconomic policies.

THE INITIATIVE'S TRADE COMPONENT

Concerning the EAI's trade component, Colombia has taken steps in two directions. On the one hand, economic foreign policy reforms have been adopted, aimed at further opening up the Colombian economy to international competition, which is an important condition in the EAI elegibility criteria. Examples of these include creating a Ministry of Foreign Trade and an Industrial Modernization Fund, stepping up tariff reductions to levels predicted for 1994, allowing free importation of almost all goods, and transforming the Export Promotion Fund—PROEXPO—into a Foreign Trade Bank. On the other hand, progress has been made in developing the institutional mechanisms contemplated in the bilateral Agreement in Principle on Trade and Investment, signed with the Joint U.S.–Colombian Commission on Trade and Investment.

Origin

Colombia signed the Agreement in Principle with the United States in July 1990, becoming the first country to do so within the framework of the Initiative. This Agreement seeks to further liberalize the Colombian market and strengthen commercial ties between the two countries. As in the agreements later signed with the other countries, stipulation is made for the formation of a Bilateral Trade and Investment Commission. This commission serves well as a watchdog on trade and investment relations, calls for consultations on related issues of interest to both parties, and promotes the elimination of barriers to the flow of trade and investment. According to the terms of the Agreement in Principle, both sides of the Bilateral Commission are authorized to request assistance from their respective private sectors, whose representatives may also participate in Commission meetings.

In addition to the Agreement, an Immediate Action Agenda was drawn up, and task forces were created to work on certain items in the Agenda. The following topics on the agenda will be given priority by the Commission: (1) the Declaration of Cartagena and the Andean Trade Initiative; (2) cooperation in the Uruguay Round of GATT negotiations; (3) liberalization of and search for new trade and investment opportunities, including formulation of policies oriented toward the eventual signing of a free trade agreement; (4) continuation of discussions on a new International Coffee Pact; and (5) increased cooperation in technical areas, especially agricultural trade, copyright protection, and relations with the private sector. Finally, several task forces were created: Customs Duties and Documentation Procedures, Technical Barriers to Agricultural Trade, Copyright Protection, and the Private Sector.

Evolution

Two technical preparatory meetings were held on September 14 and October 1, 1990. The Commission formally began functioning soon after, with the inaugural meeting held in Washington on October 3, 1990.

The Customs Task Force subsequently held its first meeting in Miami in December 1990, and met again in Washington in April 1991, before being dissolved at the request of the U.S. government. Notwithstanding the progress made in the discussion and the identification of topics of mutual interest, the United States felt that these issues could be discussed in ordinary bilateral meetings. At the end of 1991, the Task Forces on Copyright and Technical Barriers had not yet begun to meet, pending the next Commission meeting.

The Private Sector Task Force (PSTF)

This group is organized as an ad hoc committee to the Council on the Americas, and is made up of representatives of important companies and business associations from both countries. Its objectives are: (1) to facilitate trade and investment through identification of business opportunities; (2) to identify technical cooperation or infrastructure needs for projects in different sectors, and provide support for their development; and (3) to advise both governments on the elimination of obstacles to trade and investment. At its inaugural meeting in Washington on May 9, 1991, the PSTF agreed to function autonomously, free of governmental interference; to adopt as an organizational model the Mexico–U.S. Business Council, which functions more as two national groups rather than as one binational group; and to focus its short-term efforts on its third objective. In June 17, 1991, and as a result of this first meeting, the principal Colombian economic groups created the National Business Association Council, in charge of coordinating the bilateral negotiations. It was also agreed that all of the functions assigned to the PSTF-Colombian Section would be assumed in the future by the Colombia–U.S. Business Council.

Both of the national groups within the PSTF have identified topics of interest to be discussed and presented to the bilateral Commission for consideration. The following topics have been indicated by the Colombian section of the PSTF: First, conditions of access to the U.S. market, which include (1) setting expedient sanitary standards for admitting food products, (2) reducing the cost of customs procedures owing to intensive searches, (3) eliminating import quotas, (4) including a "no attachment" clause in dumping and subsidies investigations,[5] and (5) eliminating obstacles to free competition in maritime transportation services; and Second, conditions for promoting foreign investment, which include better copyright protection and promotion of visits by U.S. business missions.

The U.S. section of the PSTF has indicated the following principal topics of interest: reduction of the high direct and indirect taxes charged by Colombia; more flexibile exchange regulations; elimination of excessive protection for national industry; control of contraband; training of the labor force; improvement of personal security conditions for eventual investors and entrepreneurs; and access for other countries to the low tariffs negotiated within the Andean Pact.

FOREIGN INVESTMENT REFORMS

During 1991, President Gaviria's administration introduced a series of reforms of current foreign investment regulations in Colombia, as part of a process of internationalization and modernization of the economy. Although these reforms do not represent a direct response to the EAI, they do coincide with its proposals, and thus constitute an important step toward being able to take advantage of the opportunities offered by the Initiative in the future.

Until 1990, despite timid attempts toward greater flexibility, foreign investment in Colombia had been kept under excessive control and vigilance by the state in an effort to protect national industry from competition by foreign firms. Common restrictions were the definition of modalities of investment, the need for registration and enrollment of firms, the designation of sectors able to receive investments, the establishment of minimum percentages of national equity participation for the creation of new enterprises, and the imposition of conditions for capital refunds and remittances. This situation meant that very low amounts of foreign investment were brought into Colombia during the 1980s, which was mainly concentrated in mining and quarrying.[6] The United States is undoubtedly the principal foreign investor in Colombia, as demonstrated by the fact that from 1987 to 1990 it accounted for almost 75 percent of the total nonpetroleum foreign investment.

The new foreign investment regime, begun in January 1991 and known as Resolution 49 of January 1991, covers three basic operational criteria. First, foreign investors are guaranteed equal treatment with national investors, except with respect to transfers of resources abroad. Second, it establishes universality in the allotment of investments, excepting national defense activities and the disposition and disposal of toxic and radioactive waste. Third, it assures automatic authorization of investment, eliminating previous procedures. Such authorization will be required only for investments in public services, mining and petroleum, and portfolio investments. New modalities of investment were also created, and remission of earnings abroad and investment refunds were facilitated, guaranteeing the inalterability of these conditions.[7]

THE INITIATIVE AND DEBT REDUCTION

The EAI's proposal to reduce the official concessionary and nonconcessionary debt[8] contracted by the Latin American countries with the United States has been received with great interest by Colombian authorities. This is because, on the one hand, Colombia meets all the requirements to become an eligible candidate for the debt reduction program; on the other hand, there is a coincidence of interests in terms of the importance of adequate management of natural resources and their surroundings, which means that the Initiative could support the development of environmental projects in Colombia.

In the first instance, Colombia has considerable experience dealing with the International Monetary Fund, becoming really fruitful in the last years because it enjoys an exceptional status as a good debtor, since it has never restructured its debt and has remained within the voluntary commercial loan market on the international level. On the other hand, it has been granted loans by the World Bank to carry out reforms in different sectors, and has introduced reforms in the foreign investment regime.

In the second place, in recent years, Colombia has sought to include environmental variables in its development plans, has strengthened the institutions in charge of environmental management, has given nongovernmental organizations access to decision-making levels in this area, and has promoted environmental education throughout the country. The present government, for the first time in national history, included an environmental policy in its development plan, announced the future creation of a Ministry of the Environment to organize and structure policies in this field, and included environmental issues in the new Political Constitution promulgated on July 4, 1991.

Despite this emphasis on the environment, Colombia has encountered many obstacles in obtaining international financing for developing its environmental projects, utilizing the mechanism of exchanging debt for nature. This is because, since Colombia is an exemplary debtor, its debt is calculated at comparatively high prices on the secondary market. Therefore, the Initiative could provide financial support for undertaking these projects.

Potential Amount of Official Debt Reduction

Although the EAI contains proposals for reducing both the commercial and the offical debt, it is the latter that interests Colombia. The total amount of the country's public foreign debt in 1990—including medium and short-term loans—was $13.79 billion, the multilateral debt being the most important (42 percent of the total), followed by the commercial debt (33 percent of the total). The bilateral debt with other governments at $2.56 billion represented another 19 percent, while the debt contracted with suppliers reached only 6 percent of the total foreign debt.

The total amount of the 1990 official debt with the United States that was eligible for reduction amounted to $1.08 billion (corresponding to 7.8 percent of the total public debt), a significant figure if compared to the other important debtors in the region. Of this amount, concessional loans covered a total of $529 million (3.8 percent of the total public debt), corresponding to $525 million in U.S. AID loans, and the rest to the P.L. 480 program. Nonconcessional loans accounted for $550 million (4.0 percent of the total public debt), corresponding almost entirely to loans contracted with Exim Bank ($549 million).

The public agencies responsible for managing both the foreign debt and environmental issues have been discussing possible terms of a future proposal to the United States for reducing the debt within the framework of the EAI. Some of these terms include the deposit of funds from the EAI in a Colombian National Environmental Fund account, with an equivalent sum contributed by the Colombian government. Projects to be financed by the Fund would be selected by government agencies and nongovernmental organizations, and with the collaboration of the U.S. government, while priority would be given to projects located in areas of high vulnerability and biological diversity. Finally, priority would also be given to projects that foster environmental education and technical training, community participation in resource management, development of legal and institutional mechanisms for protecting the environment, and environmental management in urban areas.

CONCLUSION

Two years after the promulgation of the EAI, it can be said that public expectations in Colombia have far exceeded the actual results.

The actions taken by Colombia have been oriented in two directions. First, concrete activities, directly inspired by the Initiative, have been undertaken, especially concerning the bilateral task forces; and second, the present government's economic reforms, although not responding directly to the EAI, are moving the country in the right direction to meet the U.S. government's eligibility requirements.

There are at least two points where these reforms and requirements coincide. The EAI's emphasis on the free market as a development alternative coincides with the general orientation of the Colombian economic reforms. Furthermore, as a mechanism for creating a regional free trade zone, and favoring negotiations with groups of countries that have put forward integration processes among themselves, the EAI is compatible with Colombian multilateral, and predominantly economic, foreign policy.

Nevertheless—putting aside excessive official enthusiasm, the macroeconomic reforms that coincide with EAI objectives, and the progress made by the task forces, especially the PSTF—there remain some limitations to carrying out the EAI in Colombia. First, trade, investment, and debt are not the only elements on the bilateral agenda with the United States. For more than a decade, this agenda has been permeated by drug trafficking, despite efforts made during the previous and present administrations to "denarcotize" it. Second, and more importantly, the pace of implementation of the EAI is dictated by the priorities of the U.S. government. The signing of an Agreement in Principle does not mean imminent negotiation of a free trade agreement. In this sense, implementation of NAFTA and the potential negotiation of a free trade agreement with Chile could be a sufficient set of objectives for the U.S. government during the rest of the 1990s.

For the most optimistic observers in Colombia, NAFTA has been seen as the first step toward greater integration of the Americas, in which Colombian participation would be obtained through negotiations with Mexico within the ambit of the Group of Three. But the reality seems to be different. Colombia, along with other countries in Latin America, will encounter serious obstacles in its attempt to be brought into the process of integration, via NAFTA or via other bilateral agreements with the United States, such as the EAI. This, because it will probably face stiff competition from countries both within and without the Americas. In the first case, Mexico has a tremendous competitive advantage in trade with the United States.

Moreover, Colombian free trade negotiations with Mexico have been more difficult than anticipated, bringing into doubt Mexico's real commitment in negotiating other bilateral agreements with its Latin American neighbors. Finally, even in the case of an agreement with Mexico, the NAFTA's rules of origin would make it very difficult for Colombian exports to accede to North American markets via Mexico. The other serious competition faced by Colombia within Latin America comes from Chile. This country is a prime candidate for a bilateral agreement with the United States or integration within the NAFTA, not only because its promarket reforms are very advanced, but also because it is already one of the most open economies in the region. Furthermore, Chile has signed a bilateral free trade agreement with Mexico, one of the NAFTA signatories, placing it in a strong position for future negotiations with the other NAFTA members.

Another issue that worries some Colombian opinion leaders is the growing possibility of competition for access to NAFTA from countries outside the Americas. According to NAFTA's clause 2.205, other countries or groups of countries—including those outside the Americas—may be admitted to the Agreement if they fulfill all terms and conditions required, and if the NAFTA member countries agree. From the Colombian perspective, this appears to be an attempt to create a truly global free trade agreement, not just a Western Hemispheric one. For some sectors of Colombian opinion this can be seen as a U.S. effort to promote a worldwide trade mechanism different from GATT. If this were the case, Colombia would face not only intraregional competition—from Chile, for example—to be included in a free trade agreement like EAI, but also from other regions like Asia, Eastern Europe, and Oceania.

NOTES

1. From 1981 to 1989, Colombian GNP per capita growth was 13.9 percent, compared to the overall Latin American average (excluding Cuba) of 8.3 percent in the same period. The source of these figures is the Economic Commission for Latin America and the Caribbean, *Changing Production Patterns with Social Equity* (Santiago, Chile: ECLAC, 1990), 20.

2. Carlos E. Juárez, "The Politics of Trade and Development in Colombia: Export Promotion and Outward Orientation, 1967–1991," preliminary draft, Department of Political Science, University of California, Los Angeles, June 1992.

3. Marta Osorio, "La Ronda de Uruguay y la agricultura: Crónica de un conflicto anunciado," *Colombia Internacional*, 17 (February–March 1992): 14–19.

4. Marta Osorio, "Las relaciones comerciales entre Colombia y la Comunidad Europea," *Documentos Ocasionales* 18 (November–December 1990).

5. Currently, when these investigations are undertaken for the same product coming from two different countries, evaluation of damage is made taking into account the imports from both countries together rather than individually.

6. According to data from the National Planning Department, nonpetroleum investment grew from $103.6 million in 1980 to only $230.3 million in 1990, and petroleum investment in the same period grew from $168.3 million to $201.6 million.

7. Only temporary alterations are contemplated, should the country's international reserves drop to less than three months of imports.

8. The main difference between the two types of debt is in their terms (e.g., rates of interest and duration). A concessionary debt is conceived as a mechanism to spur development, with more favorable rates of interest, grace periods, and longer durations than those prevailing in nonconcessionary credit markets.

Selected Bibliography

BOOKS

Avery, William P. (ed.). *World Agriculture and the GATT*. Lynne Rienner, 1992.

Beier, Friedrich K., and Schricker, Gerhard (eds.). *GATT or WIPO? New Ways in the International Protection of Intellectual Property*. VCH Publications, 1989.

Crookell, Harold. *Canadian-American Trade and Investment Under the Free Trade Agreement*. Greenwood, 1990.

Fried, Edward R., Stone, Frank, and Trezise, Philip H. (eds.). *Building a Canadian-American Free Trade Area*. The Brookings Institution, 1987.

Green, Roy E. (ed.). *Enterprise Zones: New Directions in Economic Development*. Sage Publications, 1991.

Hart, Michael. *A North American Free-Trade Agreement: The Strategic Implications for Canada*. Ashgate, 1990.

Hudec, Robert E. *The GATT Legal System and World Trade Diplomacy* (2nd ed.). Butterworth Legal Publications, 1990.

Jackson, John H. *Restructuring the GATT System*. Council on Foreign Affairs, 1990.

Jerome, Robert W. (ed.). *World Trade at the Crossroads: The Uruguay Round: GATT and Beyond*. University Press of America, 1992.

Lustig, Nora, Bosworth, Barry P., and Lawrence, Robert L. (eds.). *North American Free Trade: Assessing the Impact*. The Brookings Institution, 1992.

Messerlin, Patrick, and Sauvant, Karl P. (eds.). *The Uruguay Round: Services in the World Economy*. The World Bank, 1990.

Milberg, William, and Bartholomew, Philip F. (eds.). *Research in International Business and Finance, Volume 8: Prospects for Canadian-United States Economic Relations Under Free Trade*. Jai Press, 1990.

Morici, Peter. *A New Special Relationship: Free Trade and U. S.–Canada Economic Relations.* Ashgate, 1991.

Nau, Henry R. (ed.). *Domestic Trade Politics and the Uruguay Round.* Columbia University Press, 1988.

Nolle, Daniel E. (ed.). *Canada–U. S. Free Trade Agreement: Implications, Opportunities and Challenges.* New York University Press, 1989.

Petersmann, Ernst-Ulrich, and Hilf, Meinhard (eds.). *The New GATT Round of Multilateral Trade Negotiations: Legal and Economic Problems* (2nd rev. ed.). Kluwer Law Tax Publications, 1991.

Riggs, A. R., and Velk, Tom (eds.). *Canadian-American Free Trade: Historical, Political and Economic Dimensions.* Ashgate, 1987.

Rode, Reinhard (ed.). *GATT and Conflict Management: A Transatlantic Strategy for a Stronger Regime.* Westview, 1990.

Rugman, Alan M. *Multinationals and Canada–United States Free Trade.* University of South Carolina Press, 1990.

Sauvant, Karl P., Weber, Jorg, and Simmonds, Kenneth R. (eds.). *Law and Practice Under the GATT and Other Trading Arrangements: The International Legal Framework for Services.* Oceana, 1992.

Schmitz, Andrew (ed.). *Free Trade and Agricultural Diversification: Canada and the United States.* Westview, 1989.

Schott, Jeffrey J., and Smith, Murray G. (eds.). *The Canada–United States Free Trade Agreement: The Global Impact.* Institute for International Economics, 1988.

Schott, Jeffrey J. (ed.). *Completing the Uruguay Round: A Results Oriented Approach to the GATT Trade Negotiations.* Institute for International Economics, 1990.

Schott, Jeffrey J., and Hufbauer, Gary C. *North American Free Trade: Issues and Recommendations.* Institute for International Economics, 1992.

Siddiqui, Fakhari (ed.). *The Economic Impact and Implications of the Canadian Free Trade Agreement.* E. Mellen, 1992.

Stern, Robert, Trezise, Philip H., and Whalley, John (eds.). *Perspectives on a U.S.– Canadian Free Trade Agreement.* The Brookings Institution, 1987.

Tussie, Diana. *The Less Developed Countries and the World Trading System: A Challenge to the GATT.* St. Martin Press, 1989.

Winham, Gilbert R. *Trading with Canada: The Canada–U. S. Free Trade Agreement.* Priority, 1988.

Wonnacott, Paul. *United States and Canada: The Quest for Free Trade.* Institute for International Economics, 1987.

ARTICLES AND PERIODICALS

Barfield, Claude. "The Americas and World Trade." *American Enterprise* 3 (July–August 1992): 10–12.

Clark, Carrie B. "The Enterprise for the Americas Initiative: Supporting a 'Silent Revolution' in Latin America." *Business America* 112 (September 23, 1991): 6–11.

Gibson, J. Eugene, and Schrenk, William J. "The Enterprise for the America's Initiative: A Second Generation of Debt-for-Nature Exchanges—With an Overview of Other Recent Exchange Initiatives." *George Washington Journal of International Law and Economics* 25 (1991): 1–70.

Gitli, Eduardo, and Ryd, Gunilla. "Latin American Integration and the Enterprise for the Americas Initiative." *Journal of World Trade* 26 (August 1992): 25–45.

Graham, Carol. "The Enterprise for the Americas Initiative." *The Brookings Review* 9 (Fall 1991): 22–27.

Hakim, Peter. "President Bush's Southern Strategy: The Enterprise for the Americas Initiative." *Washington Quarterly* 15 (Spring 1992): 93–106.

————. "The Enterprise for the Americas Initiative: What Washington Wants." *The Brookings Review* 10 (Fall 1992): 42–45.

Lewis, David E. "The North American Free Trade Agreement: Its Impact on Caribbean Basin Economies." *Caribbean Affairs* 4 (October–December 1991): 56–76.

Moran, Katy. "Debt-for-Nature Swaps: U.S. Policy Issues and Options." *Renewable Resources Journal* 9 (Spring 1991): 19–24.

Perry, William. "George Bush's Greatest Accomplishment?" *International Economy* 5 (September–October 1991): 40–43.

Porter, Roger B. "The Enterprise for the Americas Initiative: A New Approach to Economic Growth." *Journal of Interamerican Studies and World Affairs* 32, no. 4 (Winter 1990): 1–12.

Schaffer, Walt. "Enterprise for the Americas Initiative Offers New Trade, Investment Opportunities." *Business America* 113 (March 23, 1992): 2–24.

Stephenson-Glade, Skye. "The Enterprise for the Americas: An Initiative Weak on Initiative." *Business and the Contemporary World* 4 (Autumn 1991): 76–84.

Weintraub, Sidney. "The New U.S. Economic Initiative Toward Latin America." *Journal of Interamerican Studies and World Affairs* 33 (Spring 1991): 1–18.

Weiss, Mary. "The Enterprise for the Americas Initiative: An Instructive Model for International Funding for the Environment." *New York University Journal of International Law and Politics* 24 (Winter 1992): 921–55.

Xu, Shicheng. "On Bush's 'Enterprise for the Americas Initiative.' " *Foreign Affairs Journal* 20 (June 1991): 45–54.

Index

About the Editor and Contributors

ROY E. GREEN is president of REG Management Resource Group and an adjunct research professor at The George Washington University. Previously he taught public administration at the University of Colorado at Denver, the University of Oregon, and the University of Wisconsin at Milwaukee. He is the author of *The Profession of Local Government Management: Management Expertise and the American Community* (Praeger, 1989), and the editor and a contributor to *Enterprise Zones: New Directions in Economic Development* (1991).

GLADYS CRISTINA BARRERA is a researcher and lecturer, Department of Political Science, Inter-Disciplinary Center for Regional Studies (CIDER) and Center for International Studies, University of the Andes, and advisor for the Presidential Councilorship for International Relations, Republic of Columbia. Her research and publications focus on labor migration, regional and border integration, drug trafficking, and international relations.

ROBERTO BOUZAS is a senior fellow at the Department of International Relations (FLACSO/Argentina) and a research fellow at the Scientific and Technical Research National Council (CONICET). He has published extensively on international economic issues and U.S.-Latin American economic relations. His latest book (coedited with Nora Lustig) is *Trade Liberalization, Regional Integration and the Enterprise for the Americas Initiative.*

RANDALL CRANE teaches economic development, water policy, and public finance in the Urban Planning Program at the University of California at Irvine. He has published in urban economics, public economics, and international development planning journals. During 1989/90, he was a Fulbright Scholar in Economics at El Colegio de México.

MICHAEL A. GOLDBERG is dean of the Faculty of Commerce and Business Administration at the University of British Columbia and Herbert R. Fullerton Professor of Urban Land Policy. He has been at UBC since 1968. His recent work examines differences between Canadian and U.S. cities, globalization of property markets, and the development of international financial centres.

JOSEPH GRUNWALD is adjunct professor of economics at the University of California at San Diego. He was founding president of the Institute of the Americas and has been a senior fellow at the Brookings Institution and professor of economics at Yale and other universities in the United States and Chile. He has served as U.S. deputy assistant secretary of state.

MAURICE D. LEVI is Bank of Montreal Professor of International Finance at the University of British Columbia. He has held visiting positions at MIT, University of California at Berkeley, London Business School, Hebrew University of Jerusalem, National Bureau of Economic Research, and University of Exeter. Dr. Levi has written extensively in the areas of economics and finance.

PATRICK LOW is a senior economist in the International Trade Division of the World Bank, where he works on trade issues, including trade and the environment, the international trading system, and regional trade blocs. From 1988 to 1990 he was a visiting researcher at the Colegio do México, and a consultant to several governments and international agencies on trade issues. Prior to that, he was with the GATT secretariat in Geneva for eight years, and in his most recent position worked on launching the Uruguay round of multilateral trade negotiatons. He is the author of a forthcoming book on U.S. trade policy and the multilateral trading system, commissioned by the Twentieth Century Fund.

MAURICIO REINA has been a researcher and lecturer at the Center for International Studies and the Center for the Study of Economic Development, University of the Andes, since 1985. His research and publication efforts focus on international relations, Colombian trade policy, regional integration, drug trafficking, macroeconomic policy, and development aid policies.

MURRAY G. SMITH is director of the Centre for Trade Policy and Law, Carleton University and the University of Ottawa. He has also served as director of the International Economics Program at the Institute for Research on Public Policy (1987–90), as senior policy analyst at the C. D. Howe Institute, and as director of International Economic Relations in the British Columbia government. Mr. Smith serves on the roster of panelists for disputes under Chapter 18 of the Canada-U.S. FTA.

JOSEPH S. TULCHIN is director of the Latin American Program of the Woodrow Wilson International Center for Scholars in Washington, D.C. Previously he was professor of history at the University of North Carolina at Chapel Hill. He has served as associate editor and editor of the *Latin American Research Review*. His research interests are Argentine history and inter-American relations. His most recent book is *Argentina and the United States: The History of a Conflicted Relationship*.

CARLOS ALBA VEGA is a researcher at the Centro de Estudios Internacionales, El Colegio de México. His publications include: *Los empresarios y la industria de Guadalajara* (with Dirk Kruijt) (1988), *Historia y desarrollo industrial de Mexico* (editor) (1988), and "Crisis, Adjustment and Employment in the Manufacturing Industry of Jalisco" (with Bryan Roberts) (March 1990). His main fields of interest are regional development; industrialization, especially in small and medium industries; and the business community in a globalized economy.

ARLENE E. WILSON is a specialist in international trade and finance at the Congressional Research Service (CRS). Her CRS reports on the free trade agreement include: *The Effect of the Canada-U.S. Free Trade Agreement on U.S. Industries, United States-Canada Free Trade Agreement: Implementation and Elaboration*, and *U.S.-Canada Free Trade Agreement: Assessment and Implications for a U.S.-Mexico Free Trade Agreement*.

RONALD J. WONNACOTT is professor of economics at the University of Western Ontario. He has written widely on customs unions, free trade areas, and Canada-U.S. trade. He has also coauthored books on statistics and econometrics (with his brother Tom). He is a fellow of the Royal Society of Canada, was chairman of the economics department of UWO from 1969 to 1972, and was president of the Canadian Economics Association (1981–82).

MLADEN YOPO H. is director of studies at the South American Peace Commission, and is a professor at the Andres Bello and Bolivariana Universities in Chile. Mr. Yopo is an advisor to the Chilean Ministry of Foreign Relations, Economic Division. His research interests and publications are in the field of Latin American international relations.

ISBN 0-275-94266-X

90000>

EAN

9 780275 942663

HARDCOVER BAR CODE

DISCARD

DATE DUE

NORTH CAMPUS
MIAMI-DADE COMMUNITY COLLEGE
MIAMI, FLA.

DEMCO